In Another World with My Smartphone 5

Art • **Soto** Original Story • **Patora Fuyuhara**

Character Design: Eiji Usatsuka

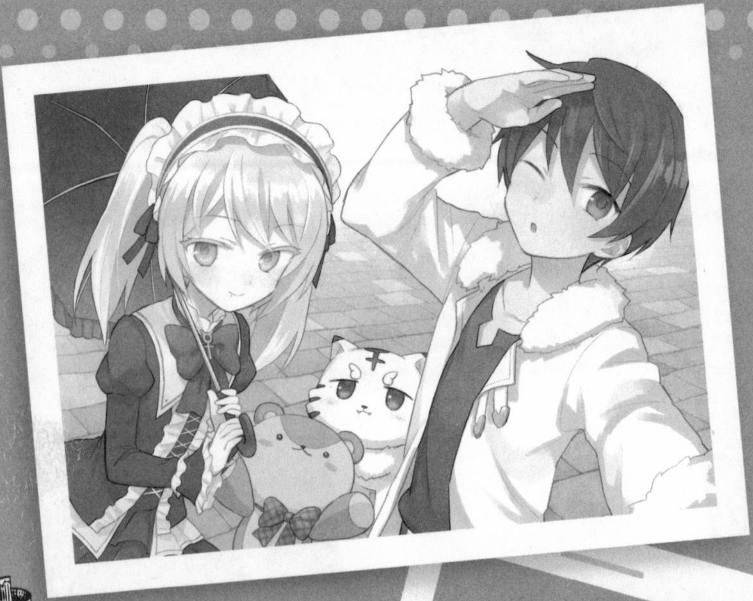

In Another World with My Smartphone

Vol. 5

«contents»

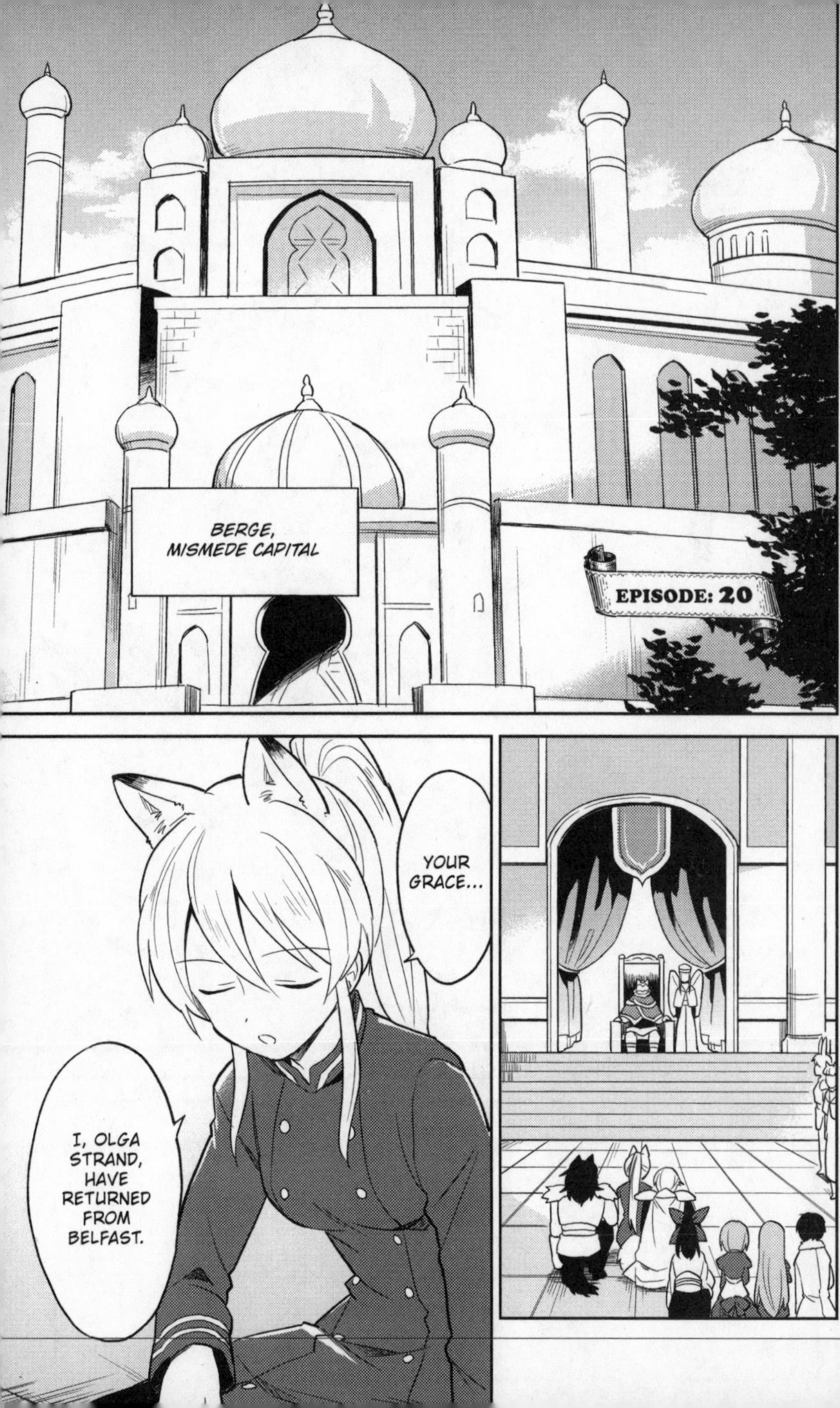
EPISODE: 20
BERGE, MISMEDE CAPITAL
YOUR GRACE...
I, OLGA STRAND, HAVE RETURNED FROM BELFAST.

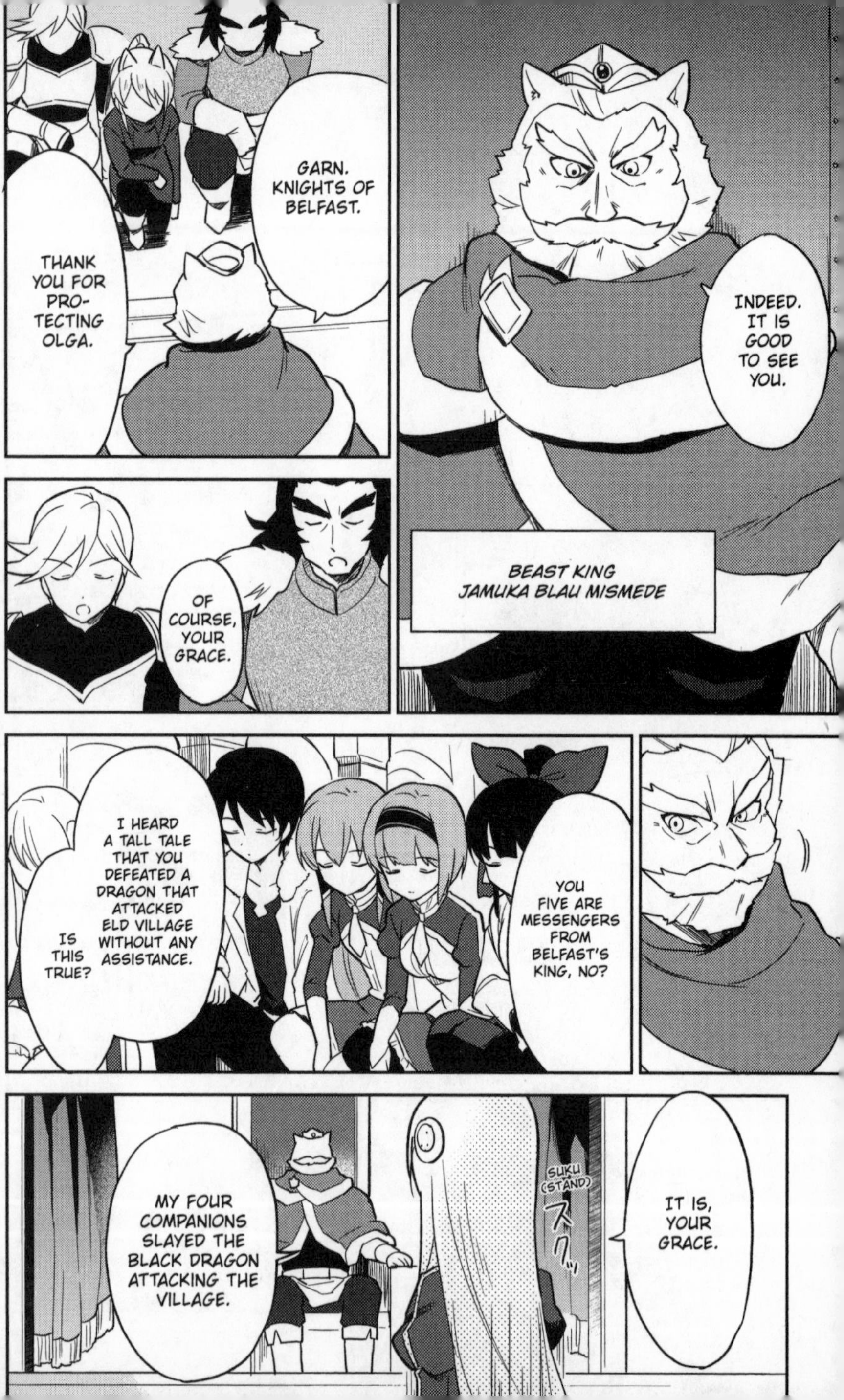
INDEED. IT IS GOOD TO SEE YOU.
BEAST KING JAMUKA BLAU MISMEDE
GARN. KNIGHTS OF BELFAST.
THANK YOU FOR PRO-TECTING OLGA.
OF COURSE, YOUR GRACE.
YOU FIVE ARE MESSENGERS FROM BELFAST'S KING, NO?
I HEARD A TALL TALE THAT YOU DEFEATED A DRAGON THAT ATTACKED ELD VILLAGE WITHOUT ANY ASSISTANCE.
IS THIS TRUE?
IT IS, YOUR GRACE.
SUKU (STAND)
スクッ
MY FOUR COMPANIONS SLAYED THE BLACK DRAGON ATTACKING THE VILLAGE.

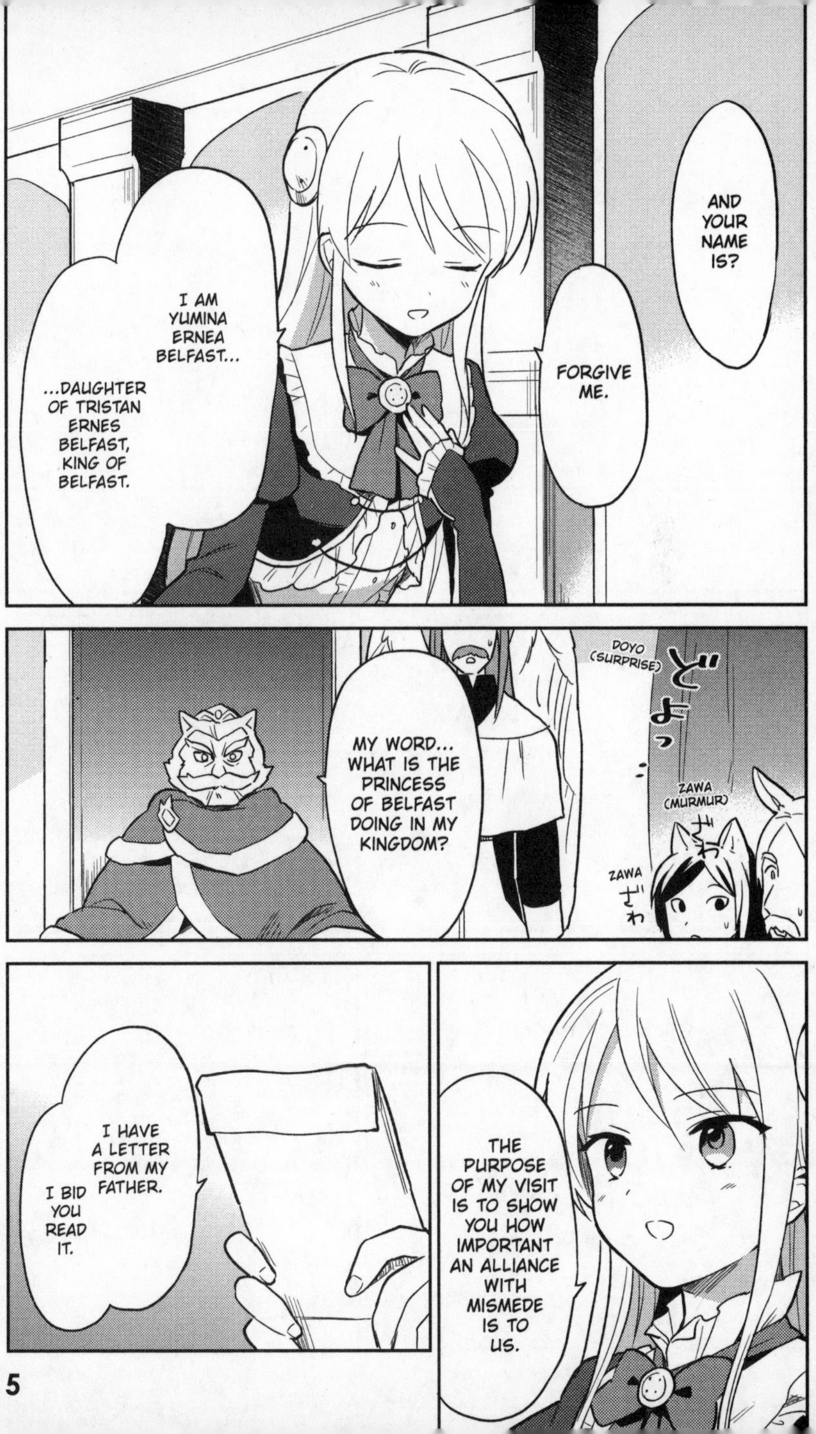
AND YOUR NAME IS?
FORGIVE ME.
I AM YUMINA ERNEA BELFAST...
...DAUGHTER OF TRISTAN ERNES BELFAST, KING OF BELFAST.
DOYO (SURPRISE)
どよっ
ZAWA (MURMUR)
ざわ
ZAWA
ざわ
MY WORD... WHAT IS THE PRINCESS OF BELFAST DOING IN MY KINGDOM?
THE PURPOSE OF MY VISIT IS TO SHOW YOU HOW IMPORTANT AN ALLIANCE WITH MISMEDE IS TO US.
I HAVE A LETTER FROM MY FATHER.
I BID YOU READ IT.

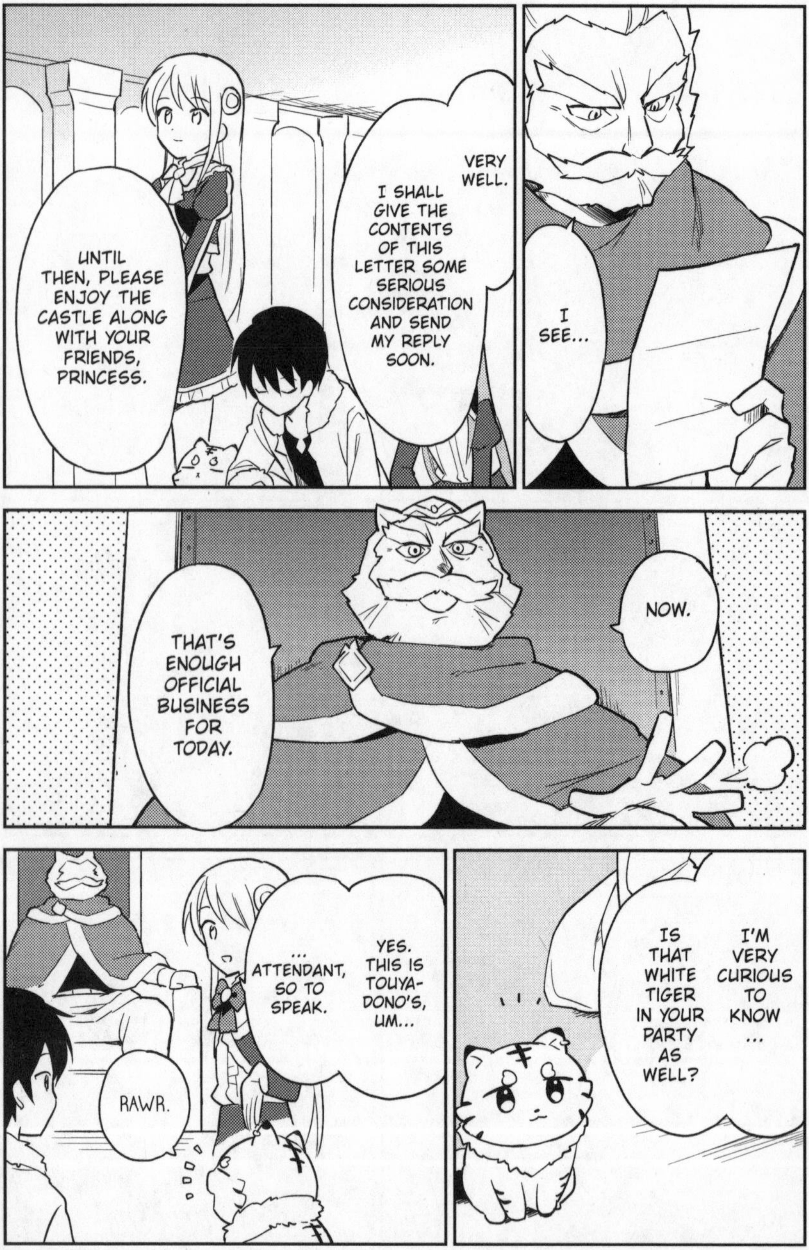
I SEE...
VERY WELL.
I SHALL GIVE THE CONTENTS OF THIS LETTER SOME SERIOUS CONSIDERATION AND SEND MY REPLY SOON.
UNTIL THEN, PLEASE ENJOY THE CASTLE ALONG WITH YOUR FRIENDS, PRINCESS.
NOW.
THAT'S ENOUGH OFFICIAL BUSINESS FOR TODAY.
I'M VERY CURIOUS TO KNOW...
IS THAT WHITE TIGER IN YOUR PARTY AS WELL?
YES. THIS IS TOUYA-DONO'S, UM...
...ATTENDANT, SO TO SPEAK.
RAWR.

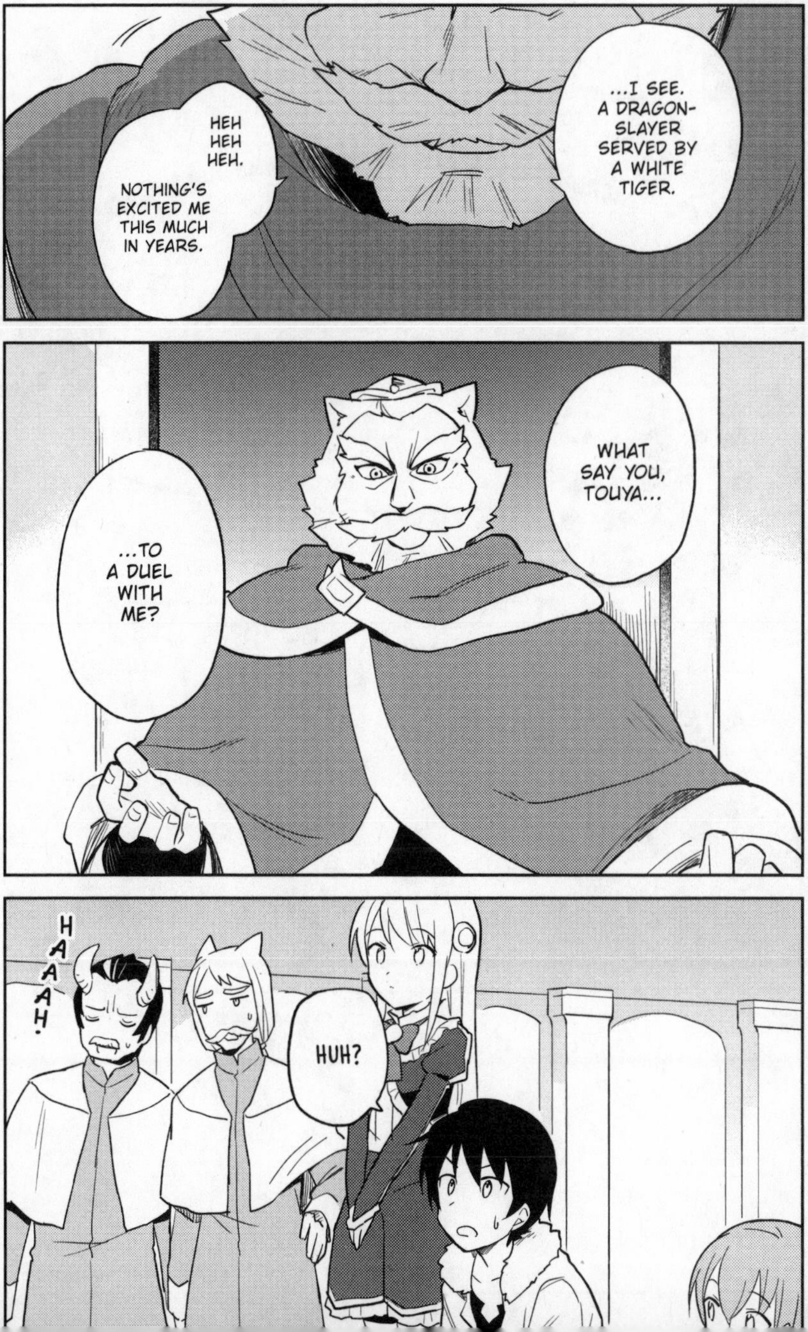
...I SEE. A DRAGON-SLAYER SERVED BY A WHITE TIGER.
HEH HEH HEH.
NOTHING'S EXCITED ME THIS MUCH IN YEARS.
WHAT SAY YOU, TOUYA...
...TO A DUEL WITH ME?
HUH?
HAAAH!

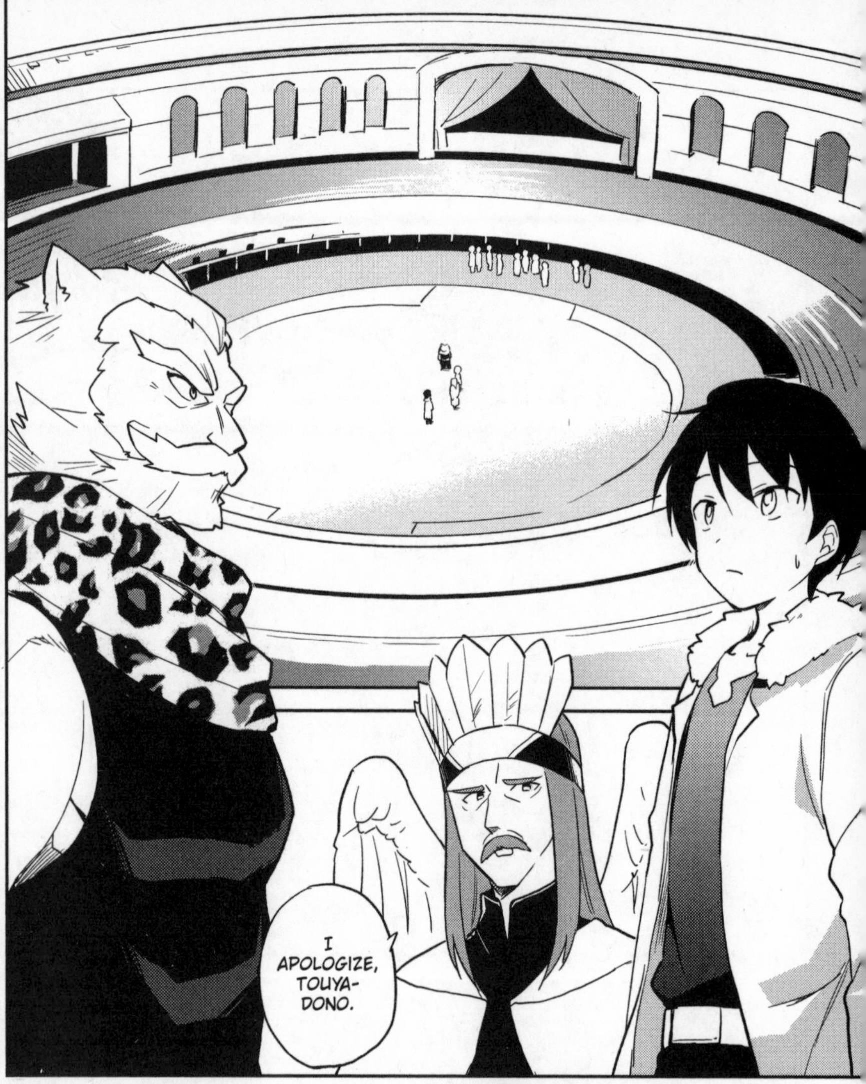
I APOLOGIZE, TOUYA-DONO.

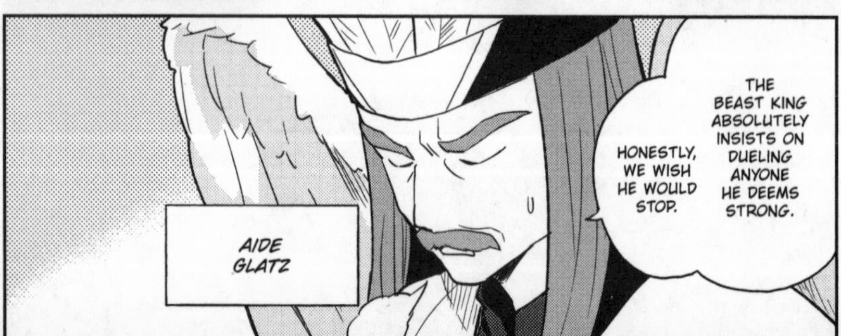
THE BEAST KING ABSOLUTELY INSISTS ON DUELING ANYONE HE DEEMS STRONG.
HONESTLY, WE WISH HE WOULD STOP.
AIDE GLATZ

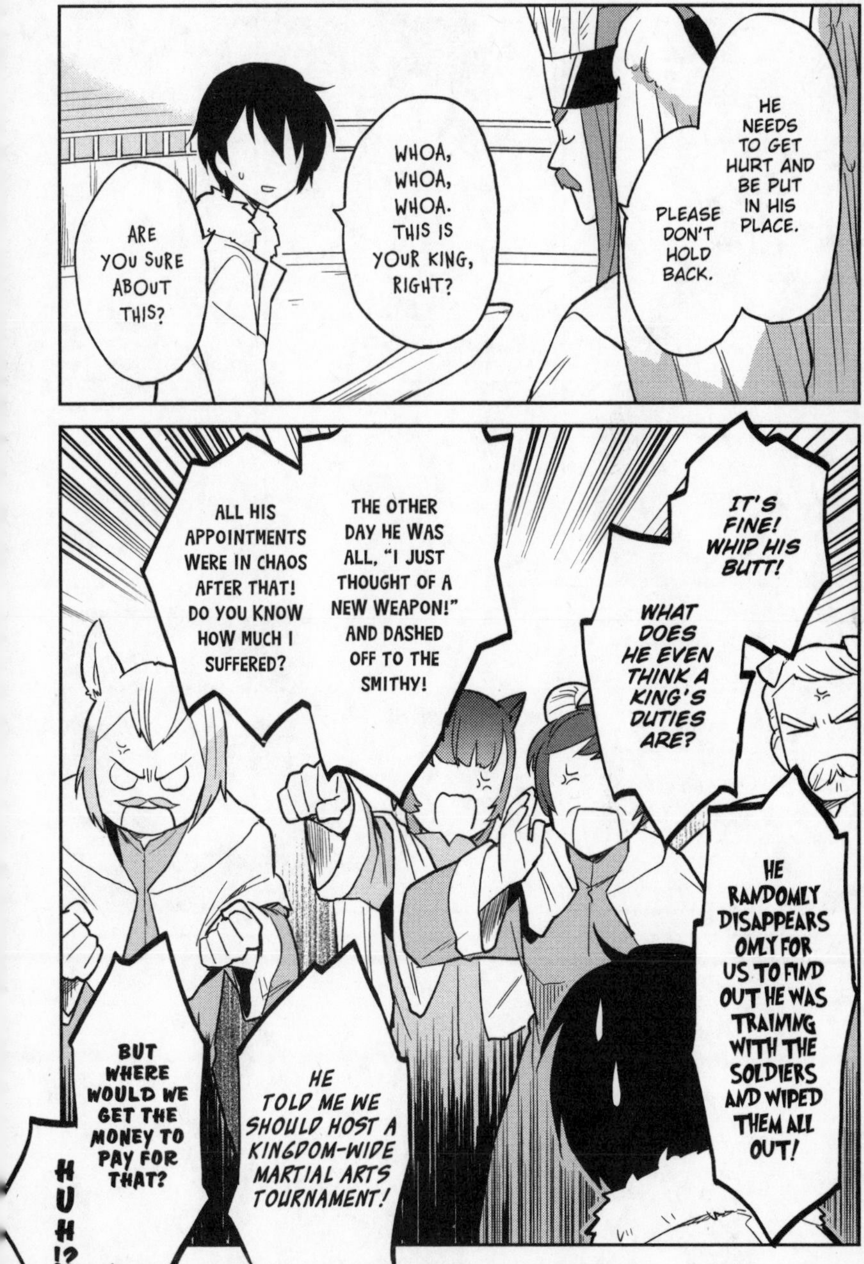
HE NEEDS TO GET HURT AND BE PUT IN HIS PLACE.
PLEASE DON'T HOLD BACK.
WHOA, WHOA, WHOA. THIS IS YOUR KING, RIGHT?
ARE YOU SURE ABOUT THIS?
IT'S FINE! WHIP HIS BUTT!
WHAT DOES HE EVEN THINK A KING'S DUTIES ARE?
THE OTHER DAY HE WAS ALL, "I JUST THOUGHT OF A NEW WEAPON!" AND DASHED OFF TO THE SMITHY!
ALL HIS APPOINTMENTS WERE IN CHAOS AFTER THAT! DO YOU KNOW HOW MUCH I SUFFERED?
HE RANDOMLY DISAPPEARS ONLY FOR US TO FIND OUT HE WAS TRAINING WITH THE SOLDIERS AND WIPED THEM ALL OUT!
HE TOLD ME WE SHOULD HOST A KINGDOM-WIDE MARTIAL ARTS TOURNAMENT!
BUT WHERE WOULD WE GET THE MONEY TO PAY FOR THAT?
HUH!?

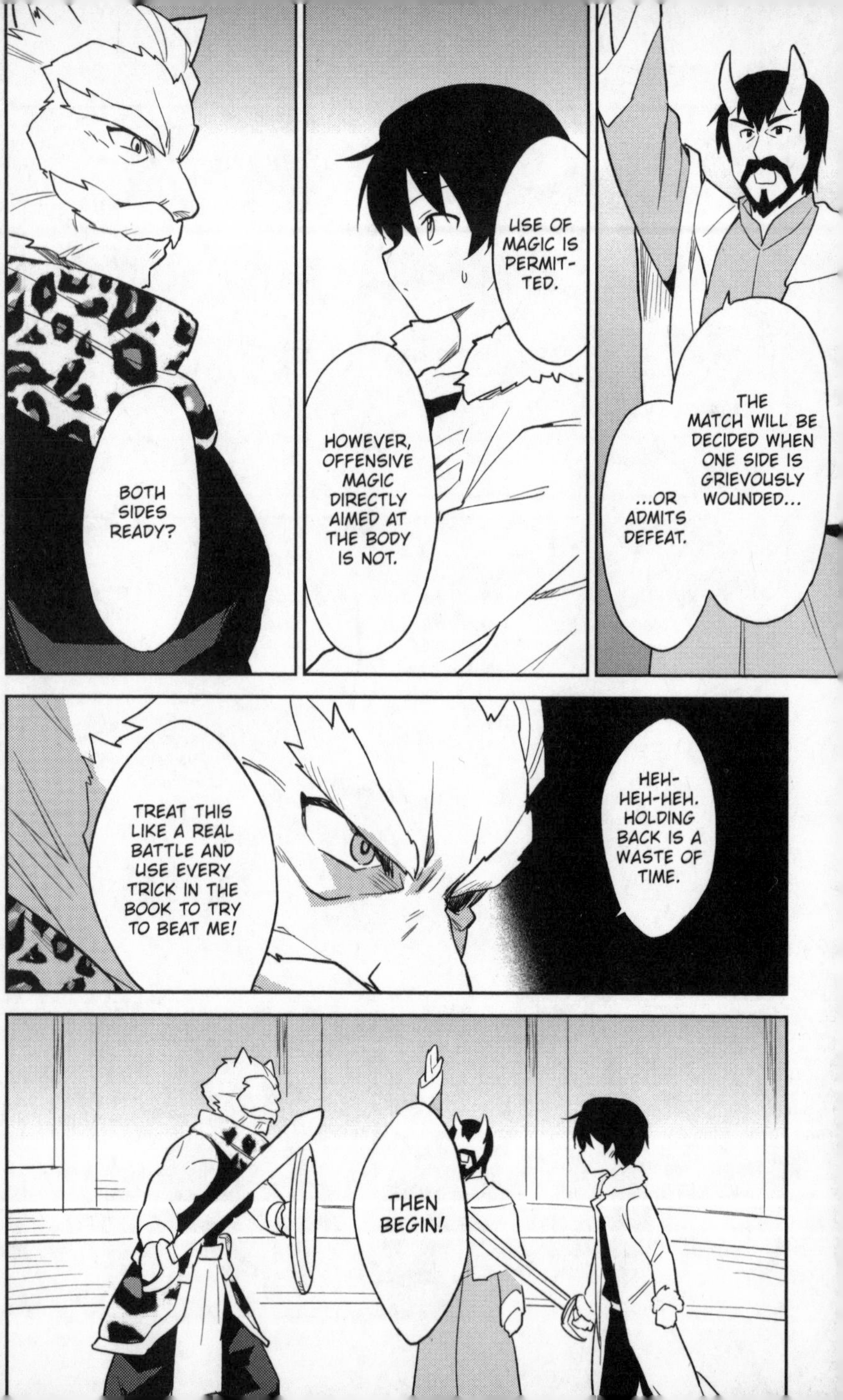
THE MATCH WILL BE DECIDED WHEN ONE SIDE IS GRIEVOUSLY WOUNDED...
...OR ADMITS DEFEAT.
USE OF MAGIC IS PERMIT-TED.
HOWEVER, OFFENSIVE MAGIC DIRECTLY AIMED AT THE BODY IS NOT.
BOTH SIDES READY?
HEH-HEH-HEH. HOLDING BACK IS A WASTE OF TIME.
TREAT THIS LIKE A REAL BATTLE AND USE EVERY TRICK IN THE BOOK TO TRY TO BEAT ME!
THEN BEGIN!

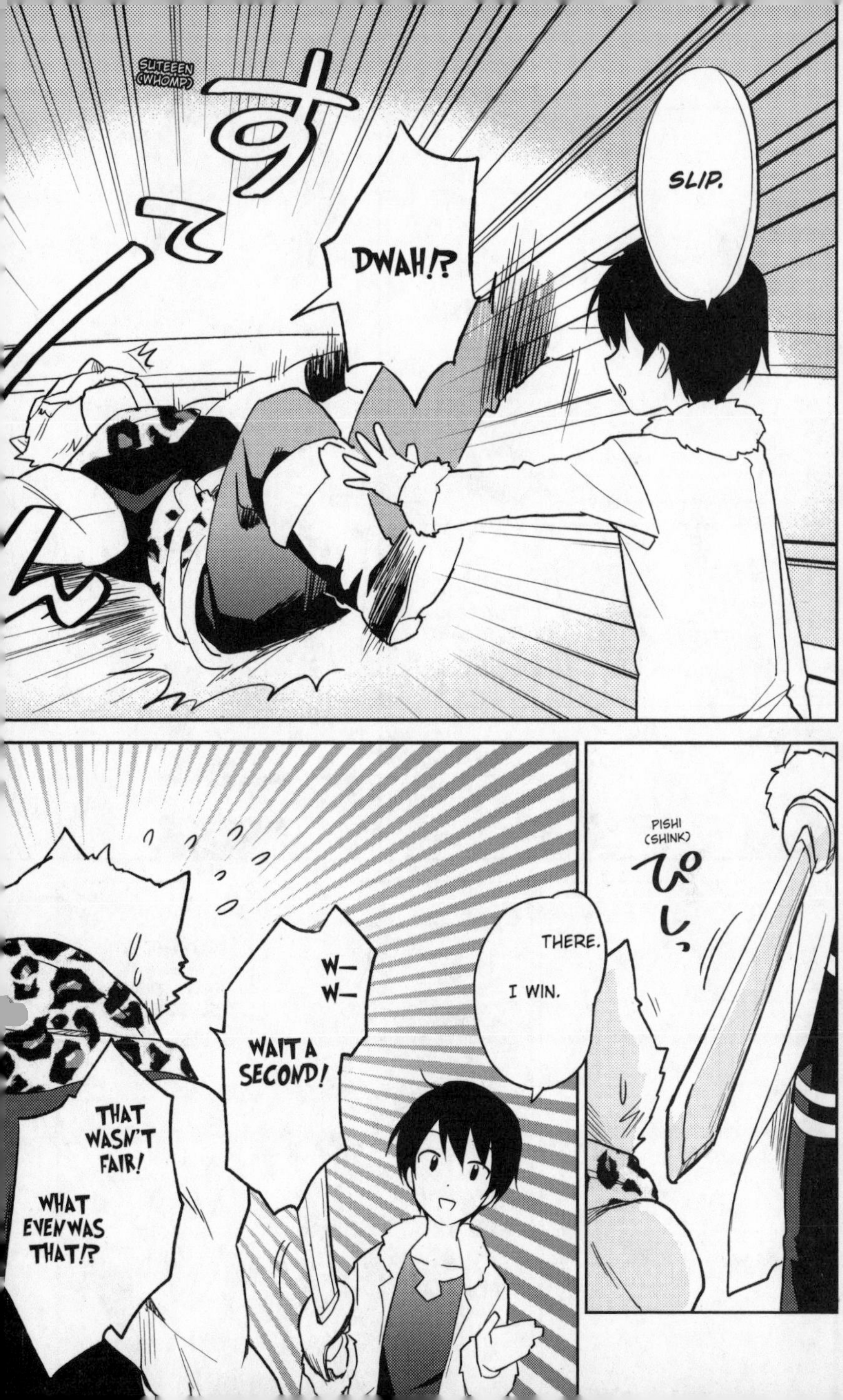
SLIP.
SUTEEEN (WHOMP)
すてーん
DWAH!?
PISHI (SHINK)
ぴしっ
THERE.
I WIN.
W— W—
WAIT A SECOND!
THAT WASN'T FAIR!
WHAT EVEN WAS THAT!?

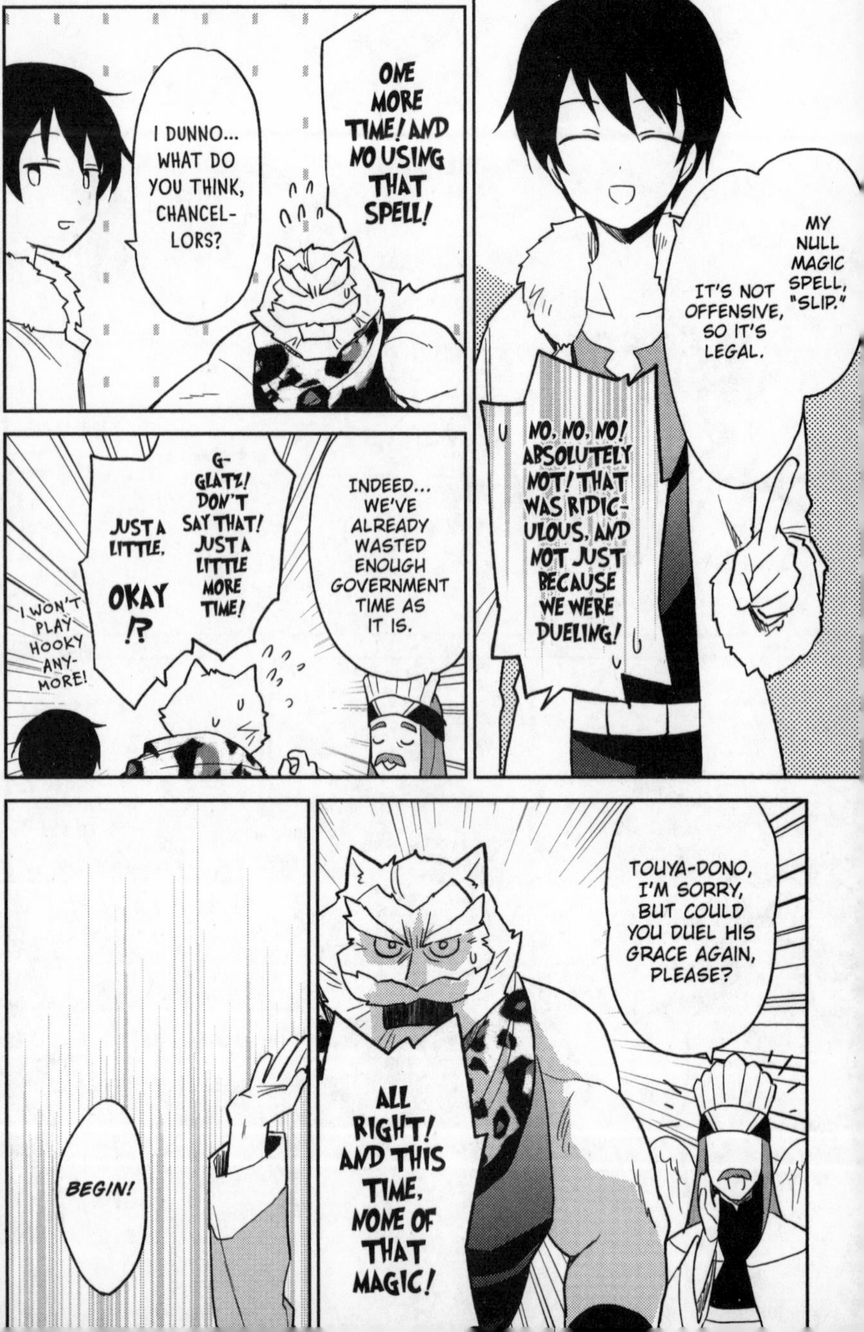
MY NULL MAGIC SPELL, "SLIP."
IT'S NOT OFFENSIVE, SO IT'S LEGAL.
NO, NO, NO! ABSOLUTELY NOT! THAT WAS RIDICULOUS, AND NOT JUST BECAUSE WE WERE DUELING!
ONE MORE TIME! AND NO USING THAT SPELL!
I DUNNO... WHAT DO YOU THINK, CHANCELLORS?
INDEED... WE'VE ALREADY WASTED ENOUGH GOVERNMENT TIME AS IT IS.
G-GLATZ! DON'T SAY THAT! JUST A LITTLE MORE TIME!
JUST A LITTLE. OKAY!?
I WON'T PLAY HOOKY ANYMORE!
TOUYA-DONO, I'M SORRY, BUT COULD YOU DUEL HIS GRACE AGAIN, PLEASE?
ALL RIGHT! AND THIS TIME, NONE OF THAT MAGIC!
BEGIN!

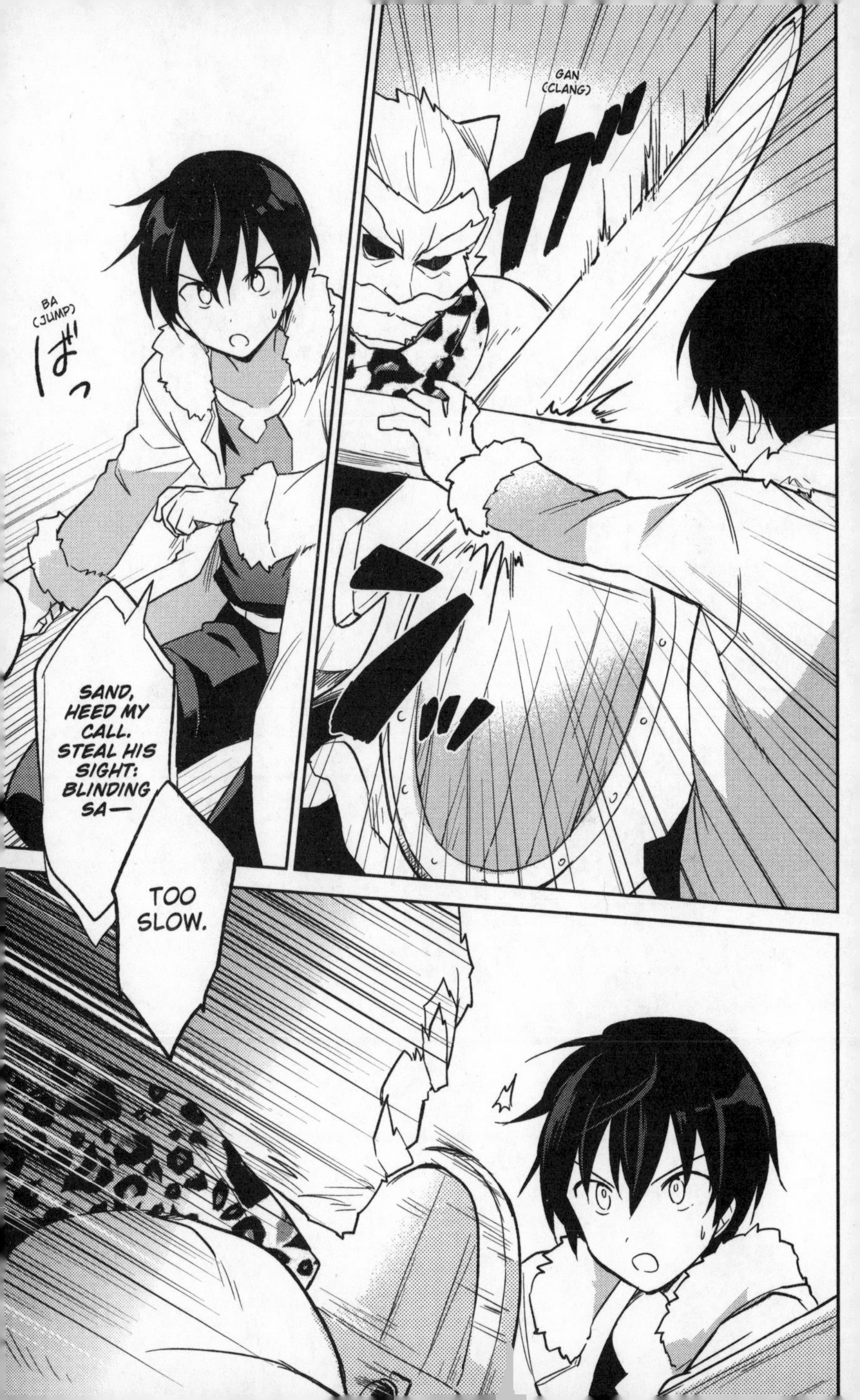
GAN
(CLANG)
BA
(JUMP)
ばっ
SAND, HEED MY CALL. STEAL HIS SIGHT: BLINDING SA—
TOO SLOW.

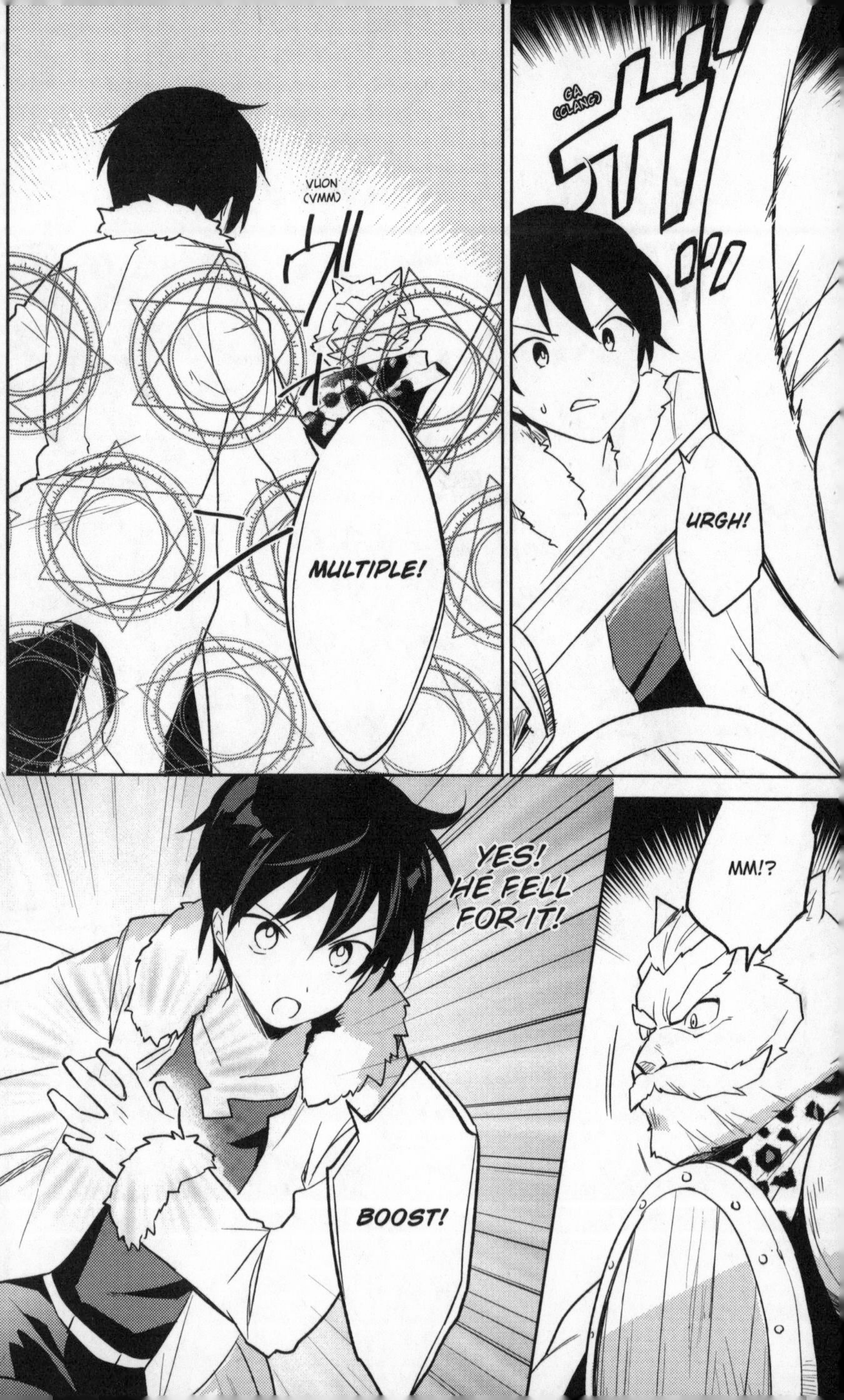
GA (CLANG)
URGH!
VUON (VMM)
MULTIPLE!
MM!?
YES! HE FELL FOR IT!
BOOST!

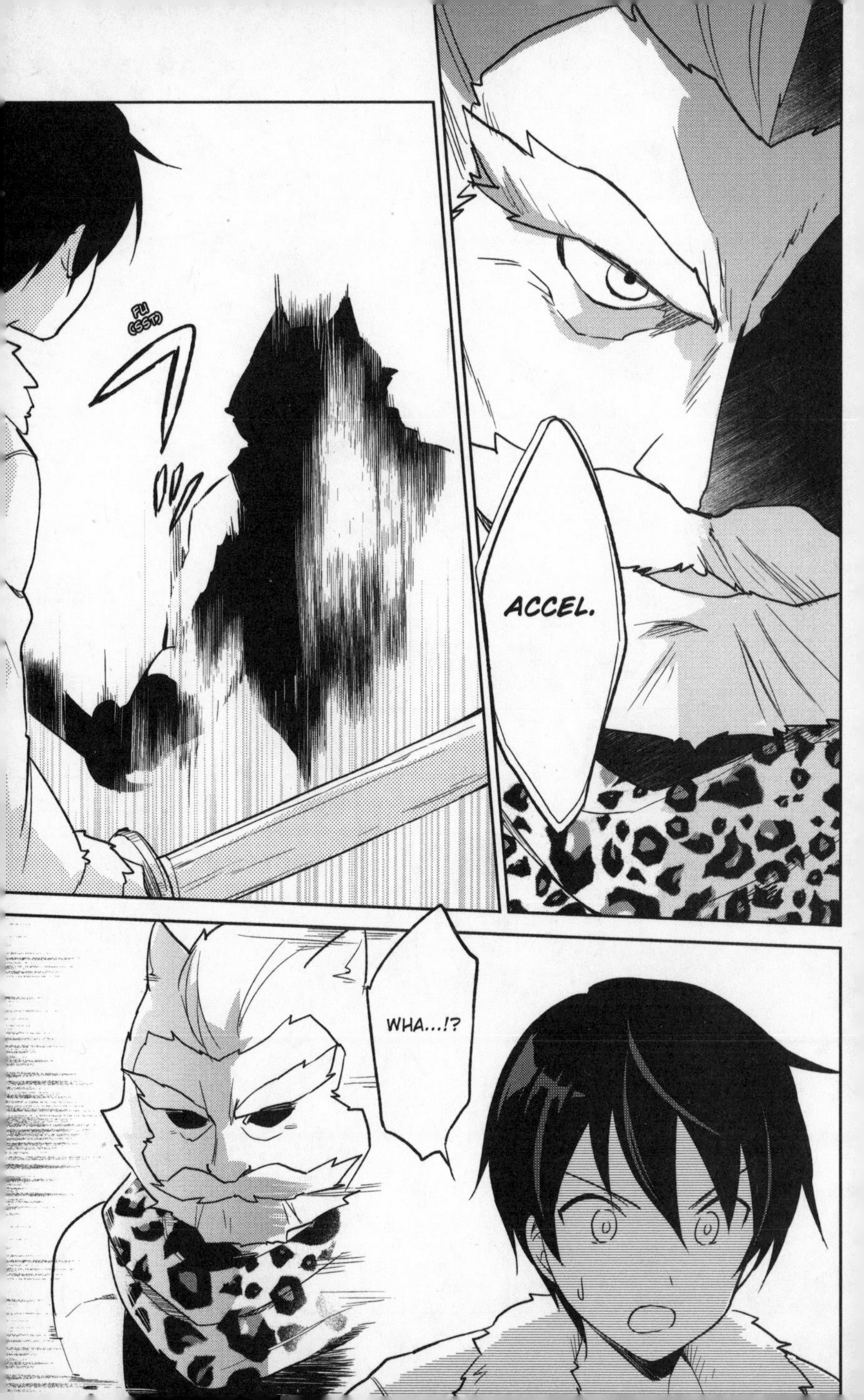
ACCEL.
FU
(SST)
WHA...!?

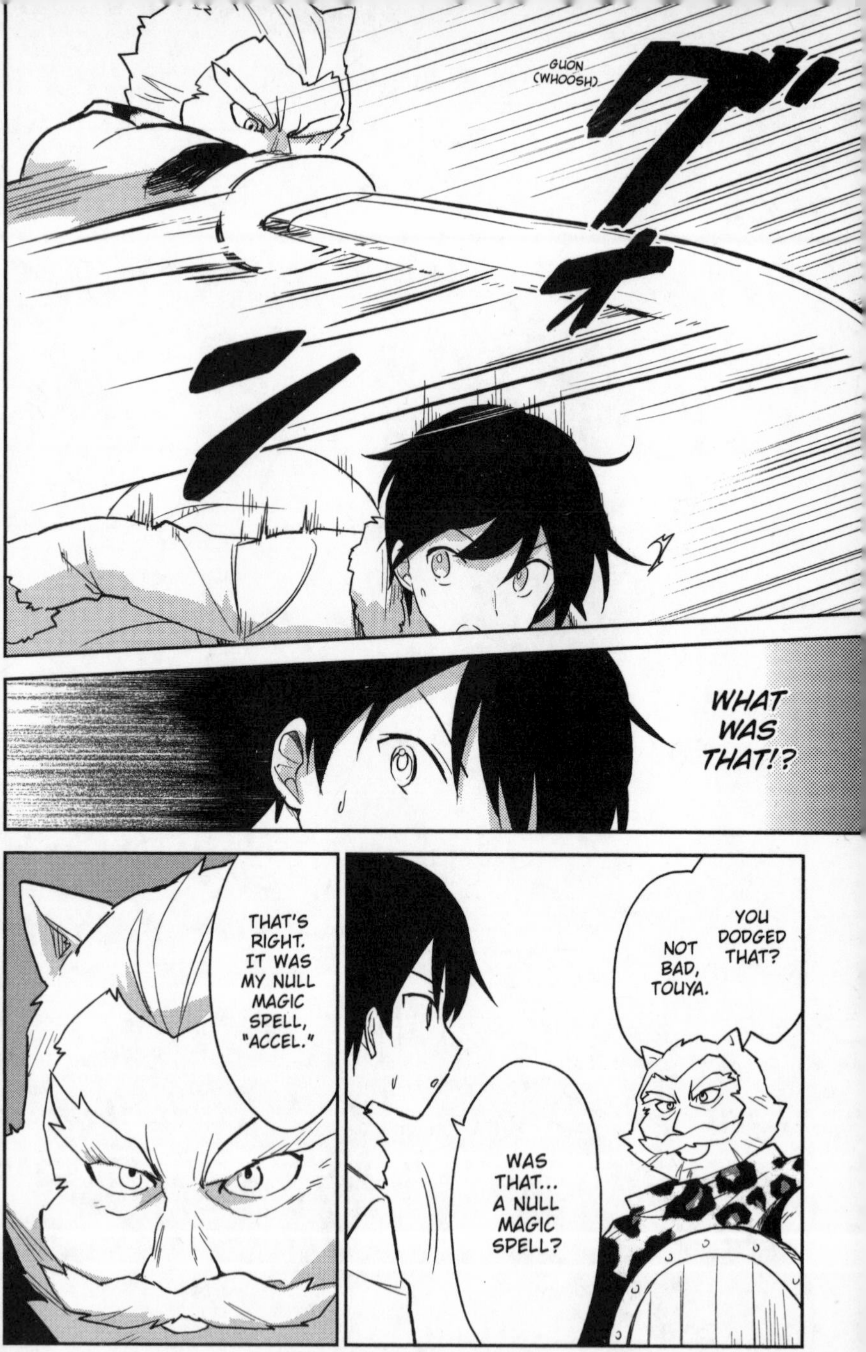
GUON (WHOOSH)
WHAT WAS THAT!?
YOU DODGED THAT?
NOT BAD, TOUYA.
WAS THAT... A NULL MAGIC SPELL?
THAT'S RIGHT. IT WAS MY NULL MAGIC SPELL, "ACCEL."

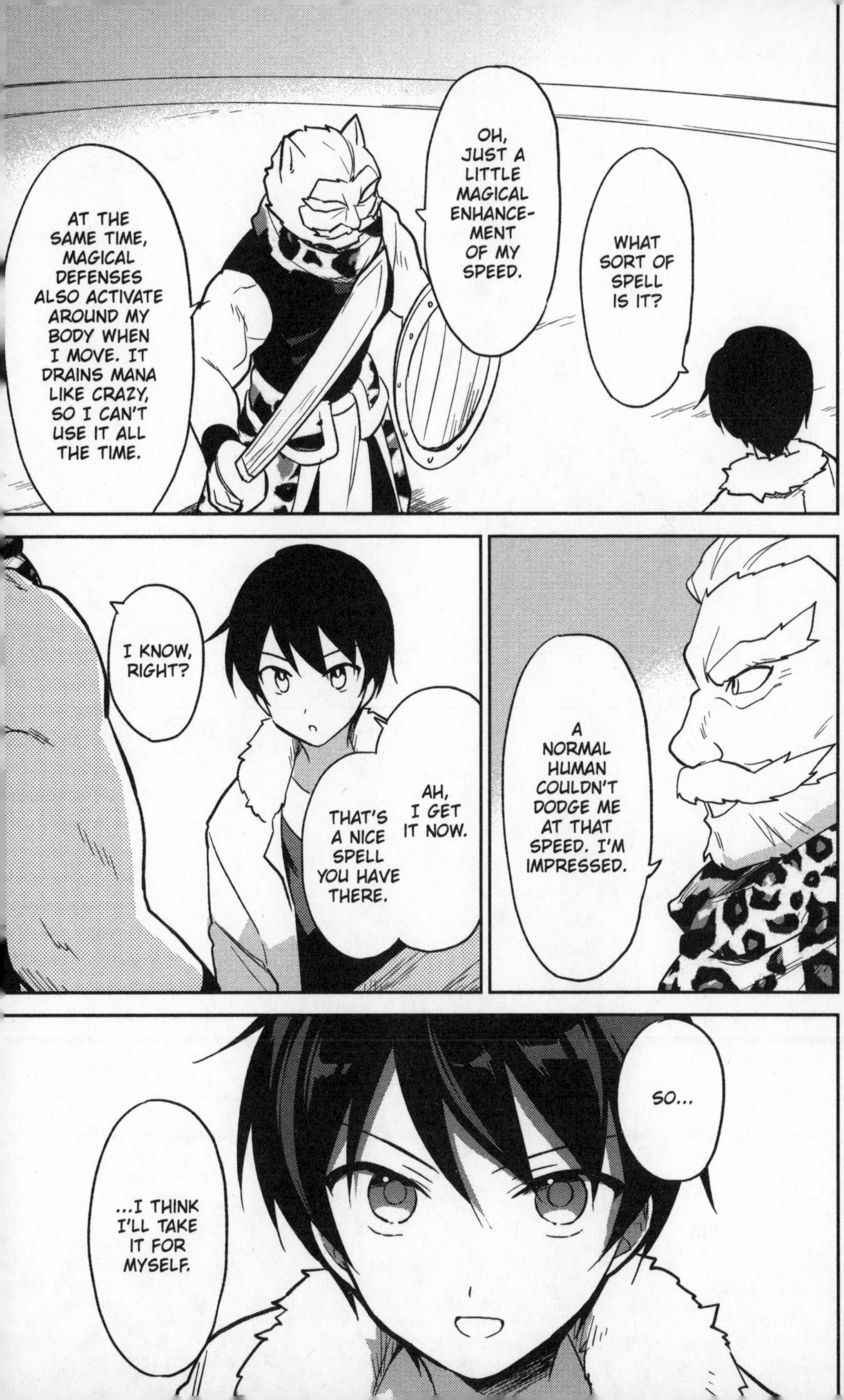
WHAT SORT OF SPELL IS IT?
OH, JUST A LITTLE MAGICAL ENHANCE-MENT OF MY SPEED.
AT THE SAME TIME, MAGICAL DEFENSES ALSO ACTIVATE AROUND MY BODY WHEN I MOVE. IT DRAINS MANA LIKE CRAZY, SO I CAN'T USE IT ALL THE TIME.
A NORMAL HUMAN COULDN'T DODGE ME AT THAT SPEED. I'M IMPRESSED.
AH, I GET IT NOW.
THAT'S A NICE SPELL YOU HAVE THERE.
I KNOW, RIGHT?
SO...
...I THINK I'LL TAKE IT FOR MYSELF.

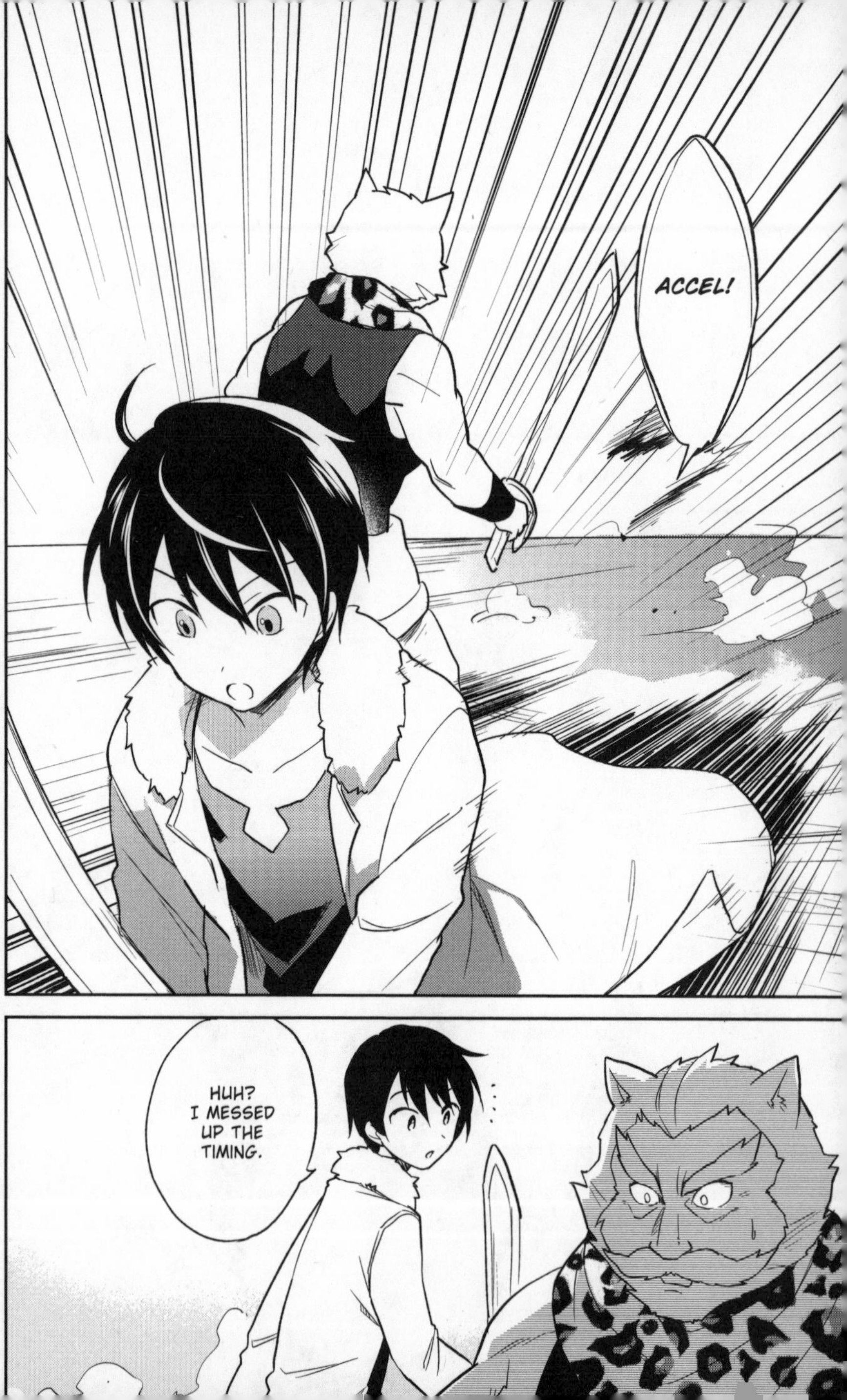
ACCEL!
HUH? I MESSED UP THE TIMING.

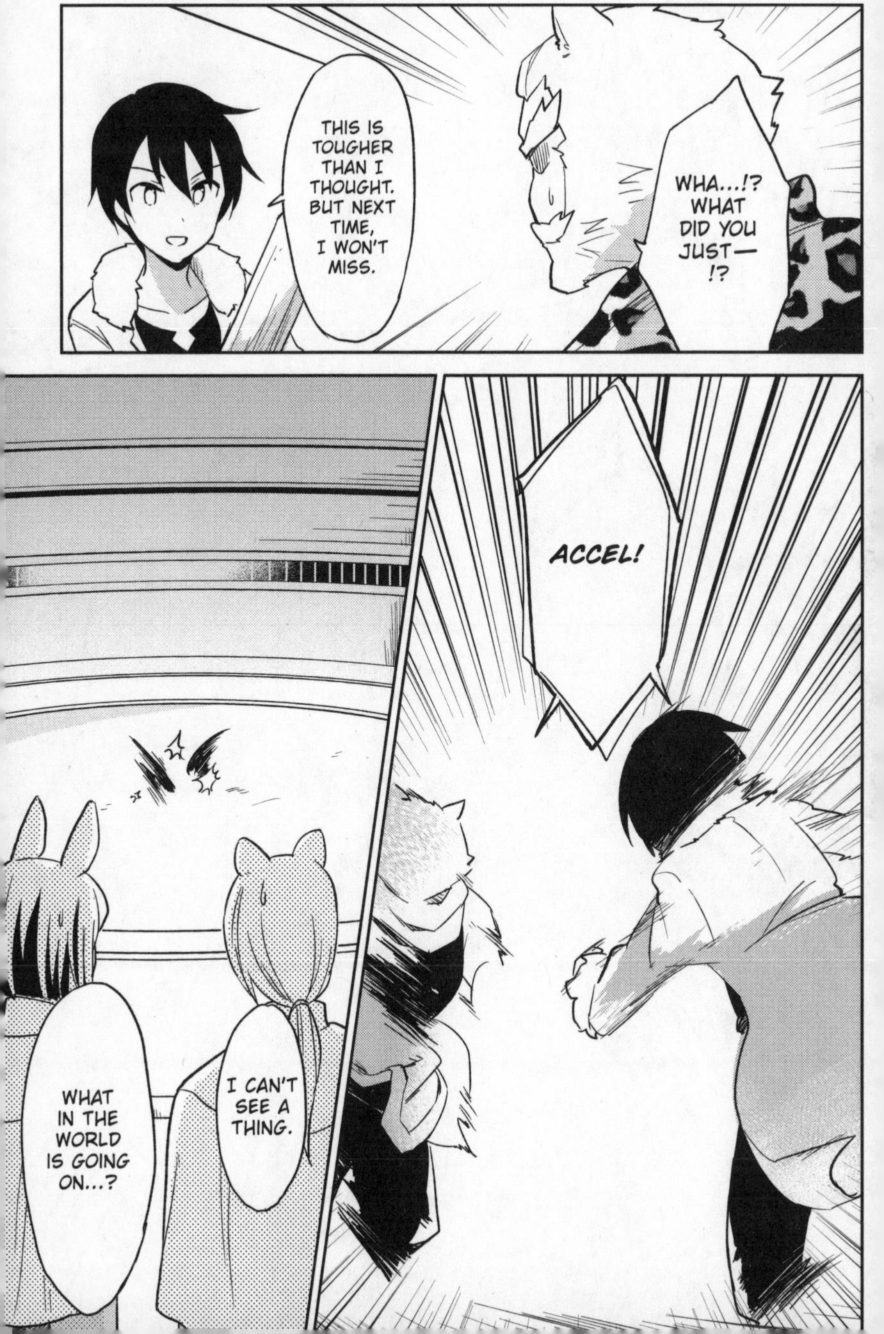
WHA...!? WHAT DID YOU JUST—!?
THIS IS TOUGHER THAN I THOUGHT. BUT NEXT TIME, I WON'T MISS.
ACCEL!
I CAN'T SEE A THING.
WHAT IN THE WORLD IS GOING ON...?

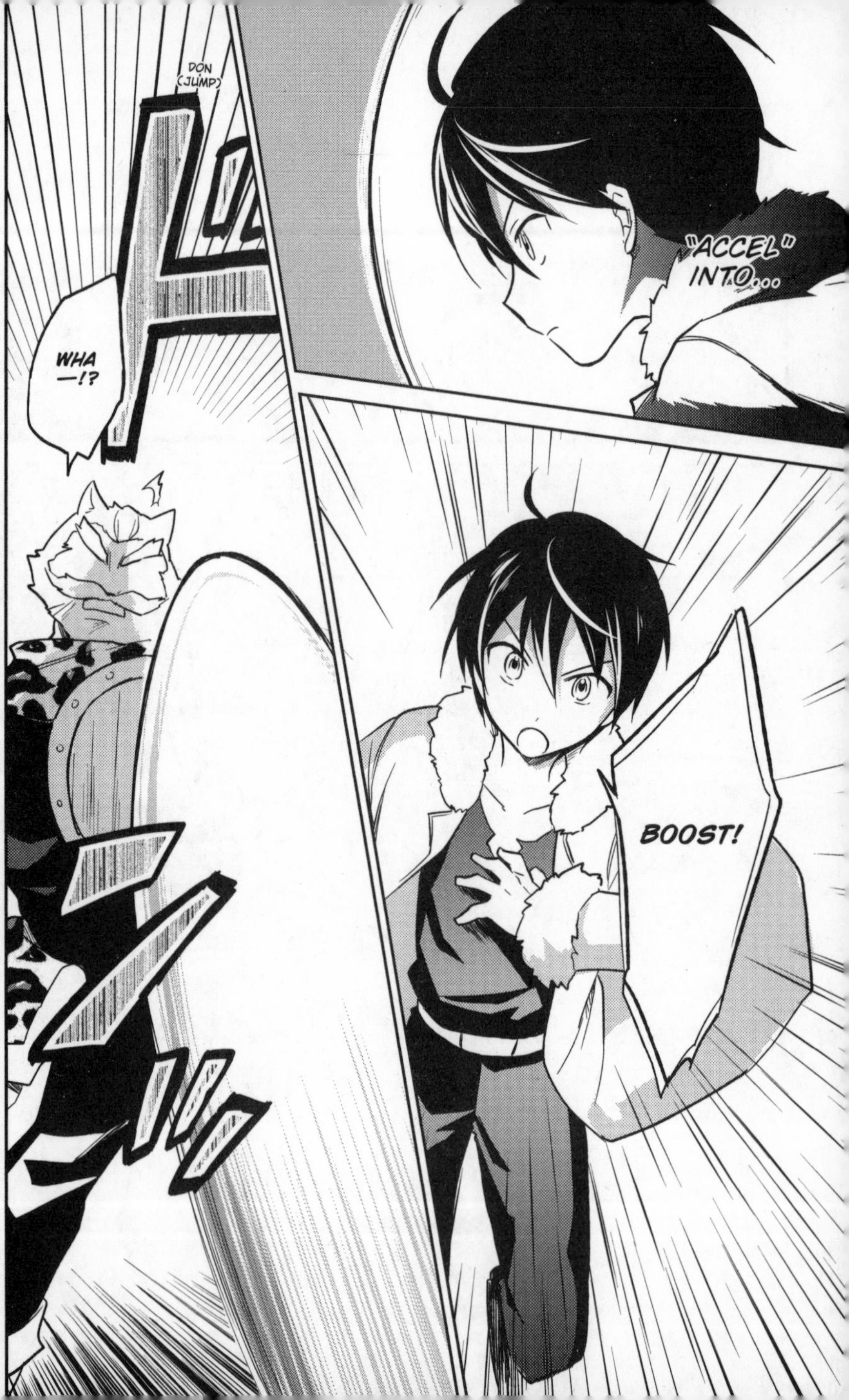
"ACCEL" INTO...
BOOST!
DON (JUMP)
WHA—!?

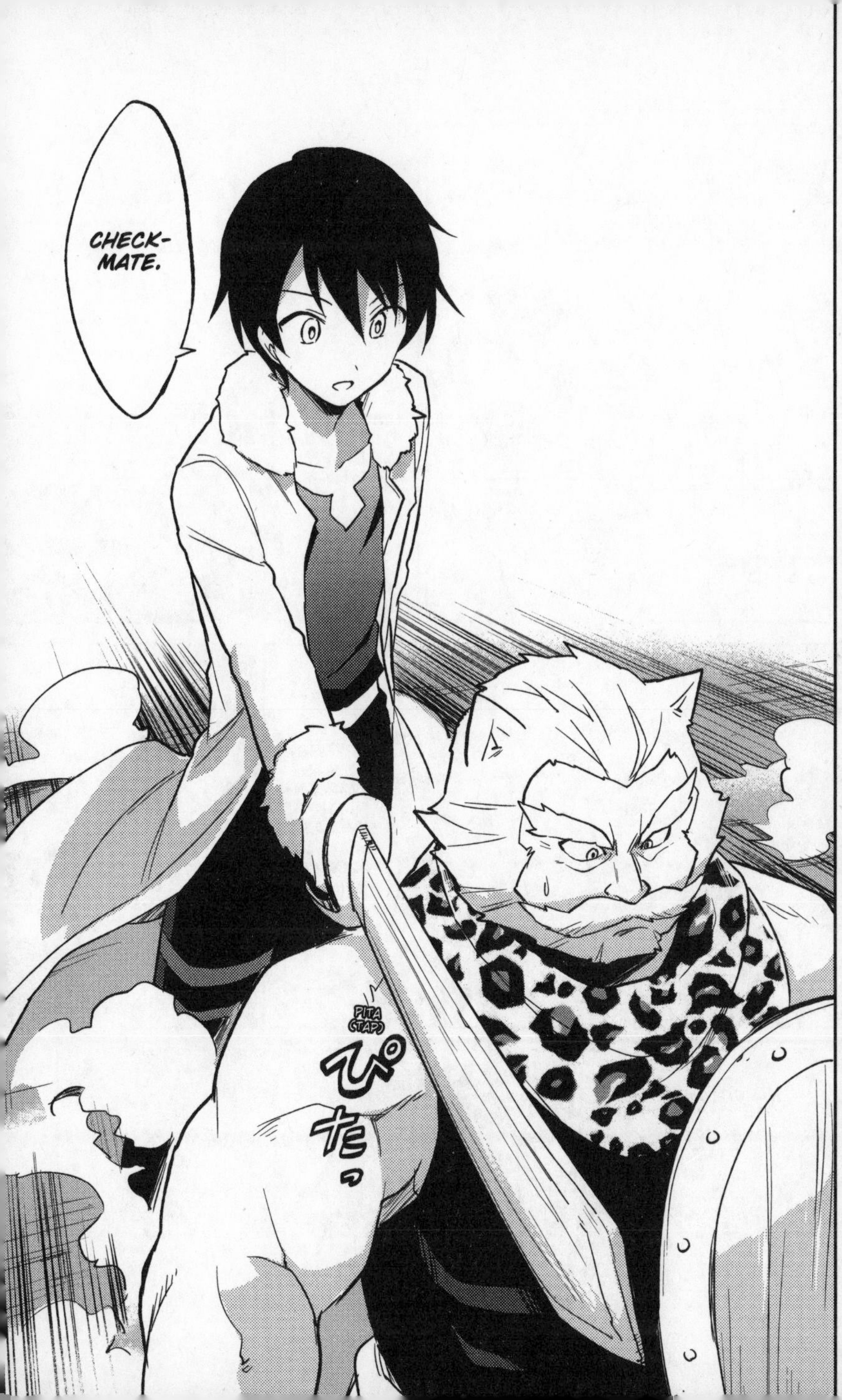
CHECK-
MATE.
PITA
(TAP)
ぴたっ

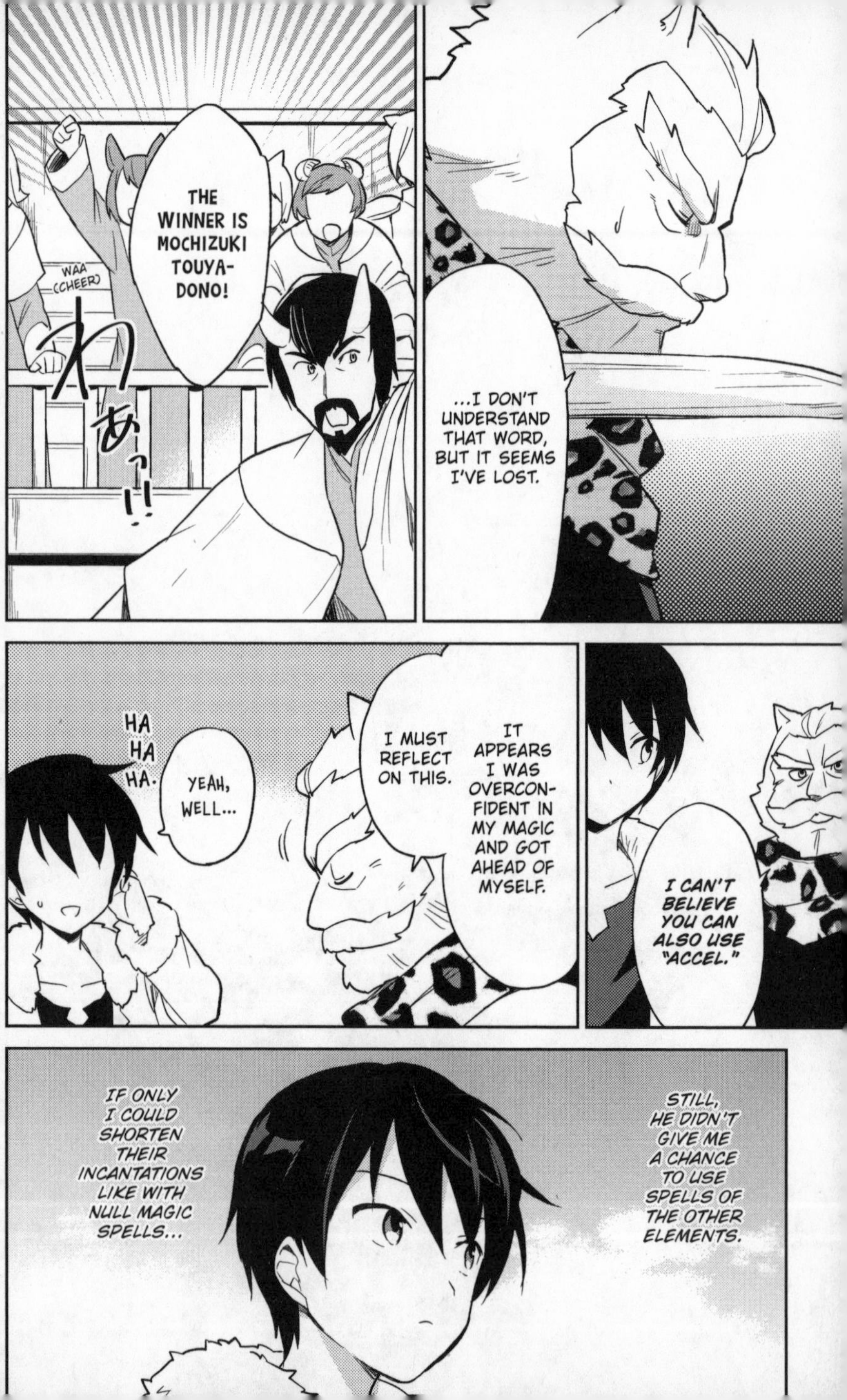
...I DON'T UNDERSTAND THAT WORD, BUT IT SEEMS I'VE LOST.
THE WINNER IS MOCHIZUKI TOUYA-DONO!
WAA (CHEER)
わあっ!!
I CAN'T BELIEVE YOU CAN ALSO USE "ACCEL."
IT APPEARS I WAS OVERCONFIDENT IN MY MAGIC AND GOT AHEAD OF MYSELF.
I MUST REFLECT ON THIS.
HA HA HA.
YEAH, WELL...
STILL, HE DIDN'T GIVE ME A CHANCE TO USE SPELLS OF THE OTHER ELEMENTS.
IF ONLY I COULD SHORTEN THEIR INCANTATIONS LIKE WITH NULL MAGIC SPELLS...

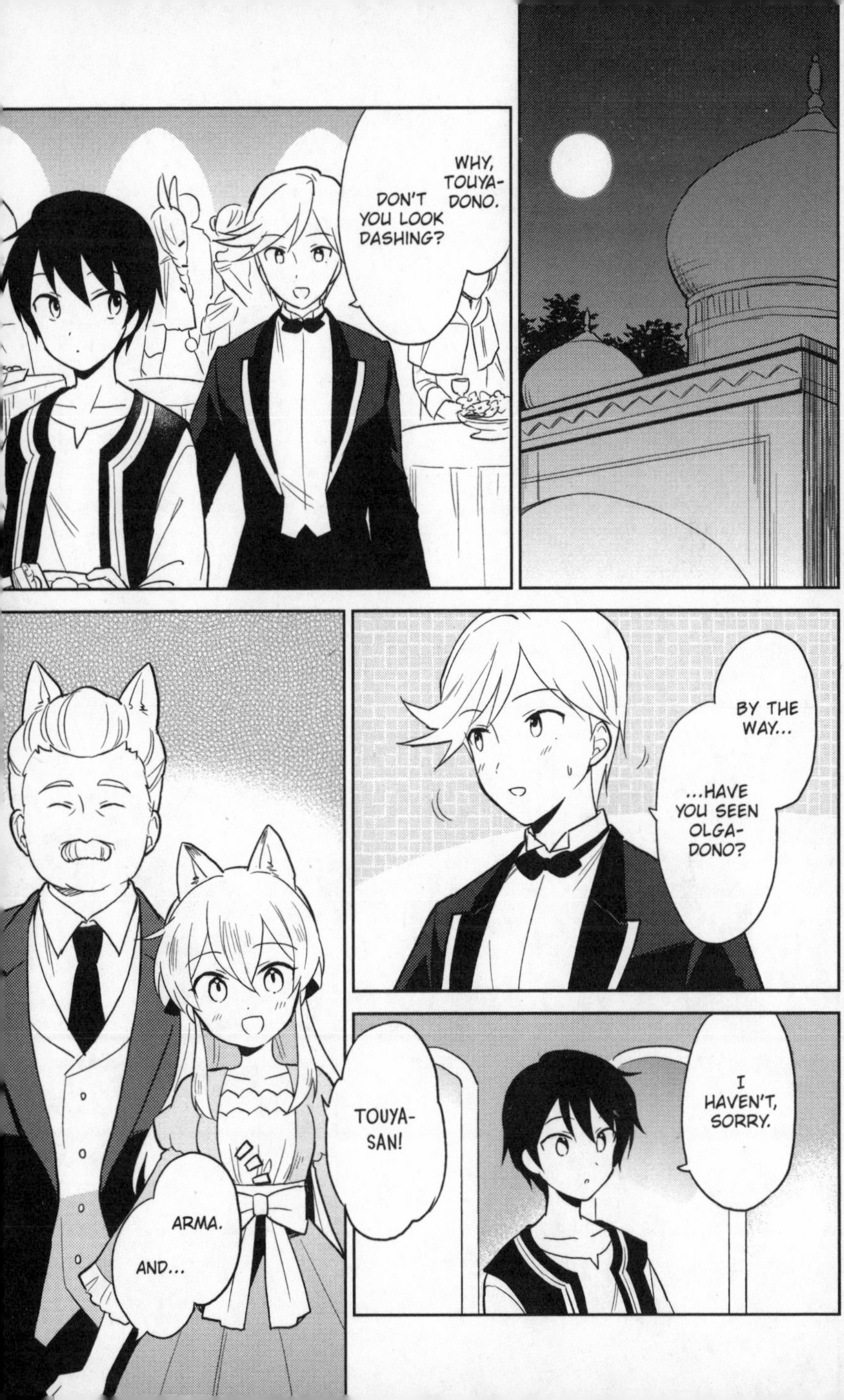
WHY, TOUYA-DONO. DON'T YOU LOOK DASHING?
BY THE WAY...
...HAVE YOU SEEN OLGA-DONO?
I HAVEN'T, SORRY.
TOUYA-SAN!
ARMA. AND...

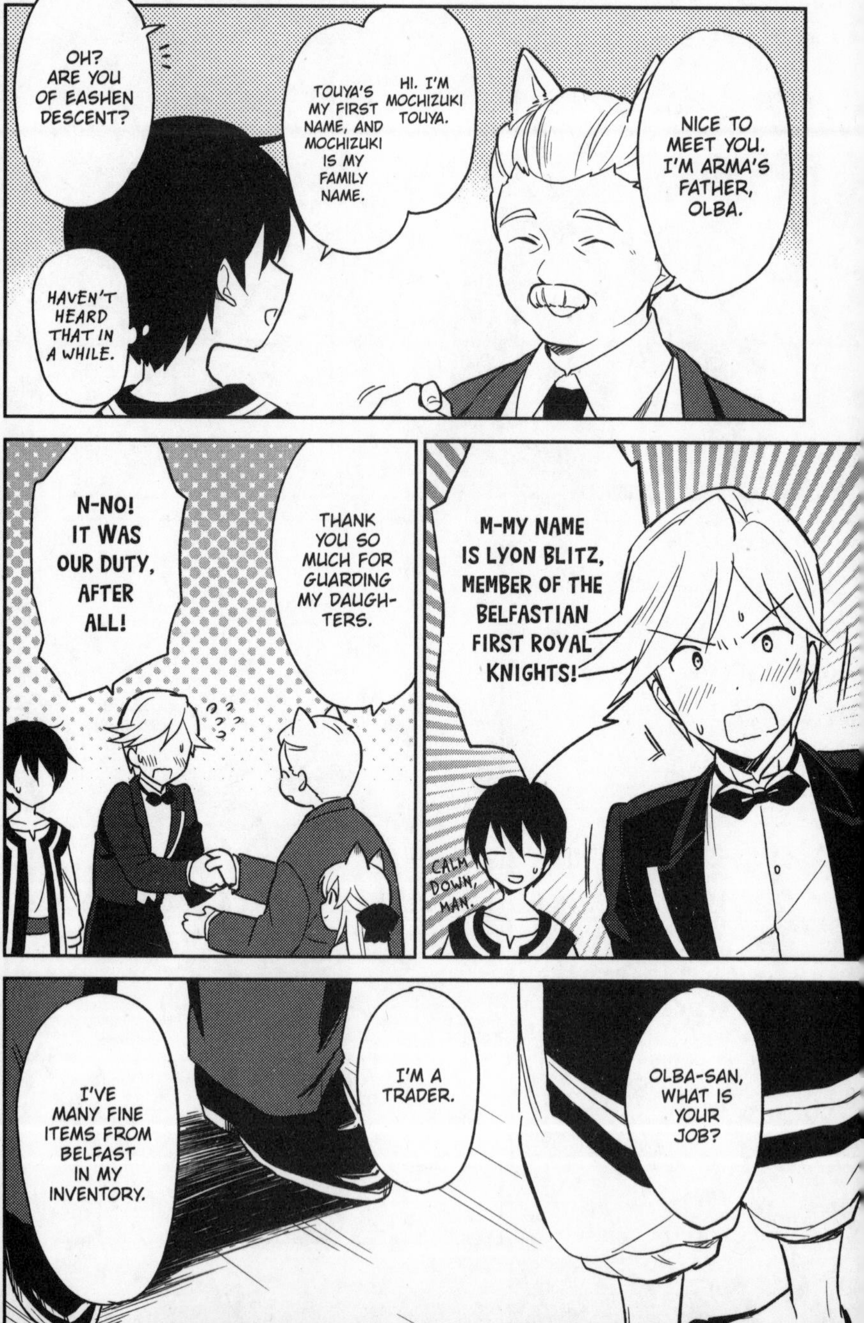
NICE TO MEET YOU. I'M ARMA'S FATHER, OLBA.
HI. I'M MOCHIZUKI TOUYA.
TOUYA'S MY FIRST NAME, AND MOCHIZUKI IS MY FAMILY NAME.
OH? ARE YOU OF EASHEN DESCENT?
HAVEN'T HEARD THAT IN A WHILE.
M-MY NAME IS LYON BLITZ, MEMBER OF THE BELFASTIAN FIRST ROYAL KNIGHTS!
CALM DOWN, MAN.
THANK YOU SO MUCH FOR GUARDING MY DAUGH-TERS.
N-NO! IT WAS OUR DUTY, AFTER ALL!
OLBA-SAN, WHAT IS YOUR JOB?
I'M A TRADER.
I'VE MANY FINE ITEMS FROM BELFAST IN MY INVENTORY.

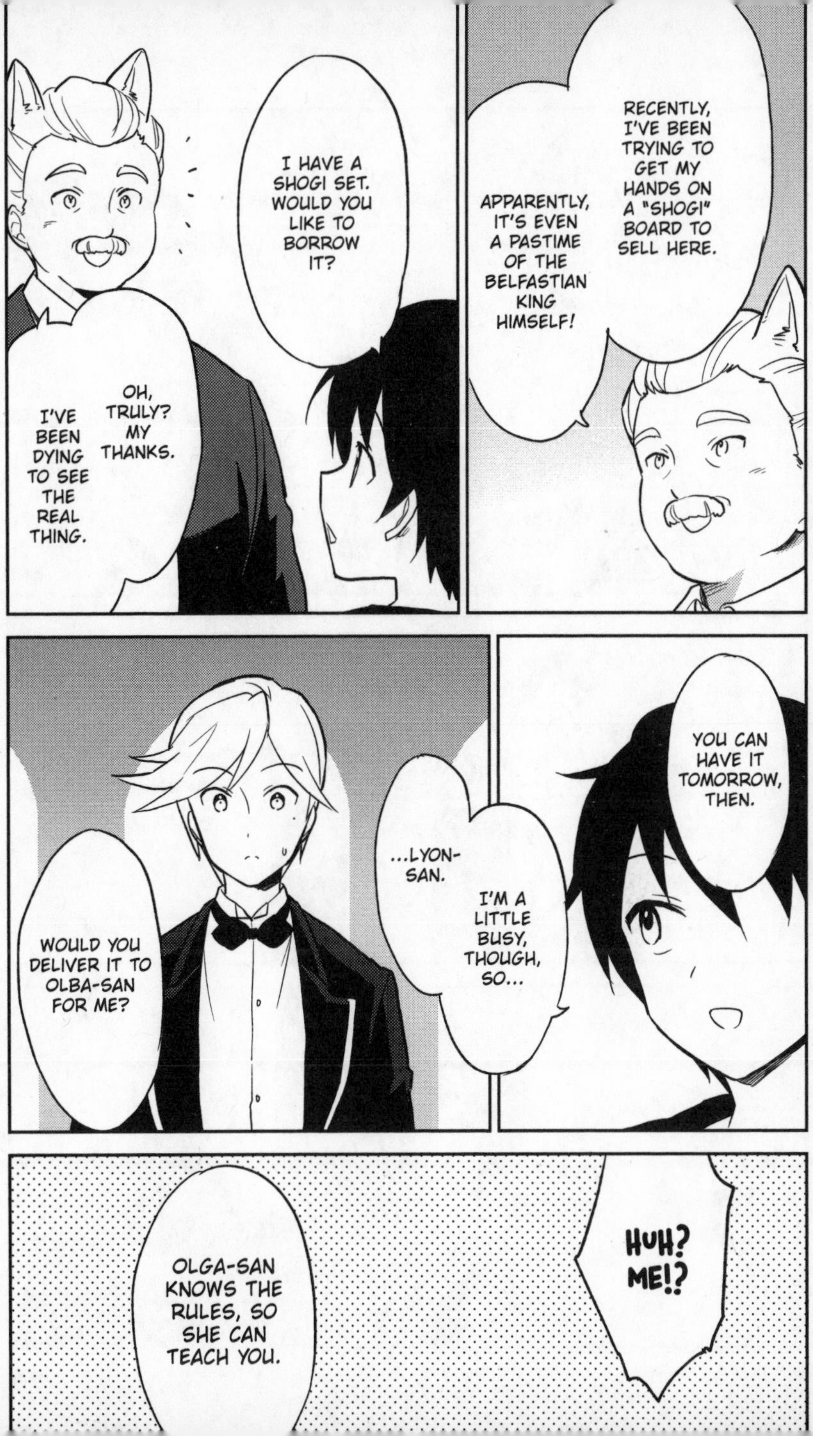
RECENTLY, I'VE BEEN TRYING TO GET MY HANDS ON A "SHOGI" BOARD TO SELL HERE.
APPARENTLY, IT'S EVEN A PASTIME OF THE BELFASTIAN KING HIMSELF!
I HAVE A SHOGI SET. WOULD YOU LIKE TO BORROW IT?
OH, TRULY? MY THANKS.
I'VE BEEN DYING TO SEE THE REAL THING.
YOU CAN HAVE IT TOMORROW, THEN.
...LYON-SAN.
I'M A LITTLE BUSY, THOUGH, SO...
WOULD YOU DELIVER IT TO OLBA-SAN FOR ME?
HUH? ME!?
OLGA-SAN KNOWS THE RULES, SO SHE CAN TEACH YOU.

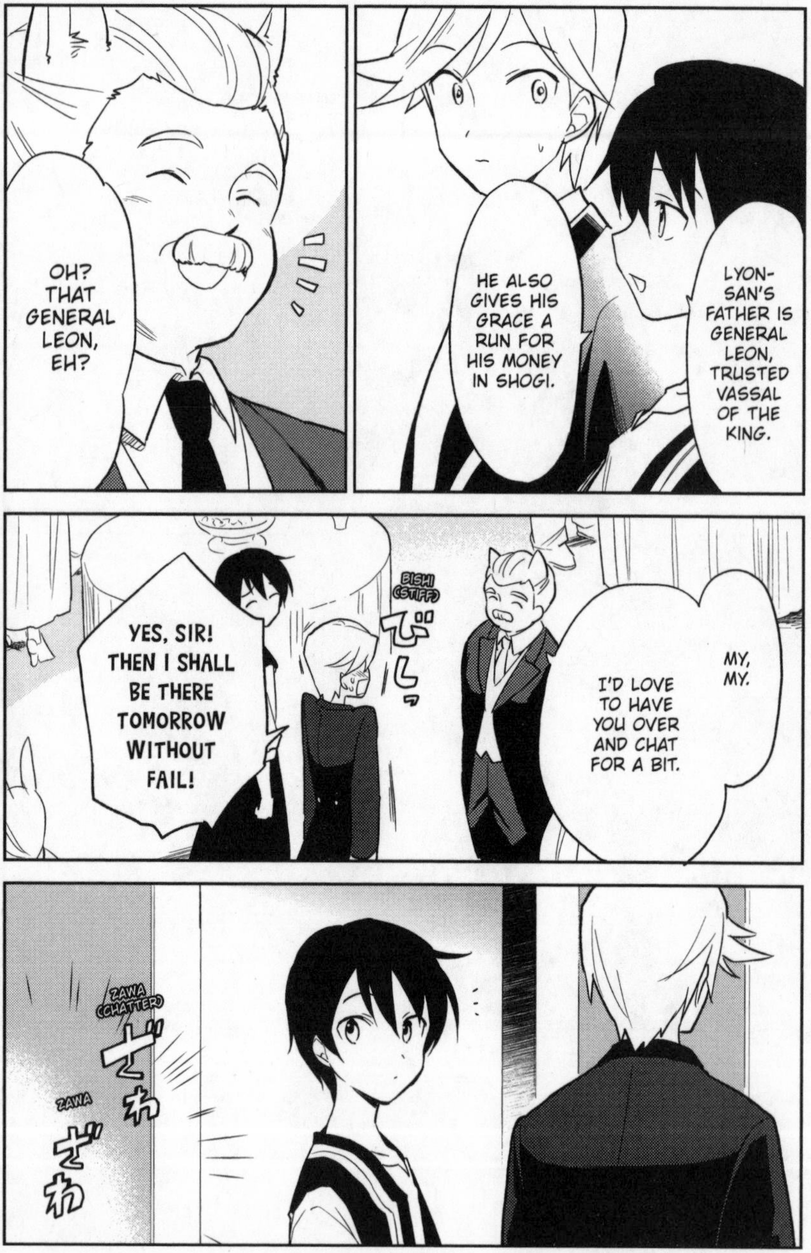
LYON-SAN'S FATHER IS GENERAL LEON, TRUSTED VASSAL OF THE KING.
HE ALSO GIVES HIS GRACE A RUN FOR HIS MONEY IN SHOGI.
OH? THAT GENERAL LEON, EH?
MY, MY.
I'D LOVE TO HAVE YOU OVER AND CHAT FOR A BIT.
BISHI (STIFF)
YES, SIR! THEN I SHALL BE THERE TOMORROW WITHOUT FAIL!
ZAWA (CHATTER)
ZAWA

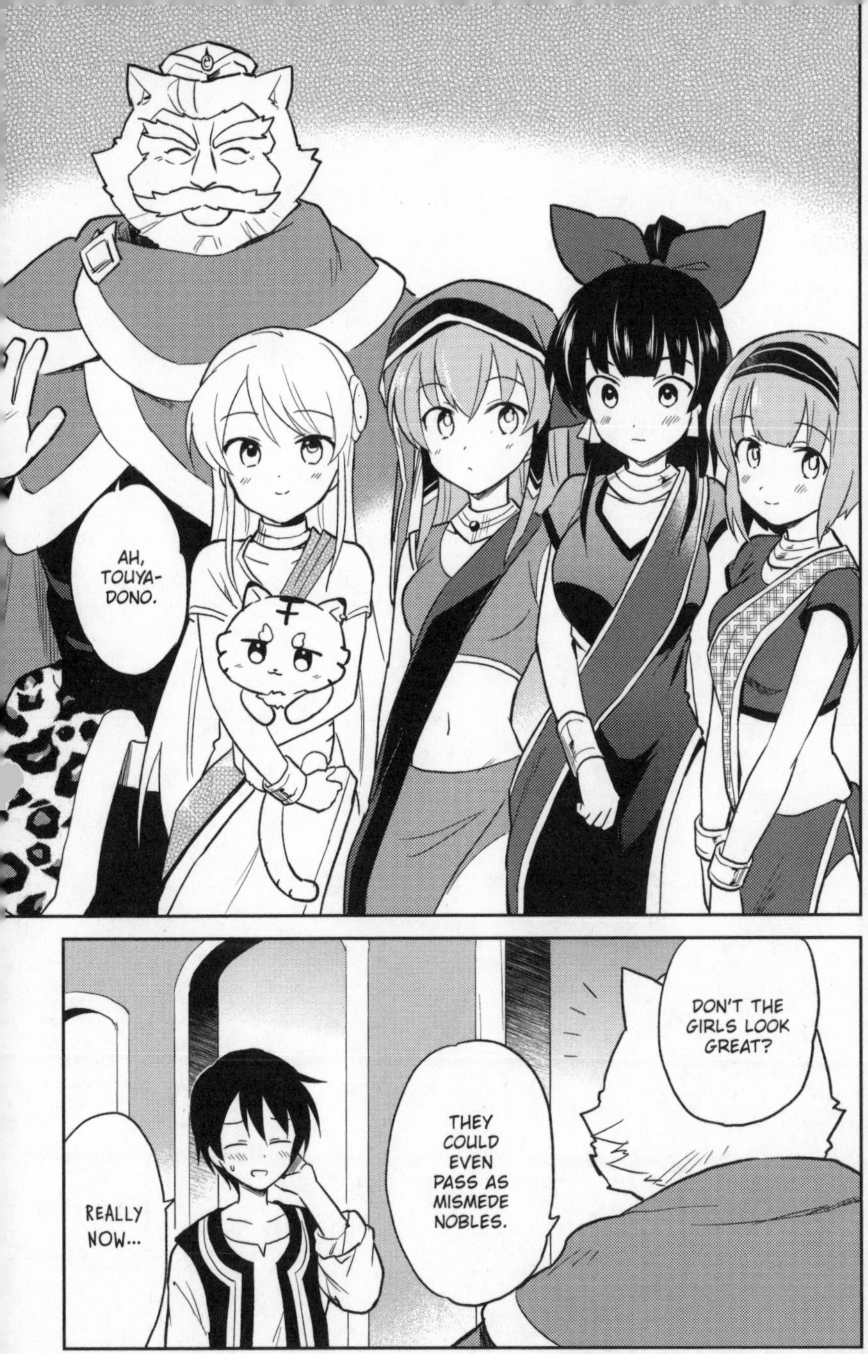
AH, TOUYA-DONO.
DON'T THE GIRLS LOOK GREAT?
THEY COULD EVEN PASS AS MISMEDE NOBLES.
REALLY NOW...

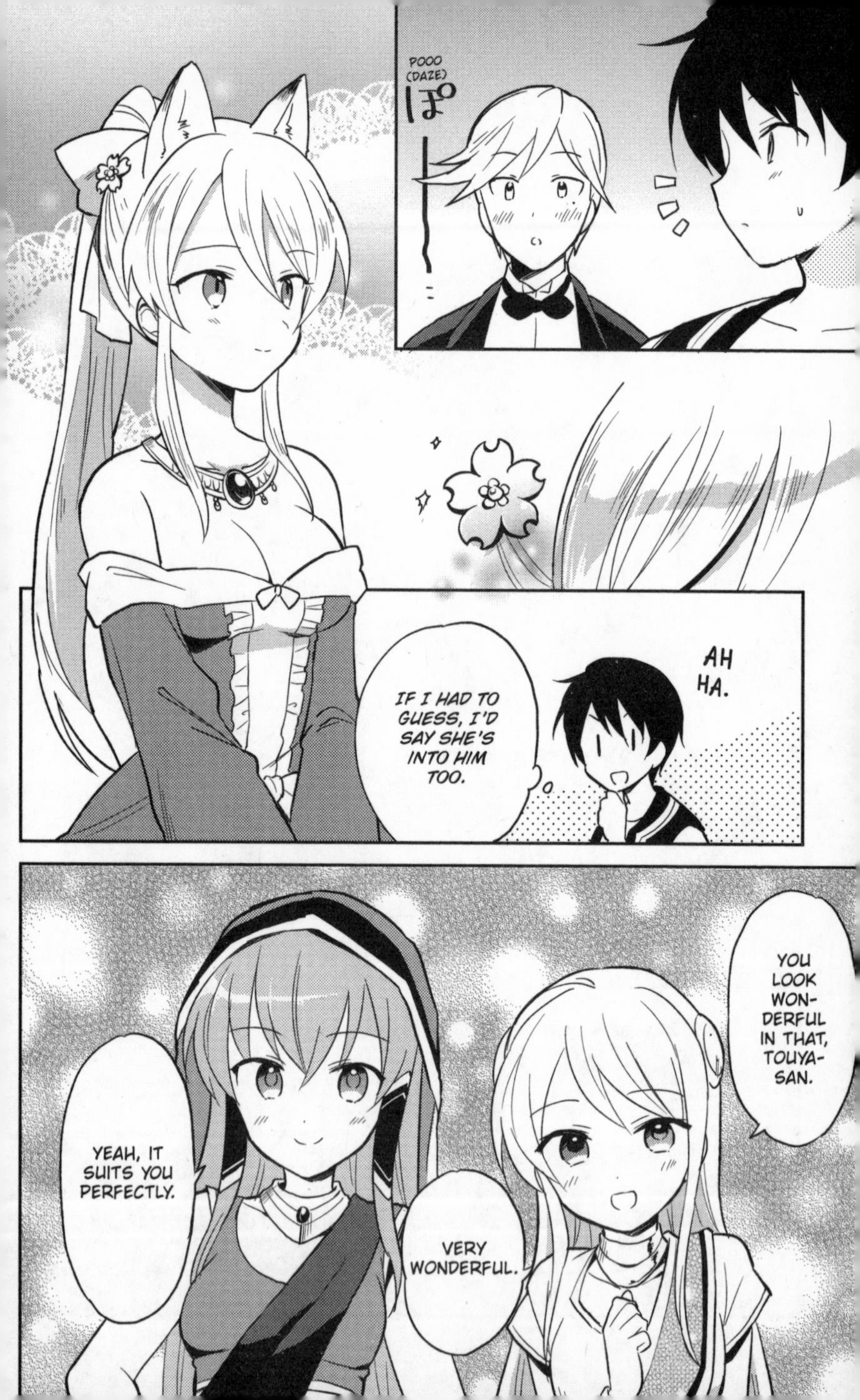
POOO (DAZE)
ぽー
AH HA.
IF I HAD TO GUESS, I'D SAY SHE'S INTO HIM TOO.
YOU LOOK WON-DERFUL IN THAT, TOUYA-SAN.
VERY WONDERFUL.
YEAH, IT SUITS YOU PERFECTLY.

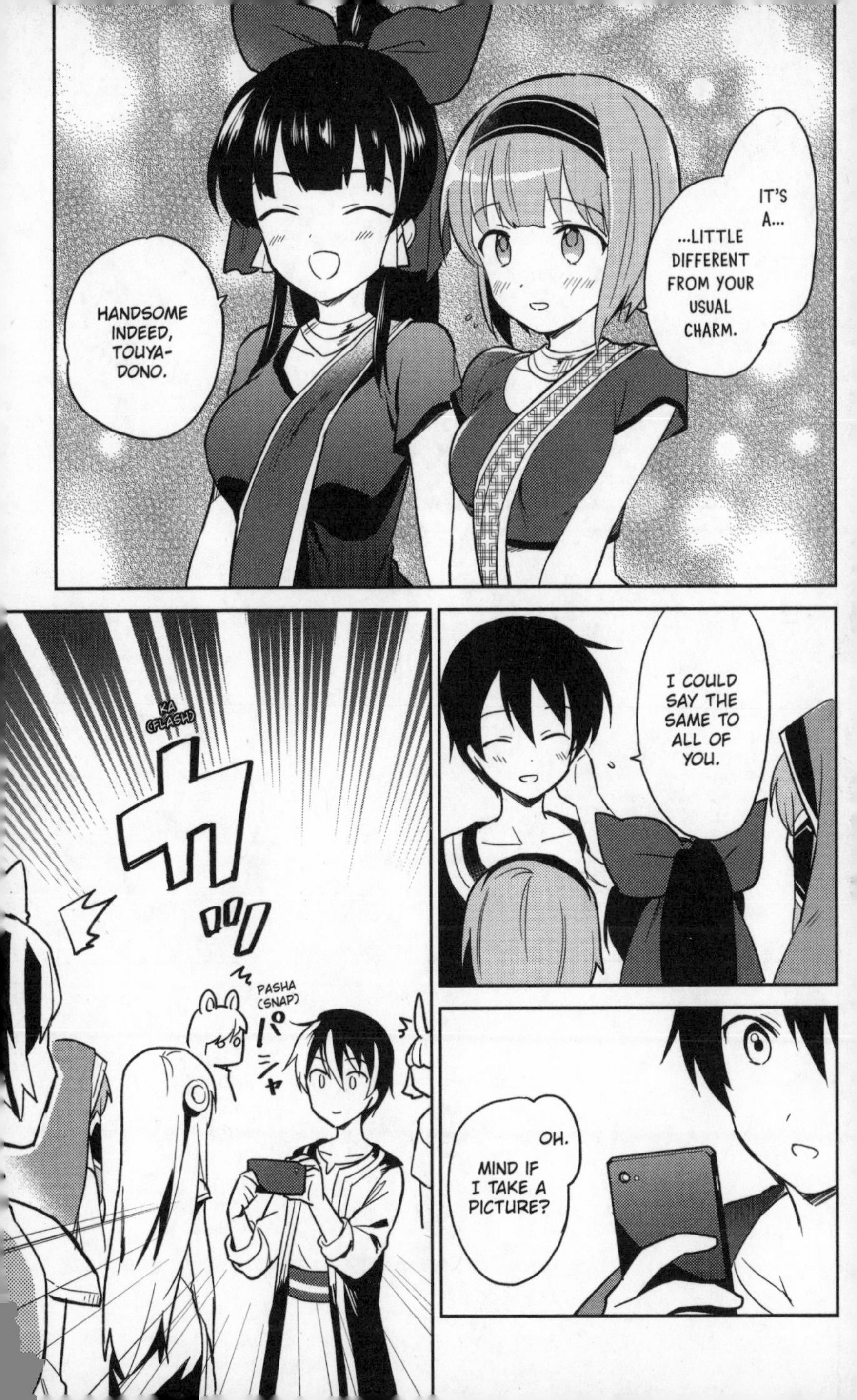
IT'S A... ...LITTLE DIFFERENT FROM YOUR USUAL CHARM.
HANDSOME INDEED, TOUYA-DONO.
I COULD SAY THE SAME TO ALL OF YOU.
OH.
MIND IF I TAKE A PICTURE?
KA (FLASH)
PASHA (SNAP)

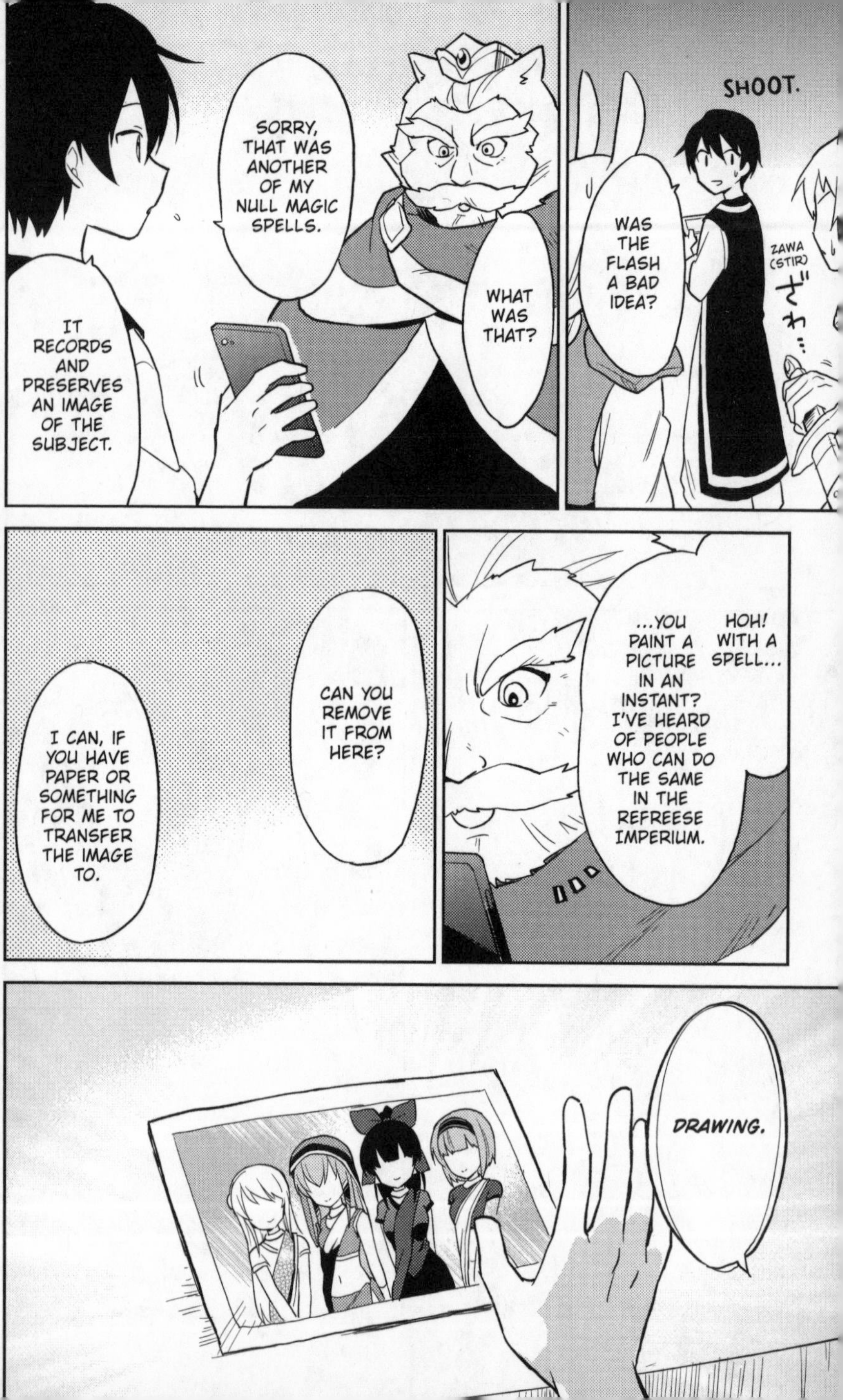
SHOOT.
WAS THE FLASH A BAD IDEA?
ZAWA (STIR)
ざわ…
WHAT WAS THAT?
SORRY, THAT WAS ANOTHER OF MY NULL MAGIC SPELLS.
IT RECORDS AND PRESERVES AN IMAGE OF THE SUBJECT.
HOH! WITH A SPELL...
...YOU PAINT A PICTURE IN AN INSTANT? I'VE HEARD OF PEOPLE WHO CAN DO THE SAME IN THE REFREESE IMPERIUM.
CAN YOU REMOVE IT FROM HERE?
I CAN, IF YOU HAVE PAPER OR SOMETHING FOR ME TO TRANSFER THE IMAGE TO.
DRAWING.

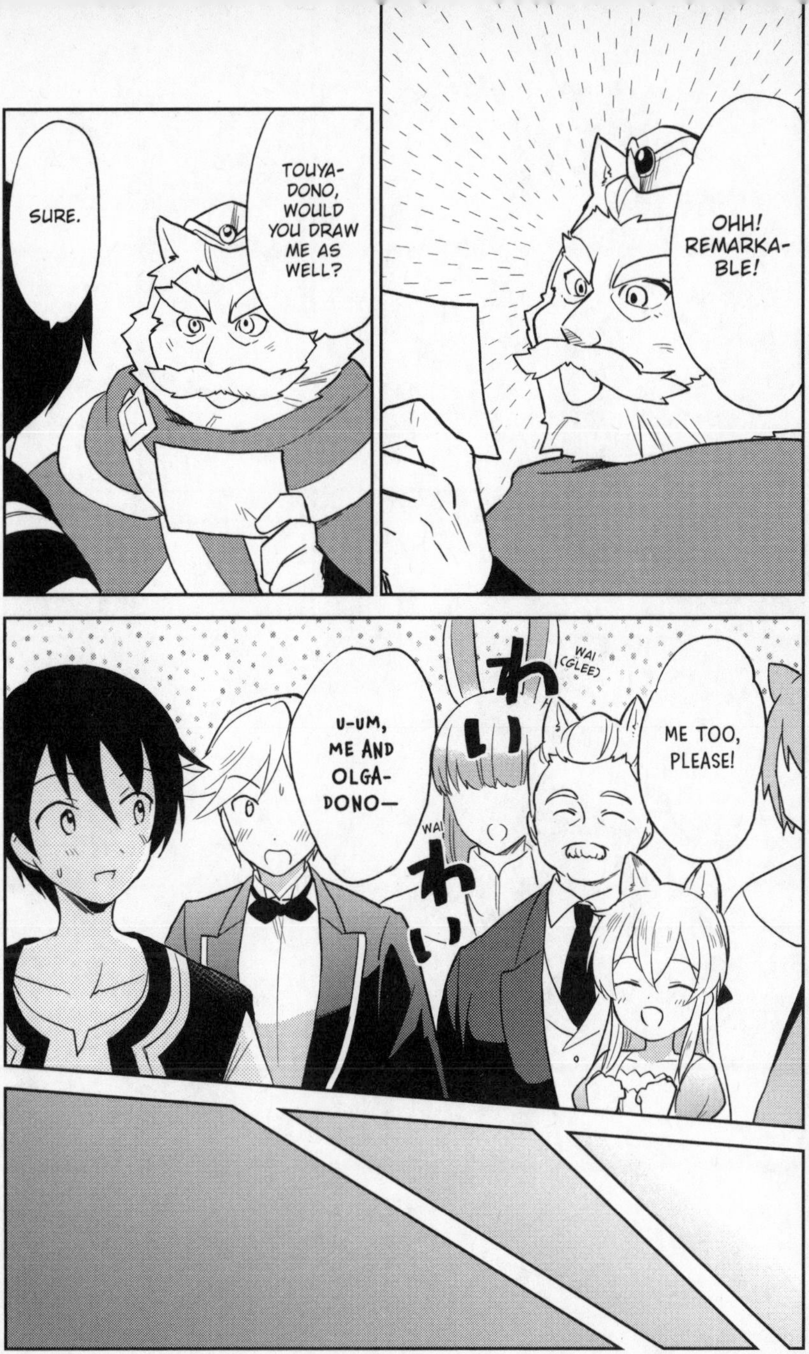
OHH! REMARKA-BLE!
TOUYA-DONO, WOULD YOU DRAW ME AS WELL?
SURE.
ME TOO, PLEASE!
WAI (GLEE)
U-UM, ME AND OLGA-DONO—
WAI

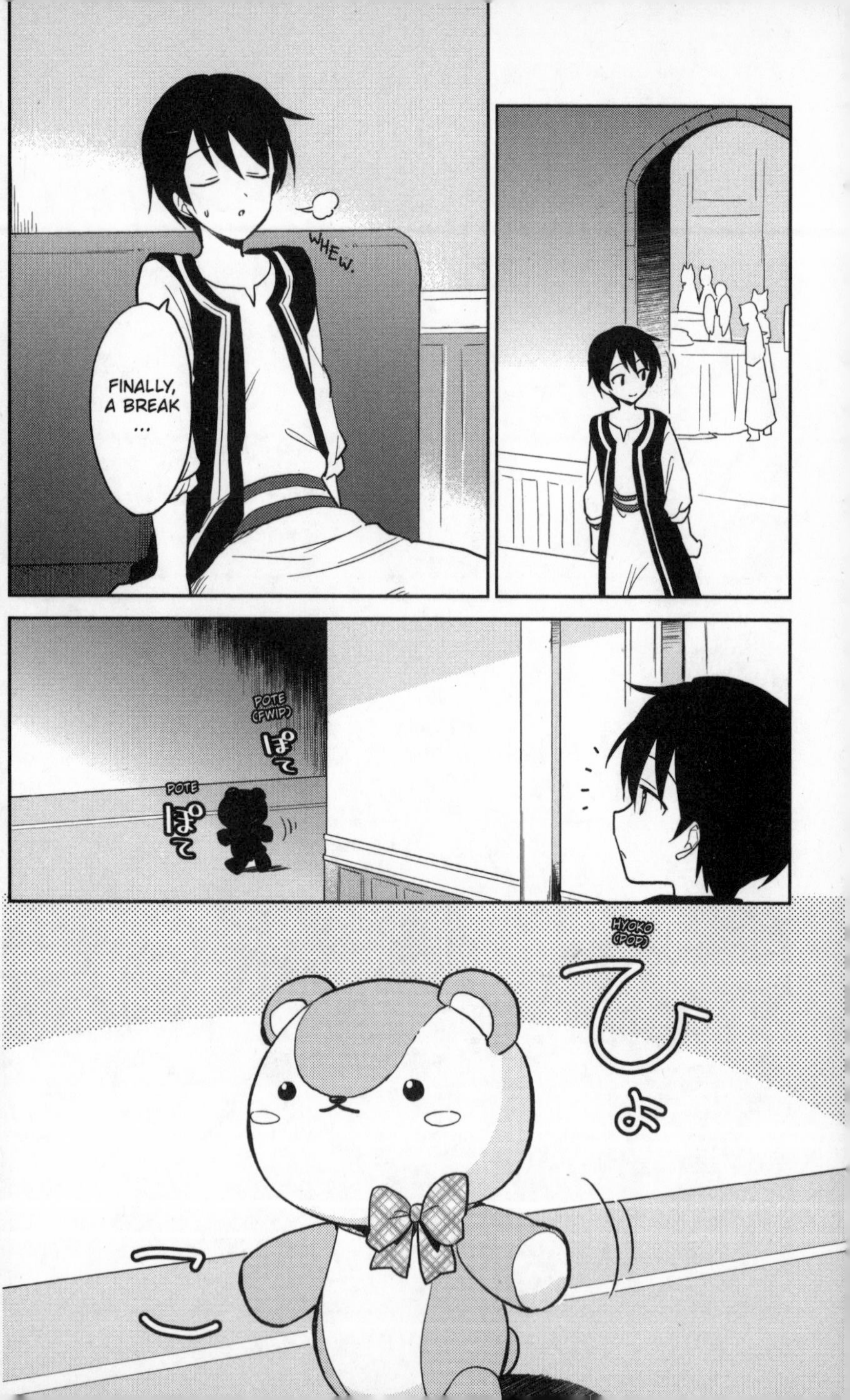
WHEW.
FINALLY, A BREAK...
POTE (FWIP)
ぽて
POTE
ぽて
HYOKO (POP)
ひょ
こ

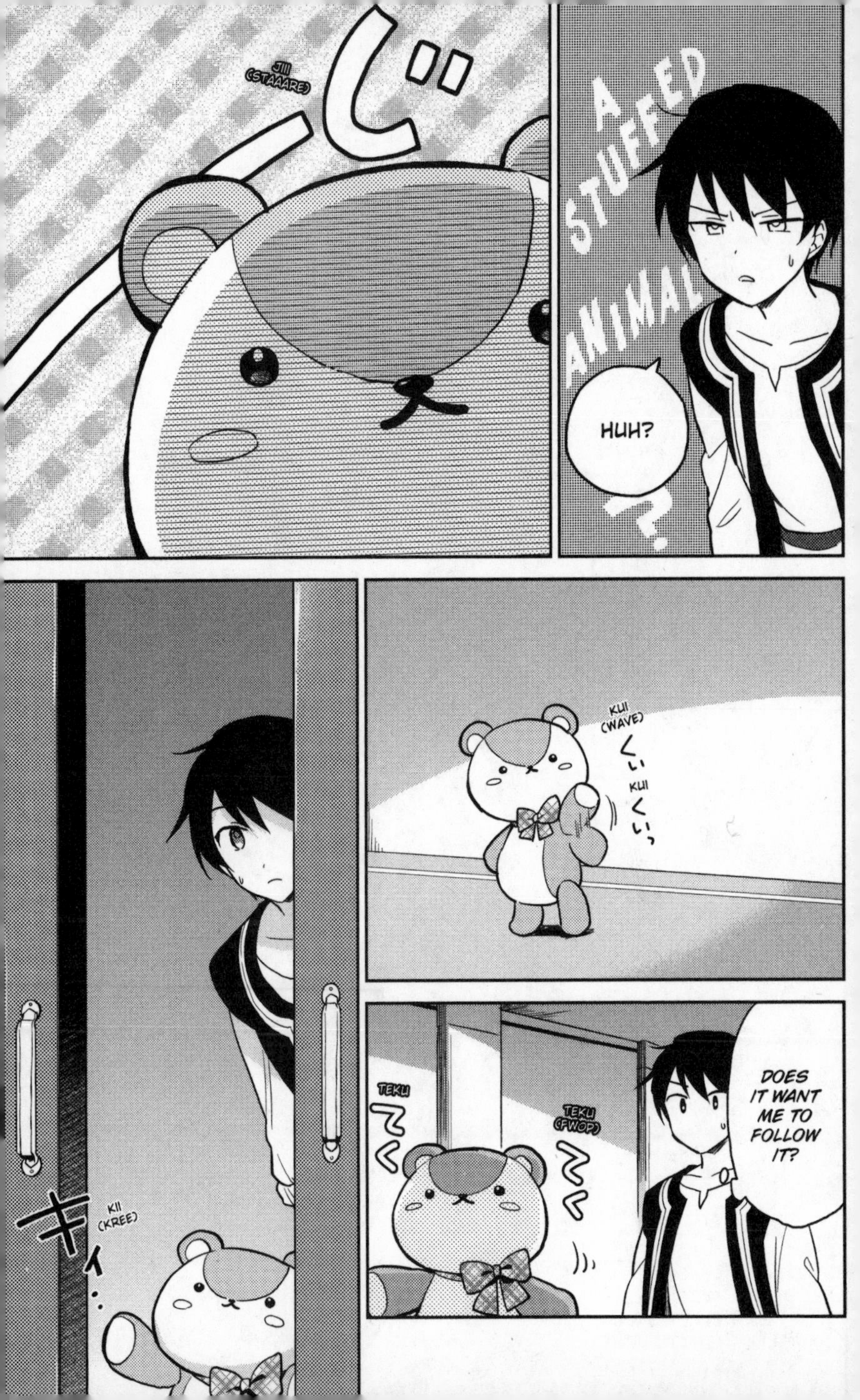
A STUFFED ANIMAL
HUH?
?
JIII (STAAARE)
KUI (WAVE)
KUI
DOES IT WANT ME TO FOLLOW IT?
TEKU (FWOP)
TEKU
KII (KREE)

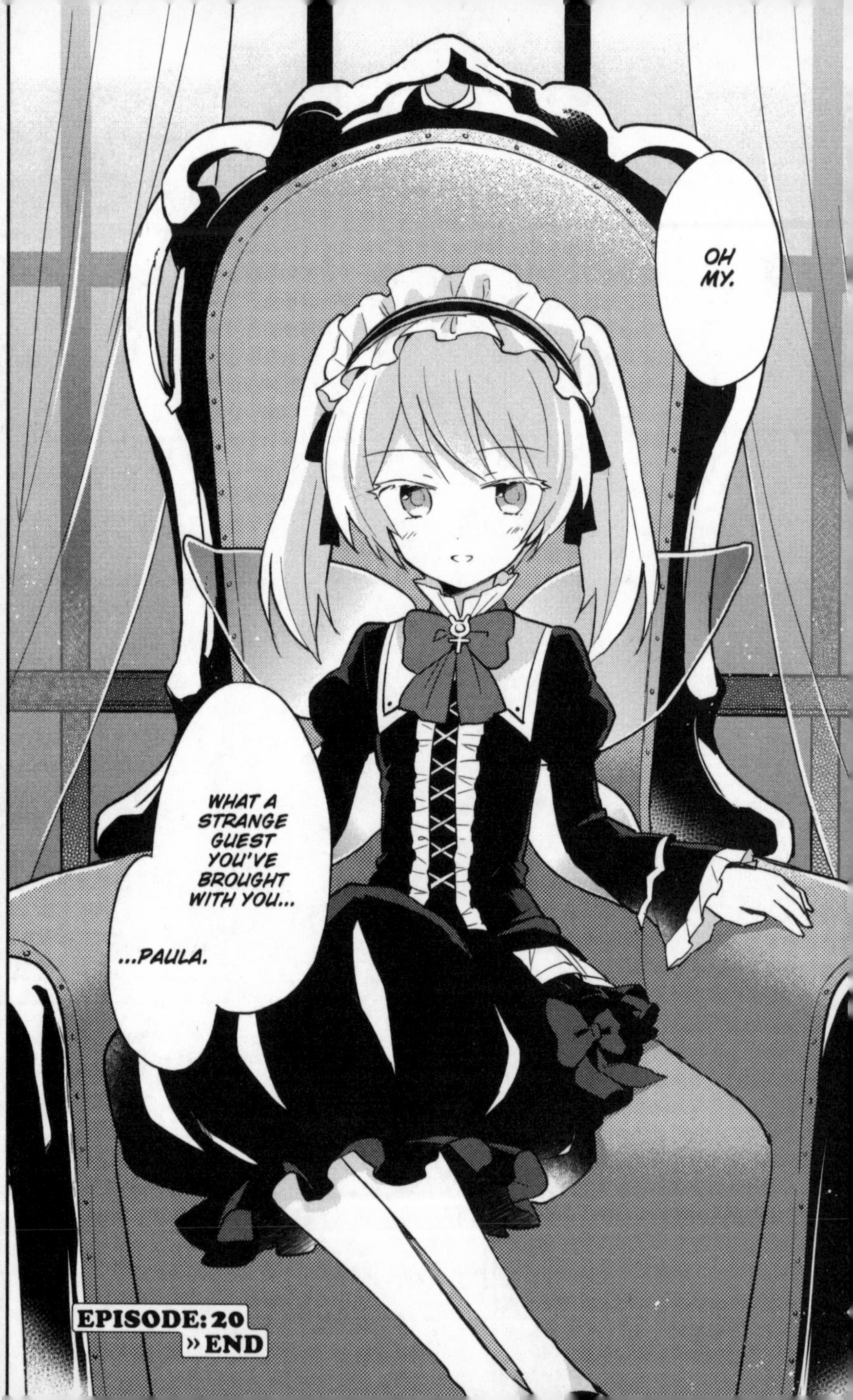
OH MY.
WHAT A STRANGE GUEST YOU'VE BROUGHT WITH YOU...
...PAULA.
EPISODE: 20 » END

In Another World With
My Smartphone

In Another World with my Smartphone

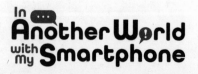

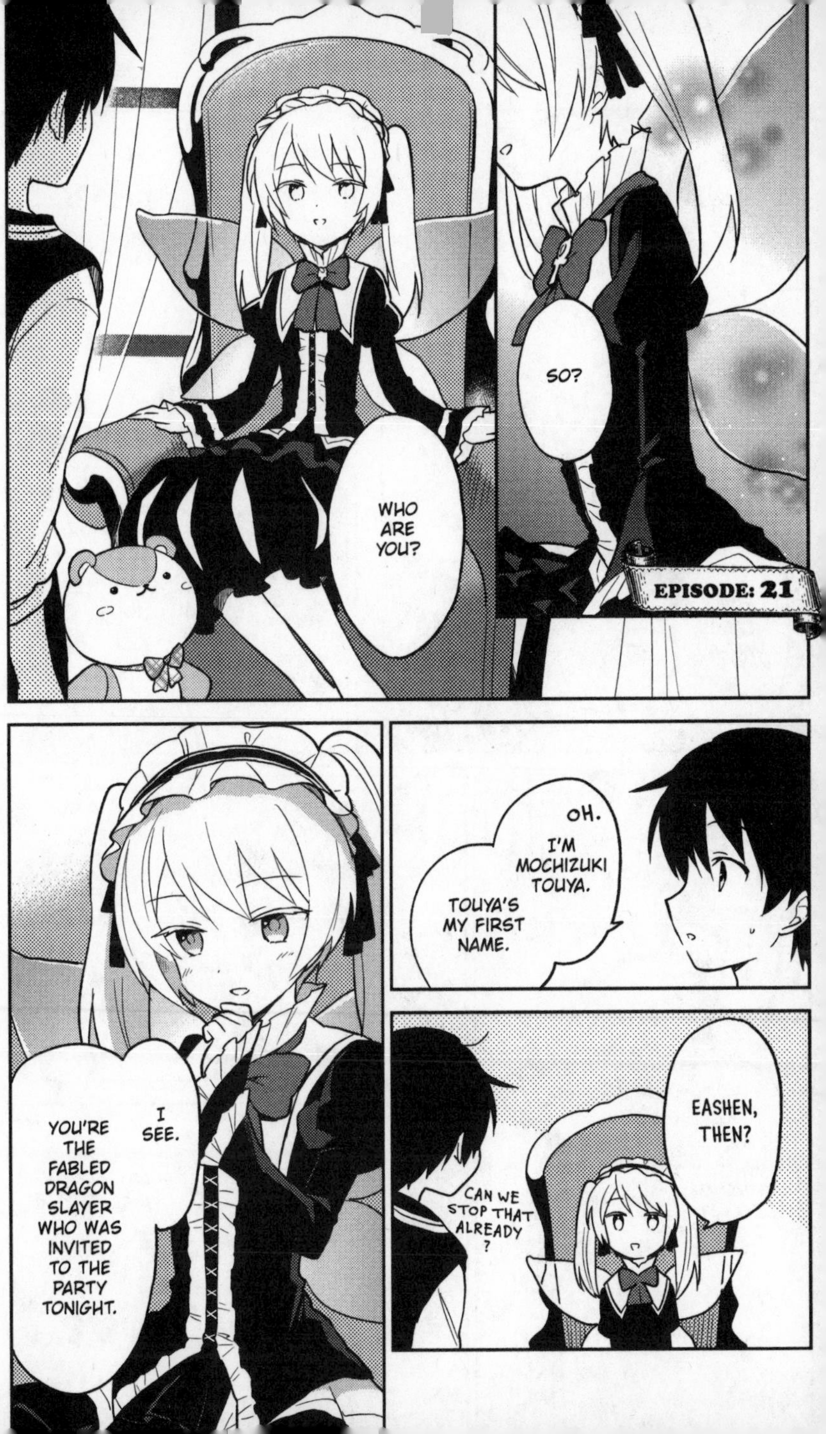
SO?
EPISODE: 21
WHO ARE YOU?
OH.
I'M MOCHIZUKI TOUYA.
TOUYA'S MY FIRST NAME.
EASHEN, THEN?
CAN WE STOP THAT ALREADY?
I SEE.
YOU'RE THE FABLED DRAGON SLAYER WHO WAS INVITED TO THE PARTY TONIGHT.

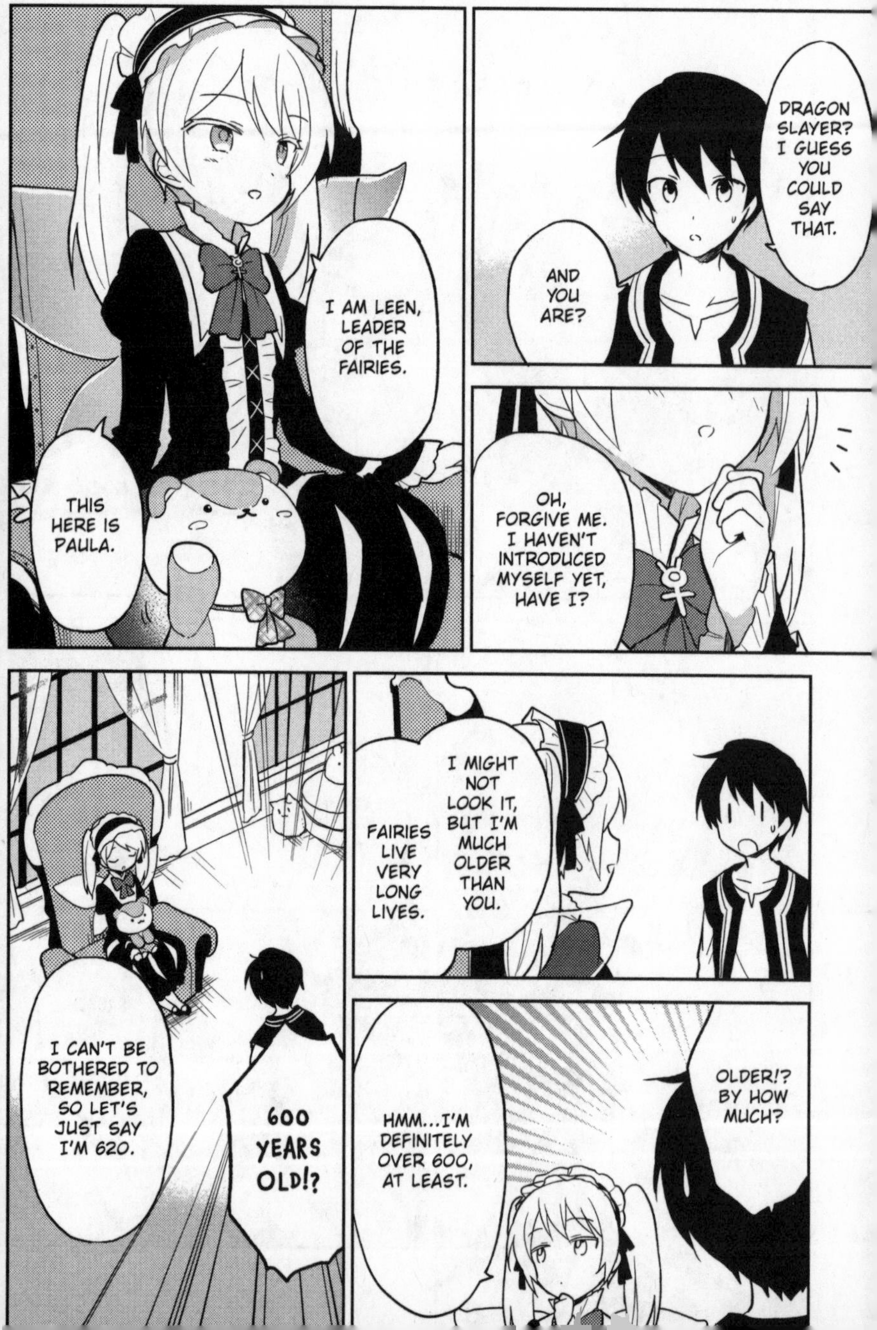
DRAGON SLAYER? I GUESS YOU COULD SAY THAT.
AND YOU ARE?
OH, FORGIVE ME. I HAVEN'T INTRODUCED MYSELF YET, HAVE I?
I AM LEEN, LEADER OF THE FAIRIES.
THIS HERE IS PAULA.
I MIGHT NOT LOOK IT, BUT I'M MUCH OLDER THAN YOU.
FAIRIES LIVE VERY LONG LIVES.
OLDER!? BY HOW MUCH?
HMM...I'M DEFINITELY OVER 600, AT LEAST.
600 YEARS OLD!?
I CAN'T BE BOTHERED TO REMEMBER, SO LET'S JUST SAY I'M 620.

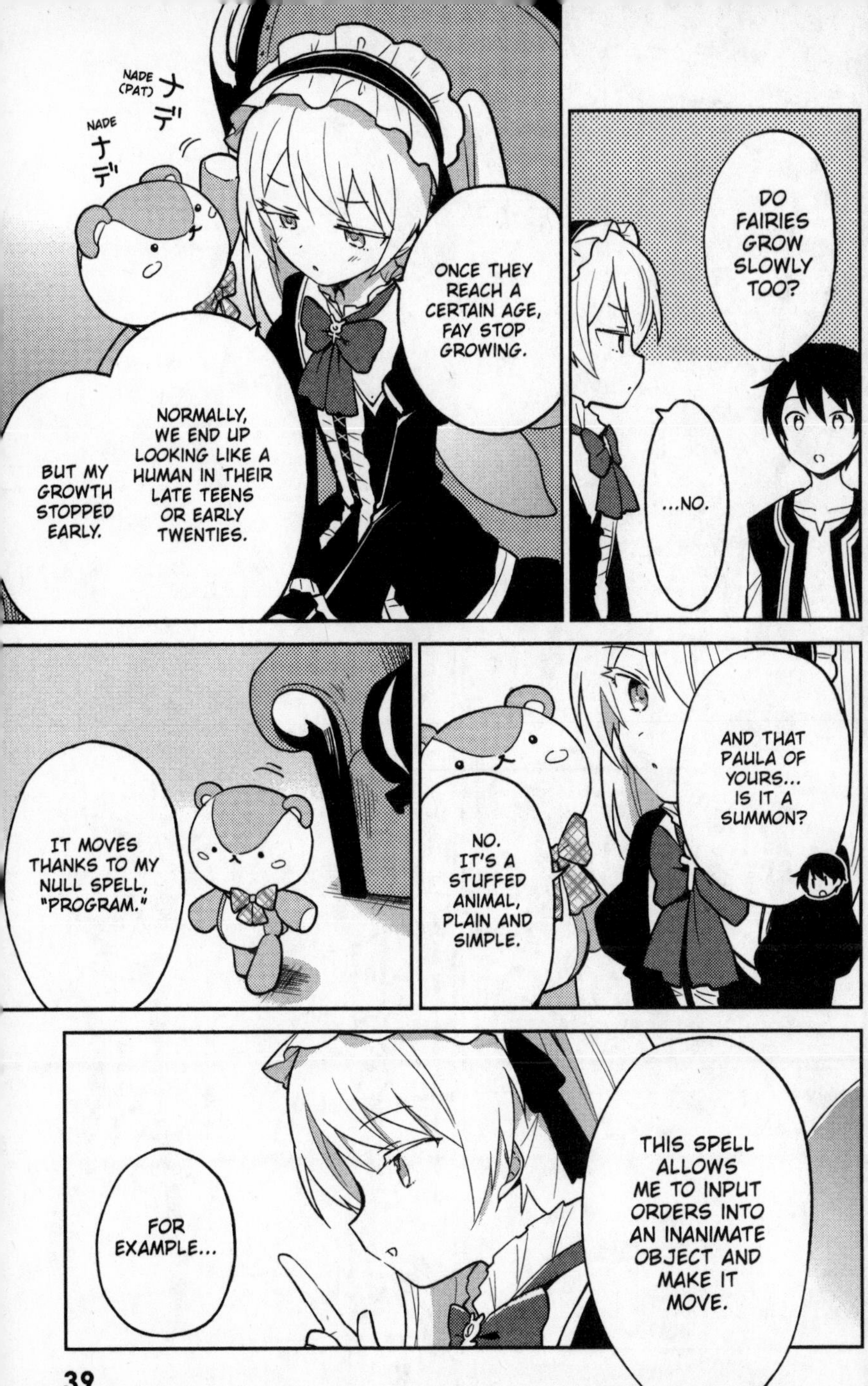
DO FAIRIES GROW SLOWLY TOO?
...NO.
NADE (PAT) ナデ
NADE ナデ
ONCE THEY REACH A CERTAIN AGE, FAY STOP GROWING.
NORMALLY, WE END UP LOOKING LIKE A HUMAN IN THEIR LATE TEENS OR EARLY TWENTIES.
BUT MY GROWTH STOPPED EARLY.
AND THAT PAULA OF YOURS... IS IT A SUMMON?
NO. IT'S A STUFFED ANIMAL, PLAIN AND SIMPLE.
IT MOVES THANKS TO MY NULL SPELL, "PROGRAM."
THIS SPELL ALLOWS ME TO INPUT ORDERS INTO AN INANIMATE OBJECT AND MAKE IT MOVE.
FOR EXAMPLE...

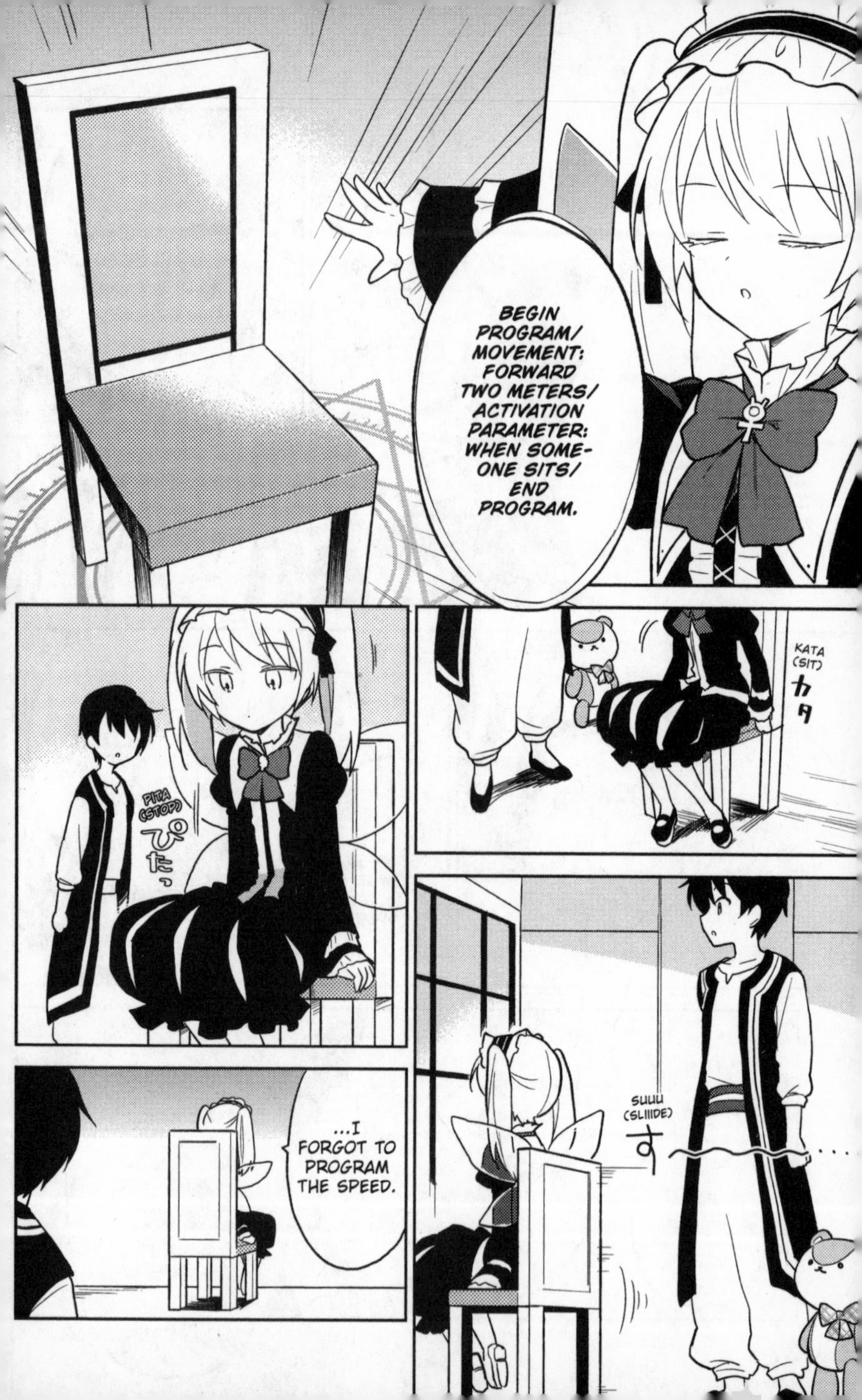
BEGIN PROGRAM/ MOVEMENT: FORWARD TWO METERS/ ACTIVATION PARAMETER: WHEN SOME-ONE SITS/ END PROGRAM.
KATA (SIT)
カタ
PITA (STOP)
ぴたっ
SUUU (SLIIIDE)
す
...I FORGOT TO PROGRAM THE SPEED.

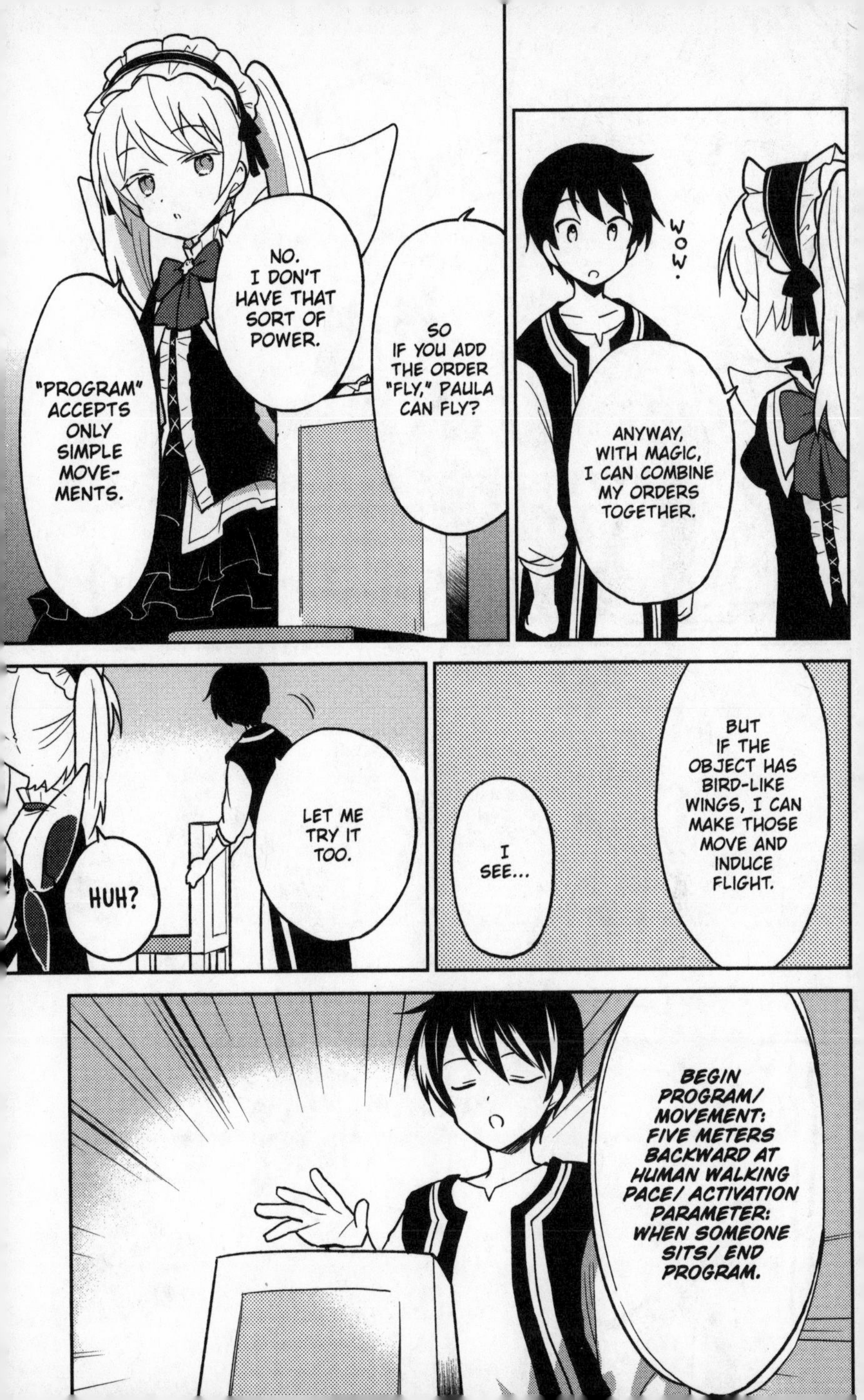
WOW.
ANYWAY, WITH MAGIC, I CAN COMBINE MY ORDERS TOGETHER.
SO IF YOU ADD THE ORDER "FLY," PAULA CAN FLY?
NO. I DON'T HAVE THAT SORT OF POWER.
"PROGRAM" ACCEPTS ONLY SIMPLE MOVE-MENTS.
BUT IF THE OBJECT HAS BIRD-LIKE WINGS, I CAN MAKE THOSE MOVE AND INDUCE FLIGHT.
I SEE...
LET ME TRY IT TOO.
HUH?
BEGIN PROGRAM/ MOVEMENT: FIVE METERS BACKWARD AT HUMAN WALKING PACE/ ACTIVATION PARAMETER: WHEN SOMEONE SITS/ END PROGRAM.

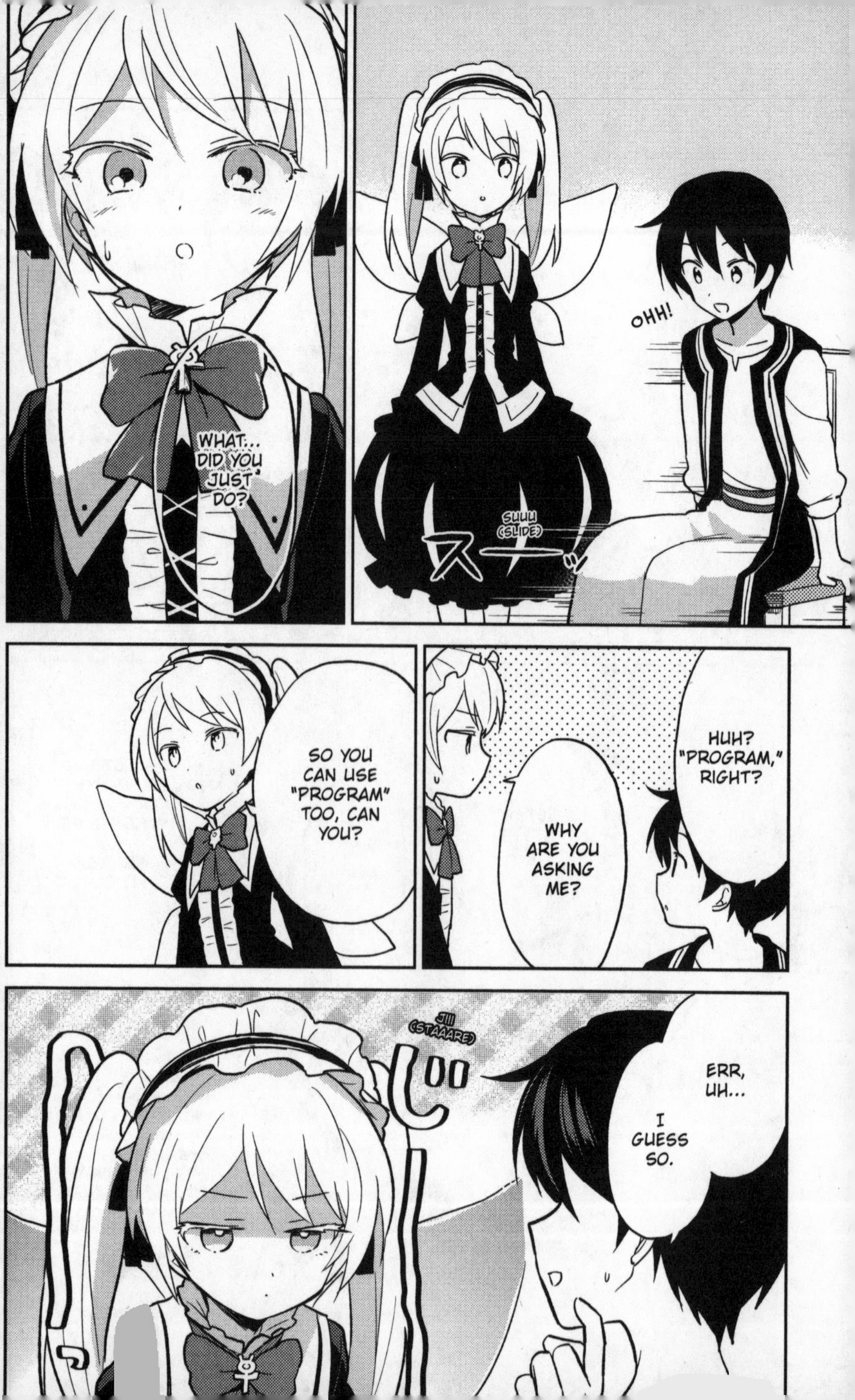
OHH!
SUUU (SLIDE)
WHAT... DID YOU JUST DO?
HUH? "PROGRAM," RIGHT?
WHY ARE YOU ASKING ME?
SO YOU CAN USE "PROGRAM" TOO, CAN YOU?
ERR, UH...
I GUESS SO.
JIII (STAAARE)

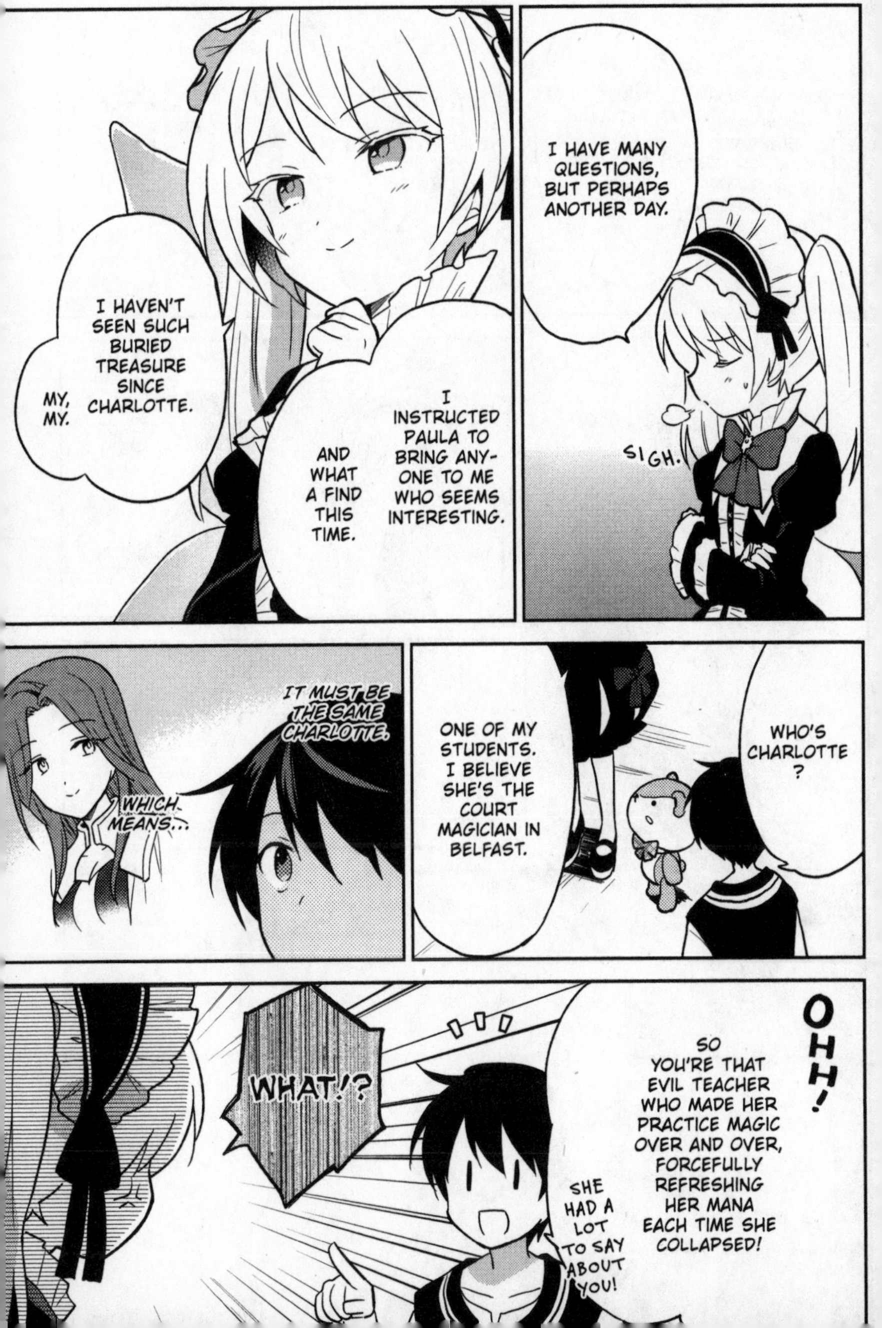
I HAVE MANY QUESTIONS, BUT PERHAPS ANOTHER DAY.
SIGH.
I INSTRUCTED PAULA TO BRING ANY-ONE TO ME WHO SEEMS INTERESTING.
AND WHAT A FIND THIS TIME.
I HAVEN'T SEEN SUCH BURIED TREASURE SINCE CHARLOTTE.
MY, MY.
WHO'S CHARLOTTE?
ONE OF MY STUDENTS. I BELIEVE SHE'S THE COURT MAGICIAN IN BELFAST.
IT MUST BE THE SAME CHARLOTTE.
WHICH MEANS...
OHH!
SO YOU'RE THAT EVIL TEACHER WHO MADE HER PRACTICE MAGIC OVER AND OVER, FORCEFULLY REFRESHING HER MANA EACH TIME SHE COLLAPSED!
SHE HAD A LOT TO SAY ABOUT YOU!
WHAT!?

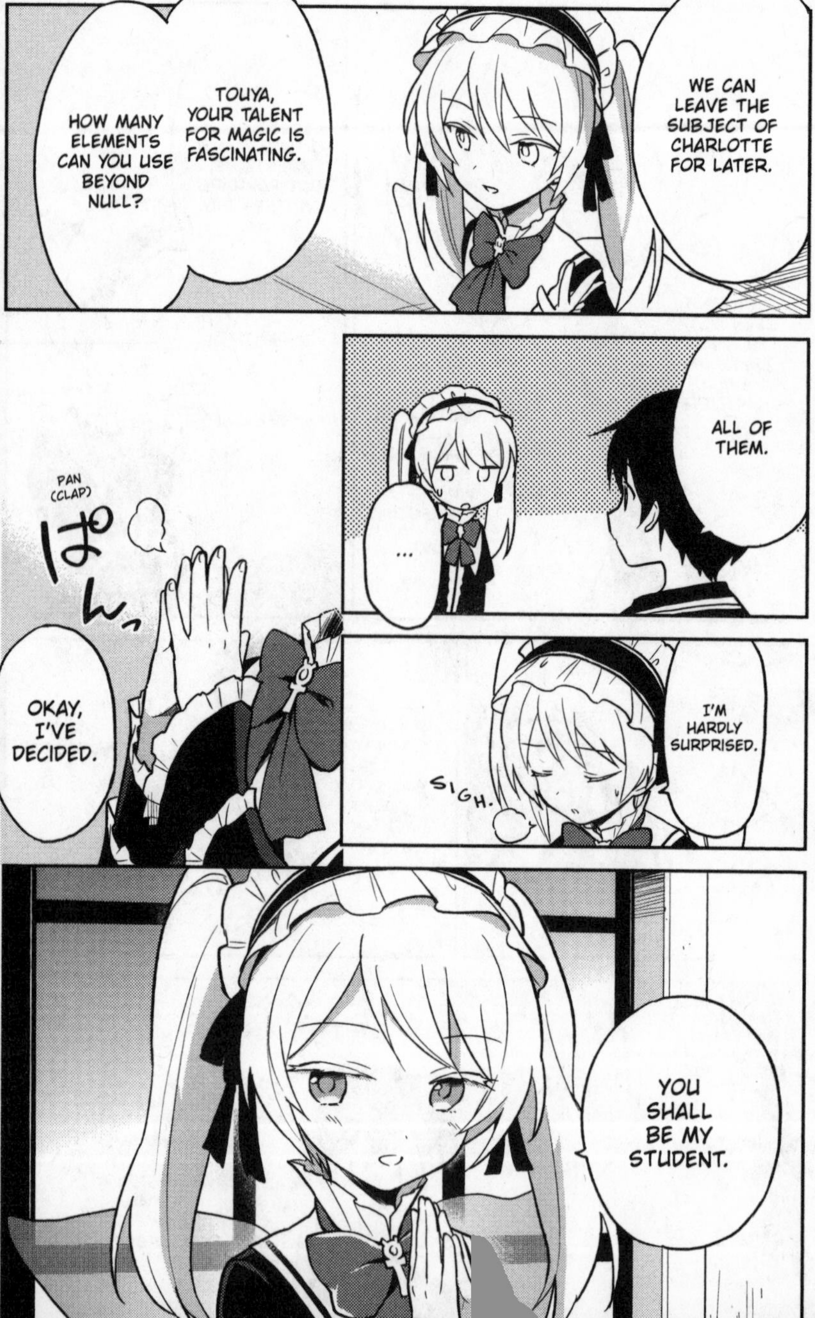
WE CAN LEAVE THE SUBJECT OF CHARLOTTE FOR LATER.
TOUYA, YOUR TALENT FOR MAGIC IS FASCINATING.
HOW MANY ELEMENTS CAN YOU USE BEYOND NULL?
ALL OF THEM.
...
I'M HARDLY SURPRISED.
SIGH.
ぱん
PAN (CLAP)
OKAY, I'VE DECIDED.
YOU SHALL BE MY STUDENT.

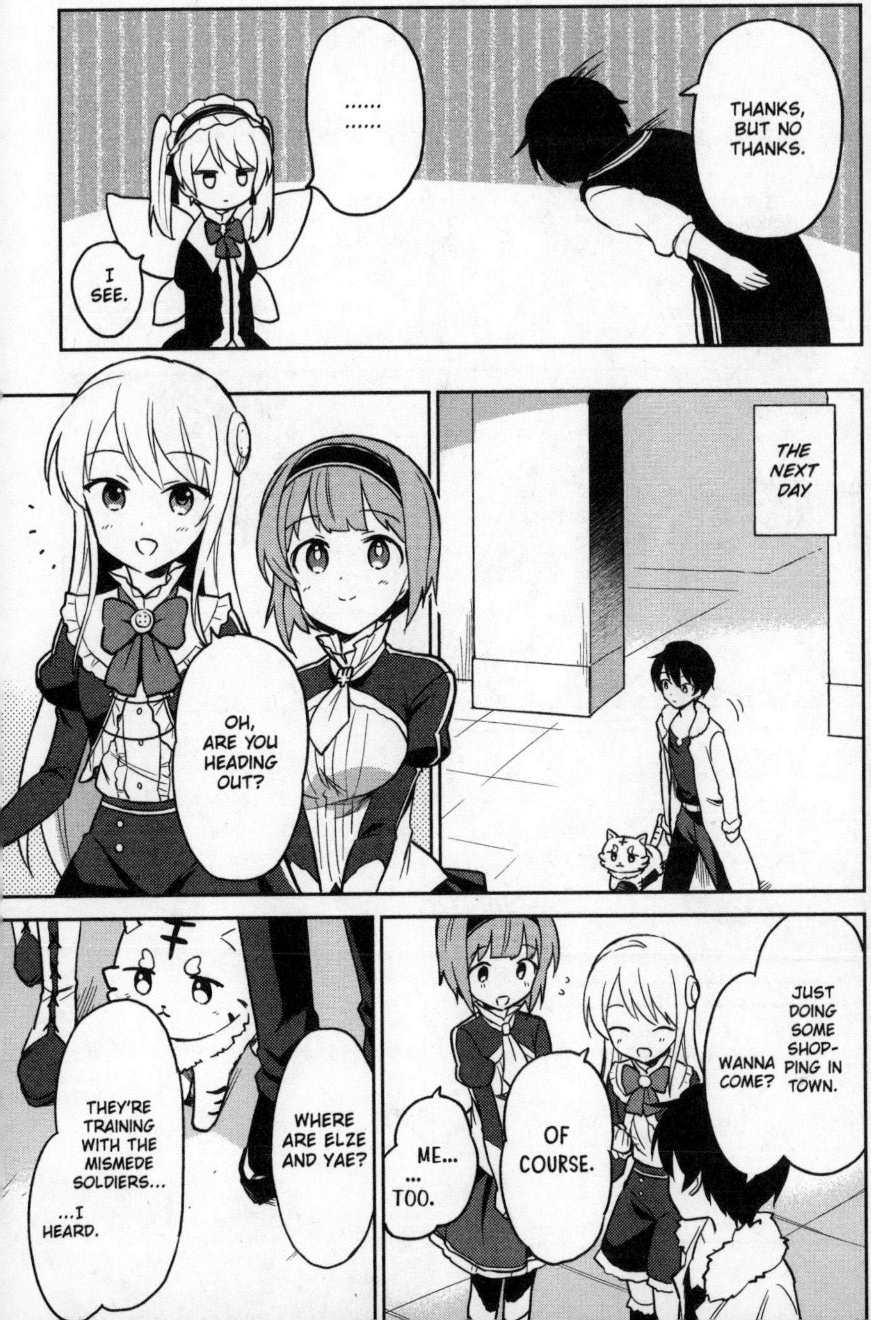
THANKS, BUT NO THANKS.
......
......
I SEE.
THE NEXT DAY
OH, ARE YOU HEADING OUT?
JUST DOING SOME SHOP-PING IN TOWN.
WANNA COME?
OF COURSE.
ME...
... TOO.
WHERE ARE ELZE AND YAE?
THEY'RE TRAINING WITH THE MISMEDE SOLDIERS...
...I HEARD.

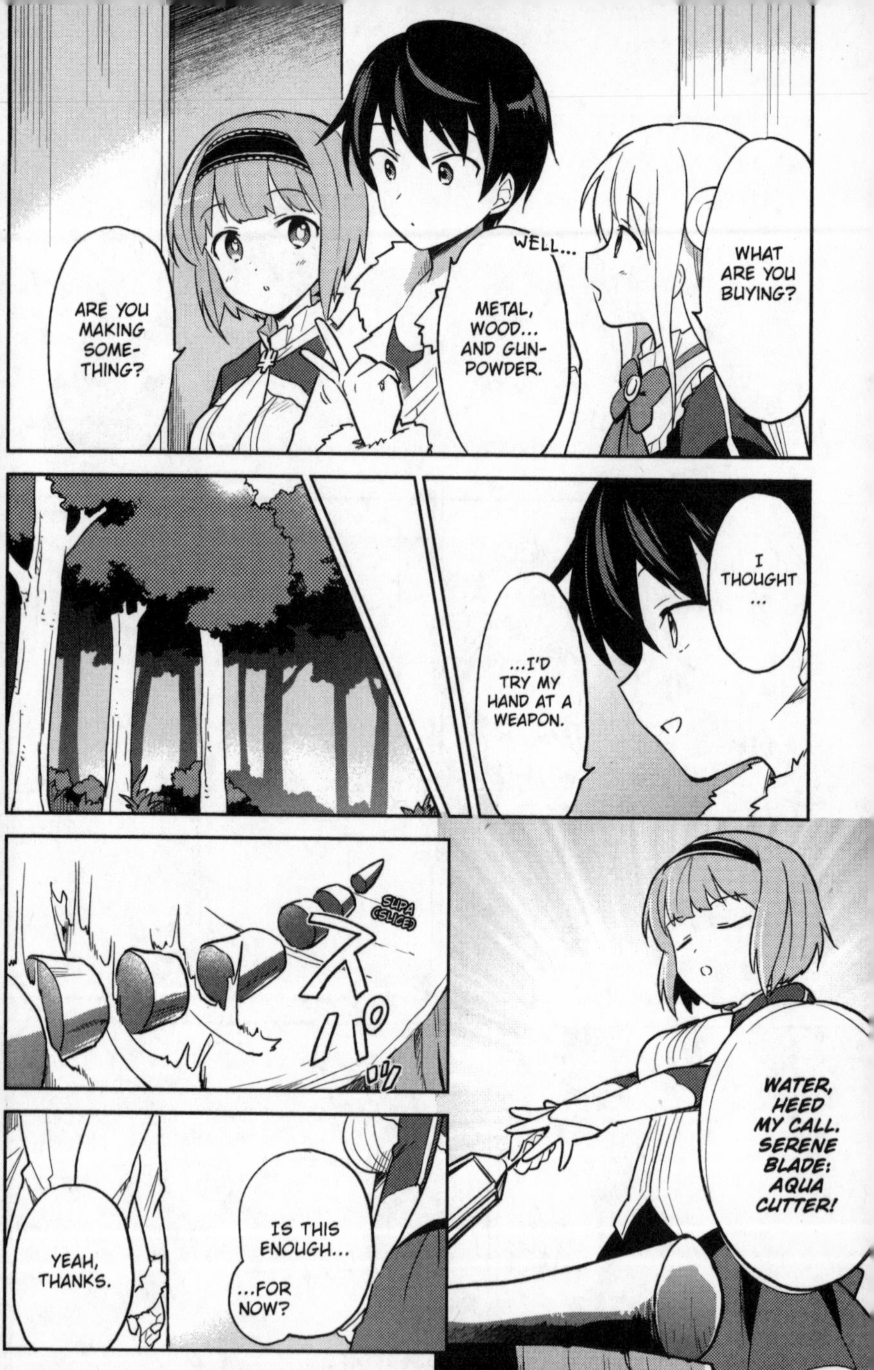
WHAT ARE YOU BUYING?
WELL...
METAL, WOOD... AND GUN-POWDER.
ARE YOU MAKING SOME-THING?
I THOUGHT ...
...I'D TRY MY HAND AT A WEAPON.
WATER, HEED MY CALL. SERENE BLADE: AQUA CUTTER!
SUPA (SLICE)
IS THIS ENOUGH...
...FOR NOW?
YEAH, THANKS.

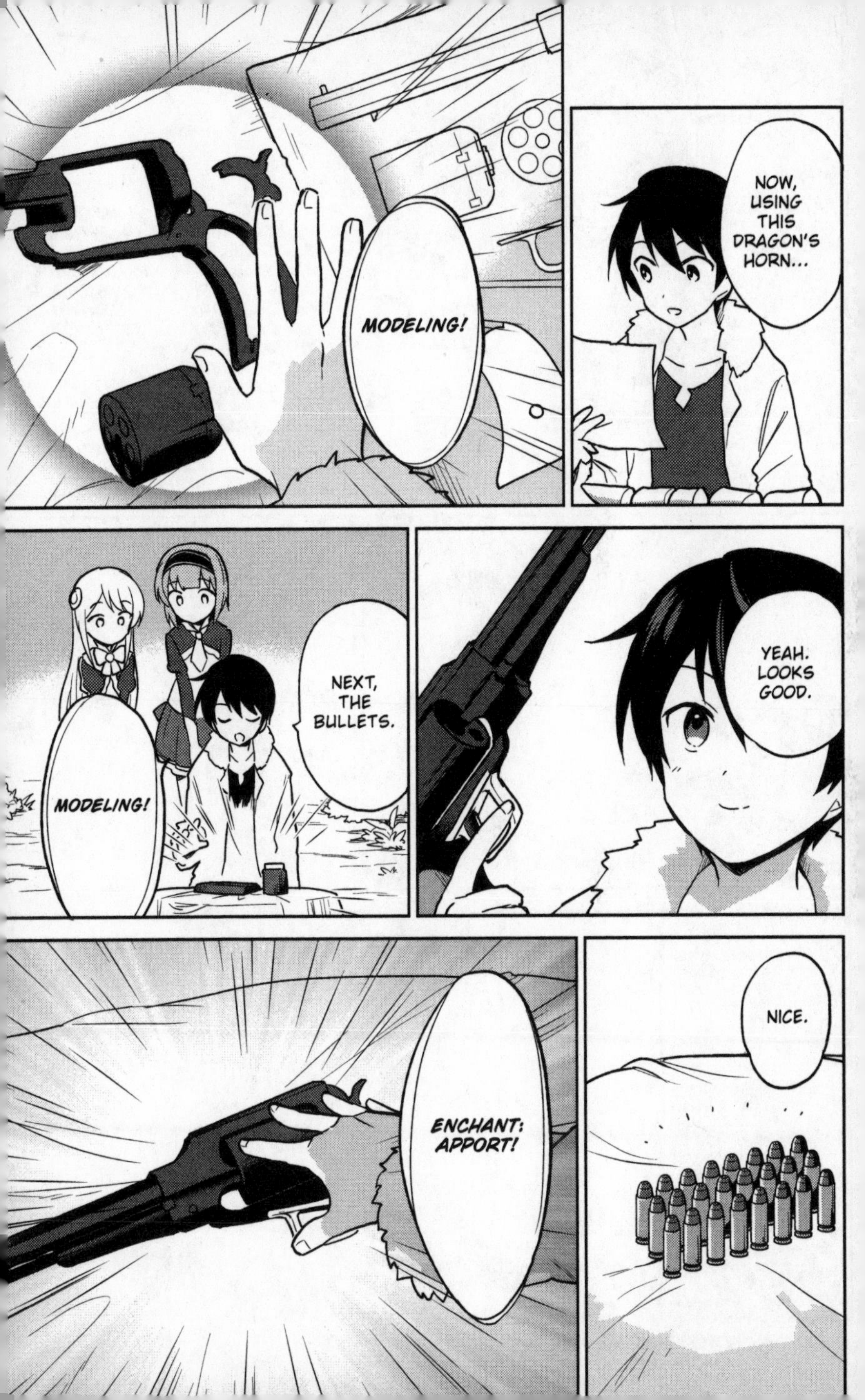
NOW, USING THIS DRAGON'S HORN...
MODELING!
YEAH. LOOKS GOOD.
NEXT, THE BULLETS.
MODELING!
NICE.
ENCHANT: APPORT!

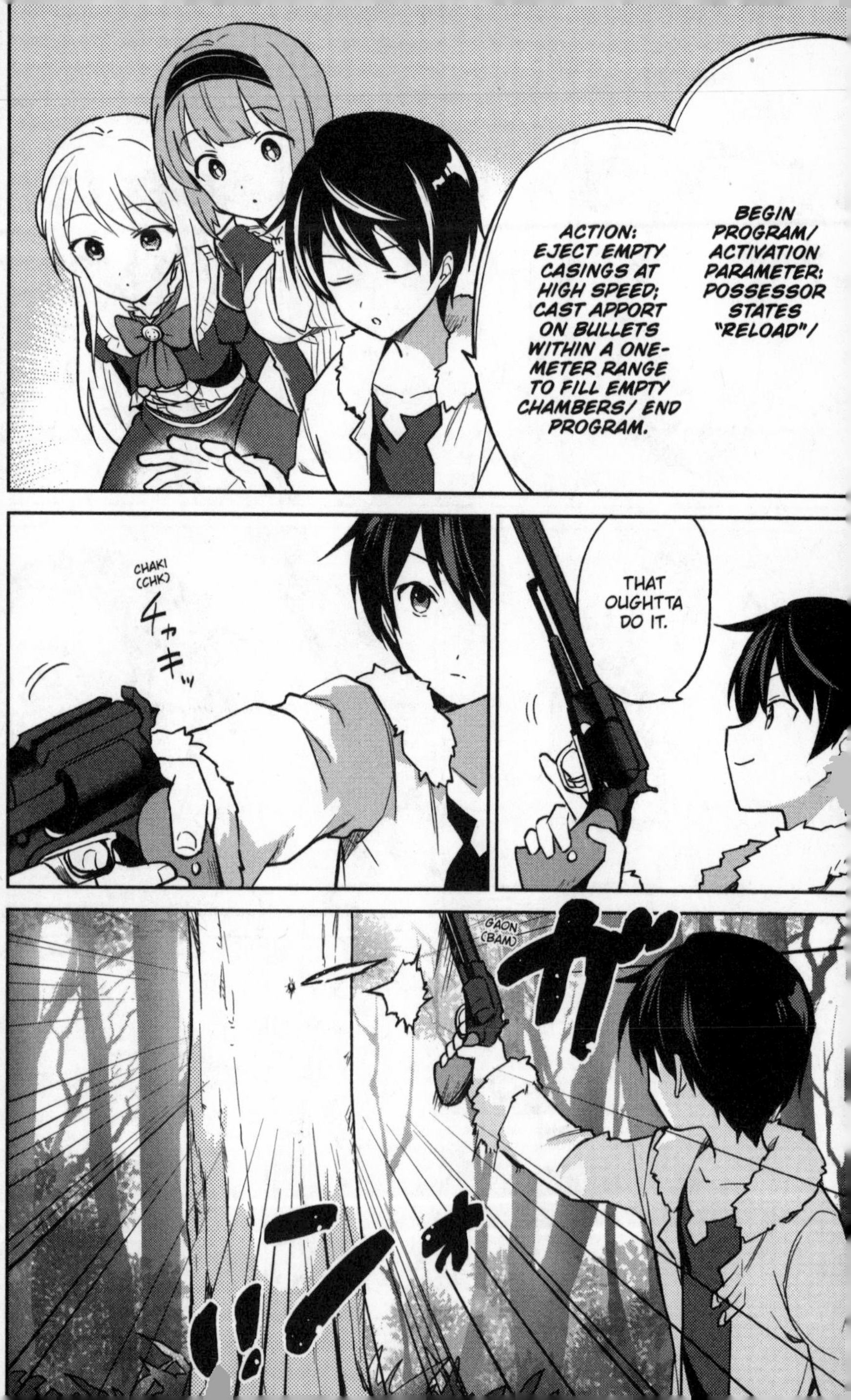
BEGIN PROGRAM/ ACTIVATION PARAMETER: POSSESSOR STATES "RELOAD"/
ACTION: EJECT EMPTY CASINGS AT HIGH SPEED; CAST APPORT ON BULLETS WITHIN A ONE-METER RANGE TO FILL EMPTY CHAMBERS/ END PROGRAM.
THAT OUGHTTA DO IT.
CHAKI (CHK)
チャキッ
GAON (BAM)

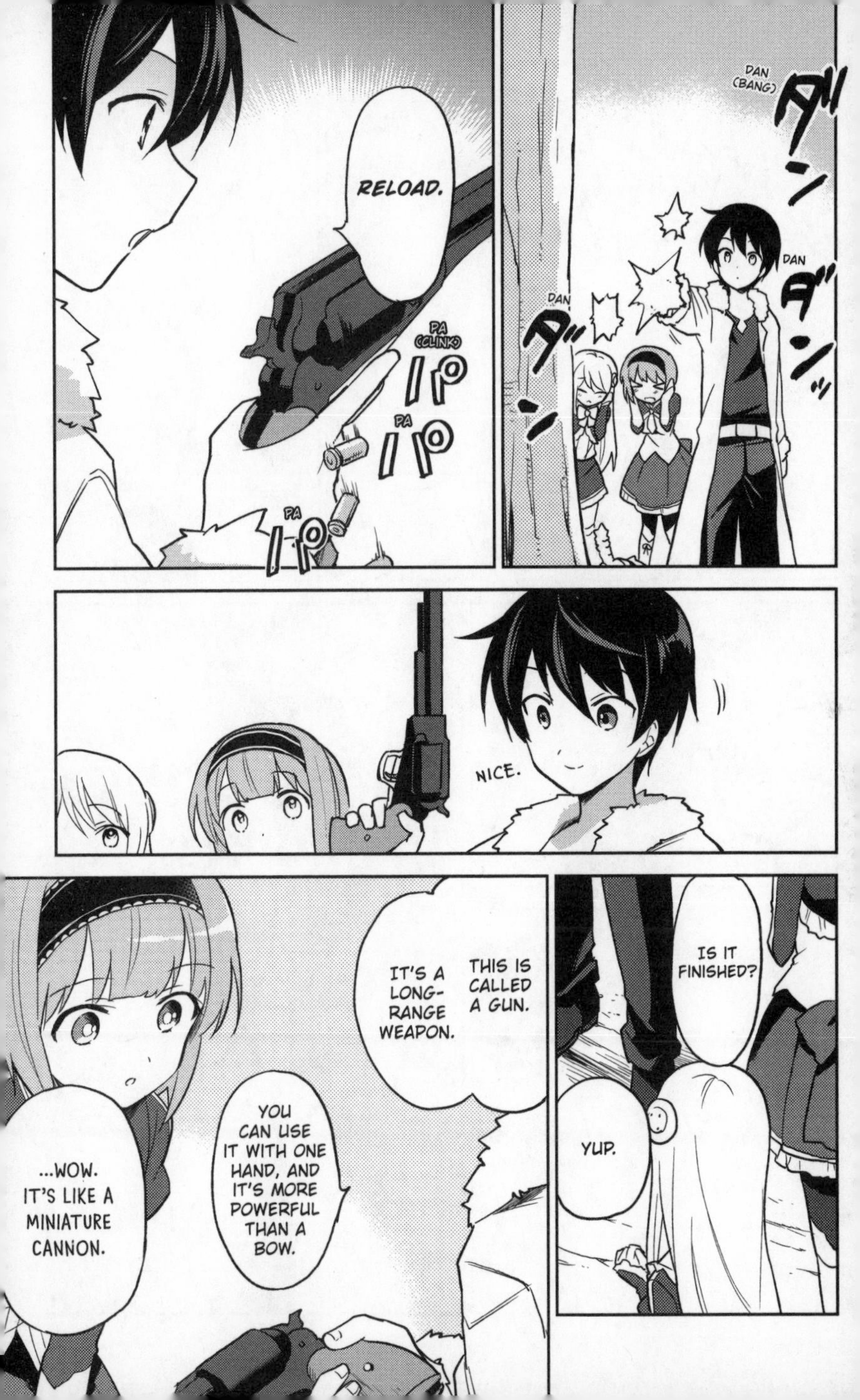

DAN (BANG)
DAN
DAN
RELOAD.
PA (CLINK)
PA
PA
NICE.
IS IT FINISHED?
YUP.
THIS IS CALLED A GUN.
IT'S A LONG-RANGE WEAPON.
YOU CAN USE IT WITH ONE HAND, AND IT'S MORE POWERFUL THAN A BOW.
...WOW. IT'S LIKE A MINIATURE CANNON.

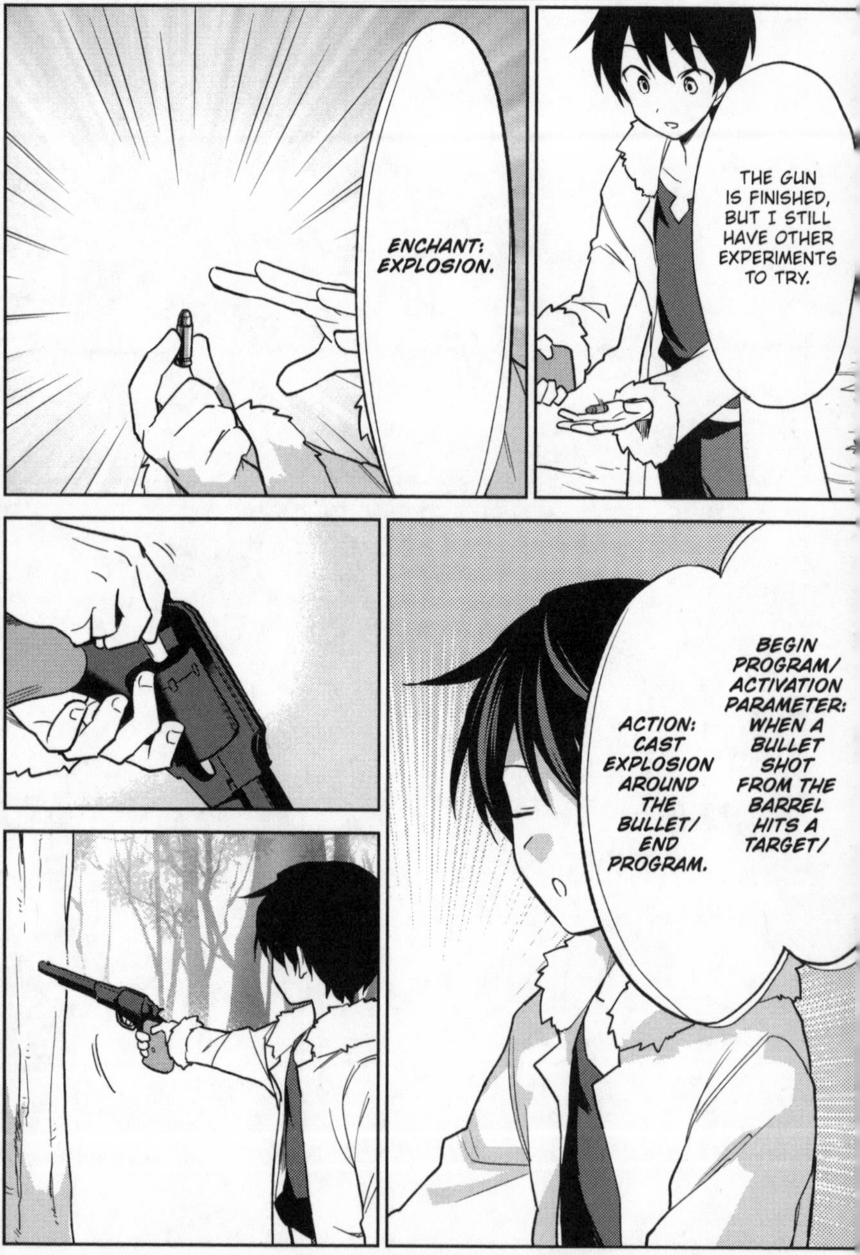
THE GUN IS FINISHED, BUT I STILL HAVE OTHER EXPERIMENTS TO TRY.
ENCHANT: EXPLOSION.
BEGIN PROGRAM/ ACTIVATION PARAMETER: WHEN A BULLET SHOT FROM THE BARREL HITS A TARGET/
ACTION: CAST EXPLOSION AROUND THE BULLET/ END PROGRAM.

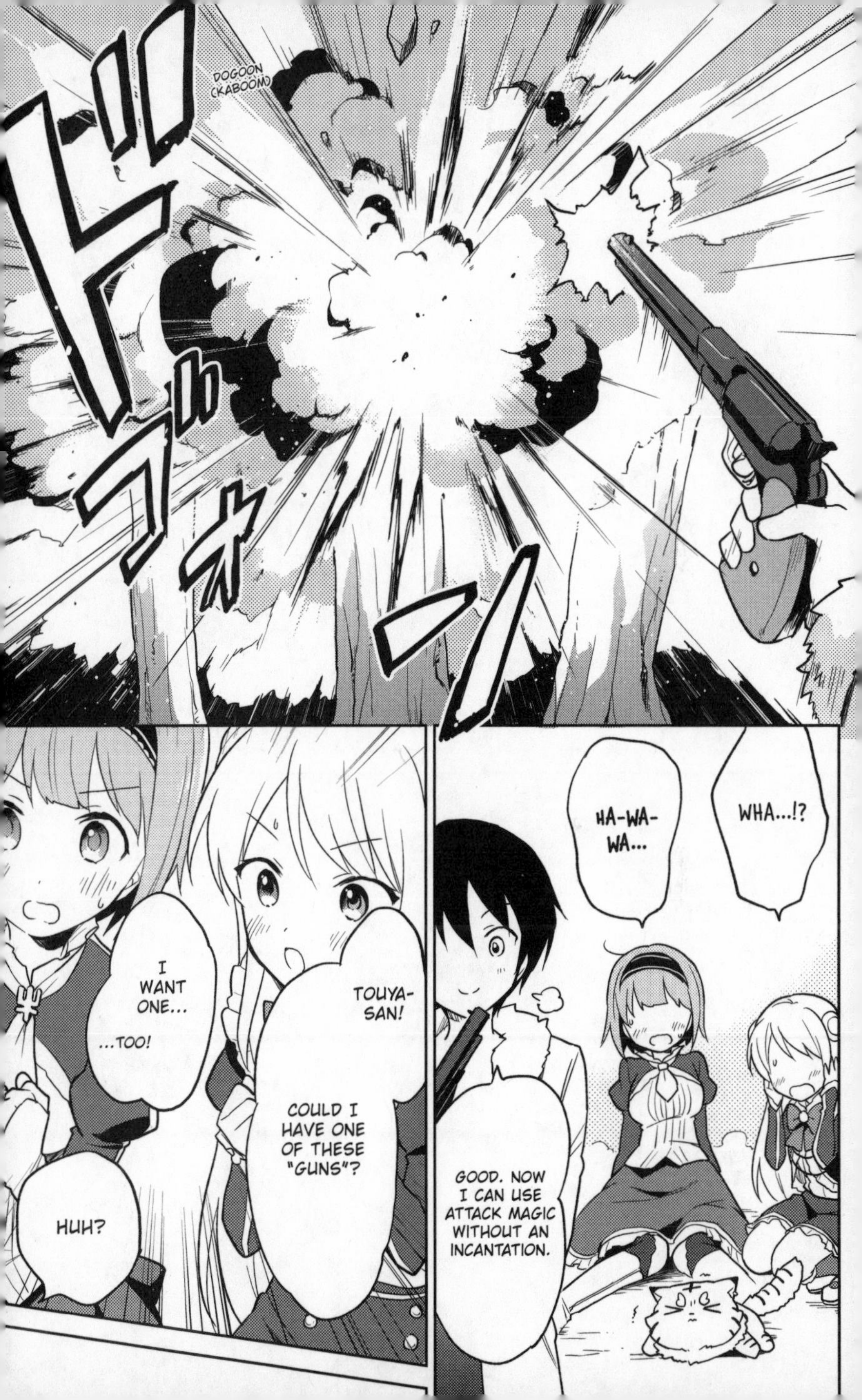
DOGOON (KABOOM)
WHA...!?
HA-WA-WA...
GOOD. NOW I CAN USE ATTACK MAGIC WITHOUT AN INCANTATION.
TOUYA-SAN!
COULD I HAVE ONE OF THESE "GUNS"?
I WANT ONE...
...TOO!
HUH?

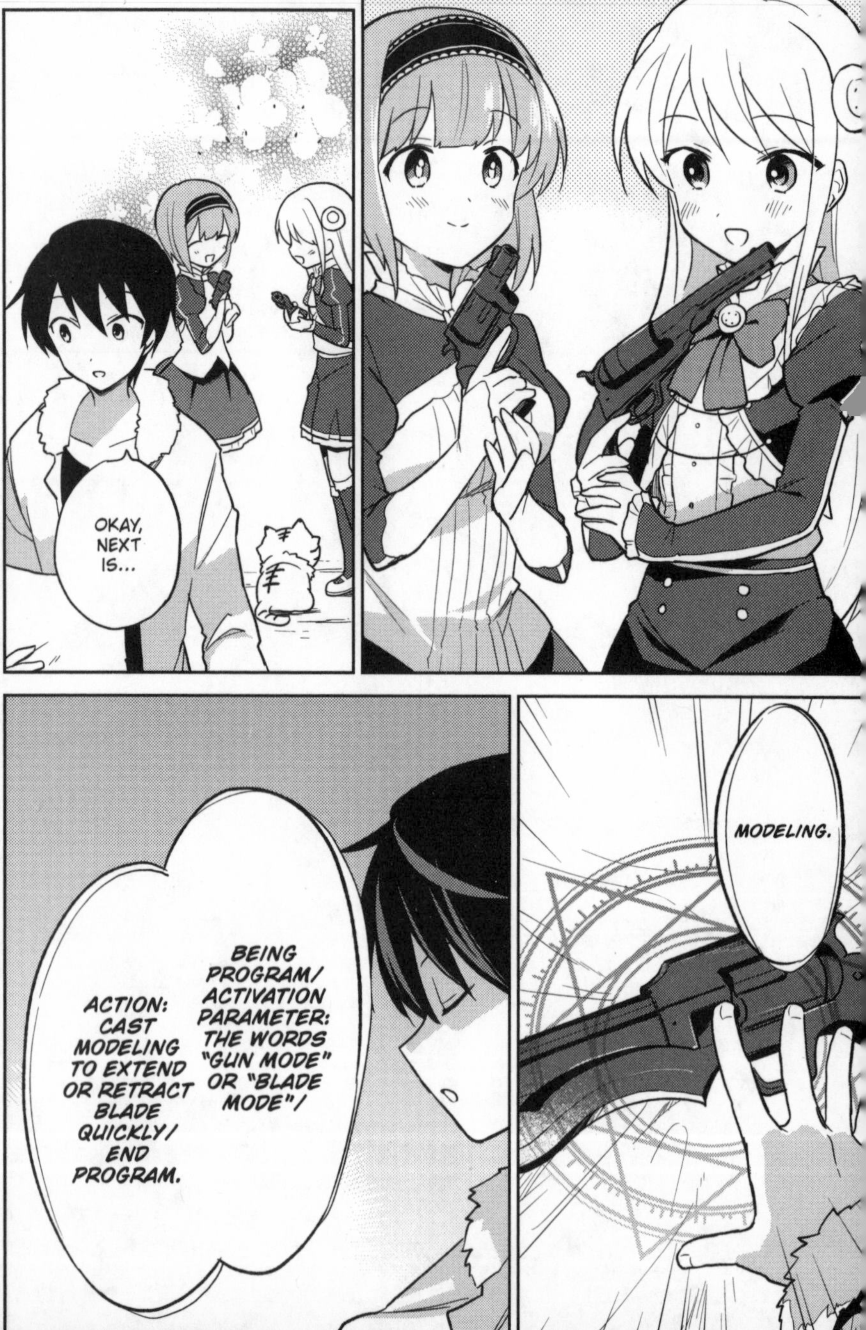
OKAY, NEXT IS...
MODELING.
BEING PROGRAM/ ACTIVATION PARAMETER: THE WORDS "GUN MODE" OR "BLADE MODE"/
ACTION: CAST MODELING TO EXTEND OR RETRACT BLADE QUICKLY/ END PROGRAM.

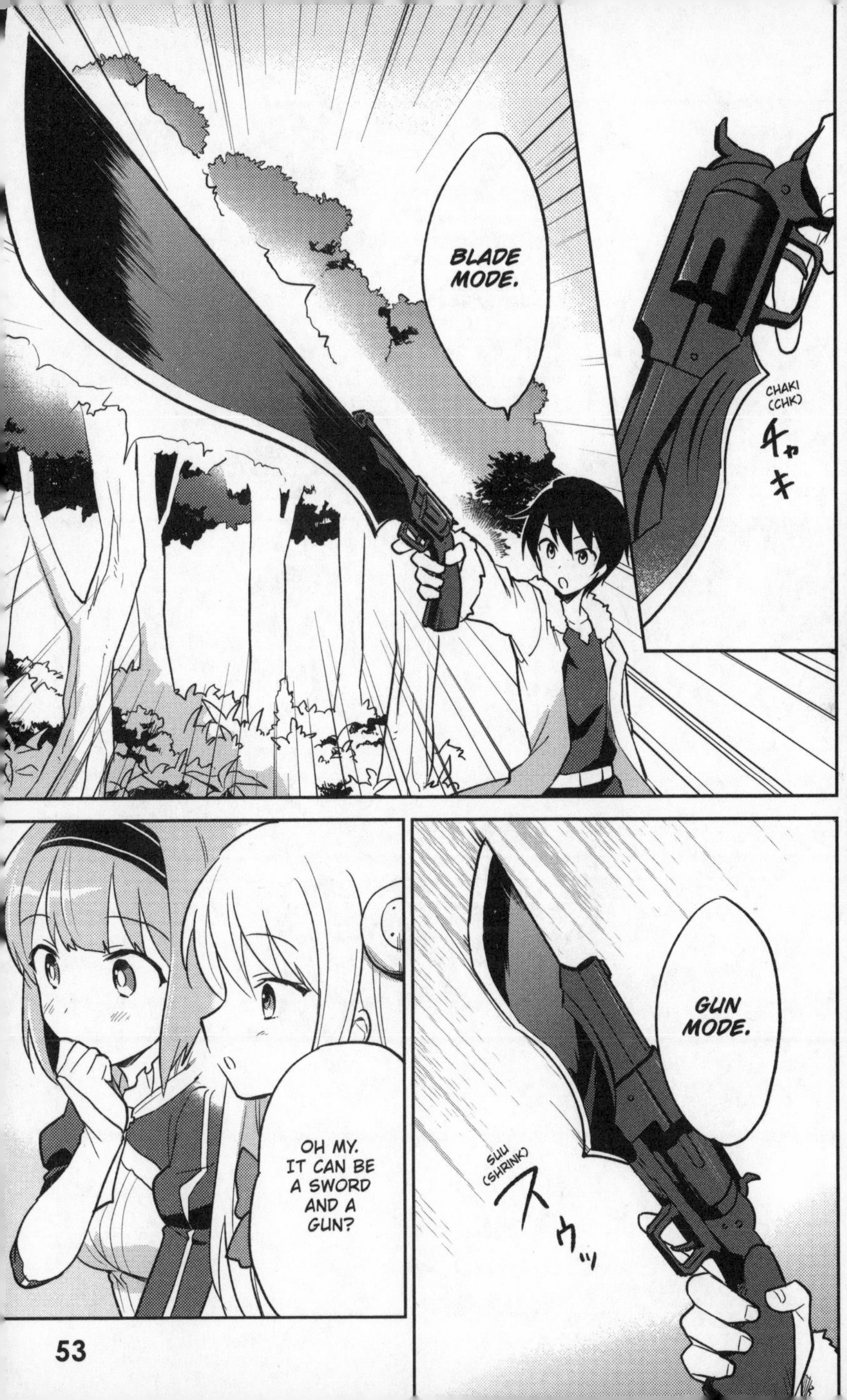
BLADE MODE.
CHAKI (CHK)
チャキ
GUN MODE.
SUU (SHRINK)
スウッ
OH MY. IT CAN BE A SWORD AND A GUN?

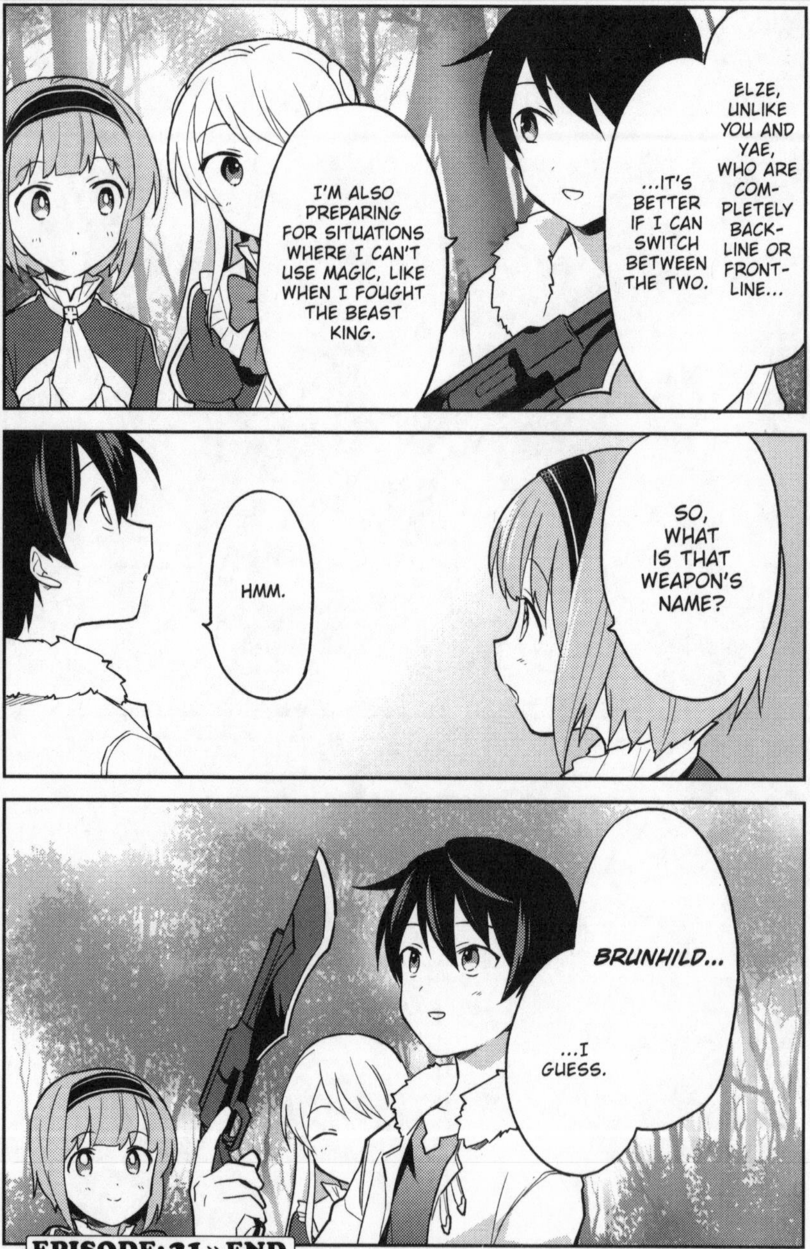
ELZE, UNLIKE YOU AND YAE, WHO ARE COMPLETELY BACK-LINE OR FRONT-LINE...
...IT'S BETTER IF I CAN SWITCH BETWEEN THE TWO.
I'M ALSO PREPARING FOR SITUATIONS WHERE I CAN'T USE MAGIC, LIKE WHEN I FOUGHT THE BEAST KING.
SO, WHAT IS THAT WEAPON'S NAME?
HMM.
BRUNHILD...
...I GUESS.

EPISODE: 21 » END

In Another World With My Smartphone

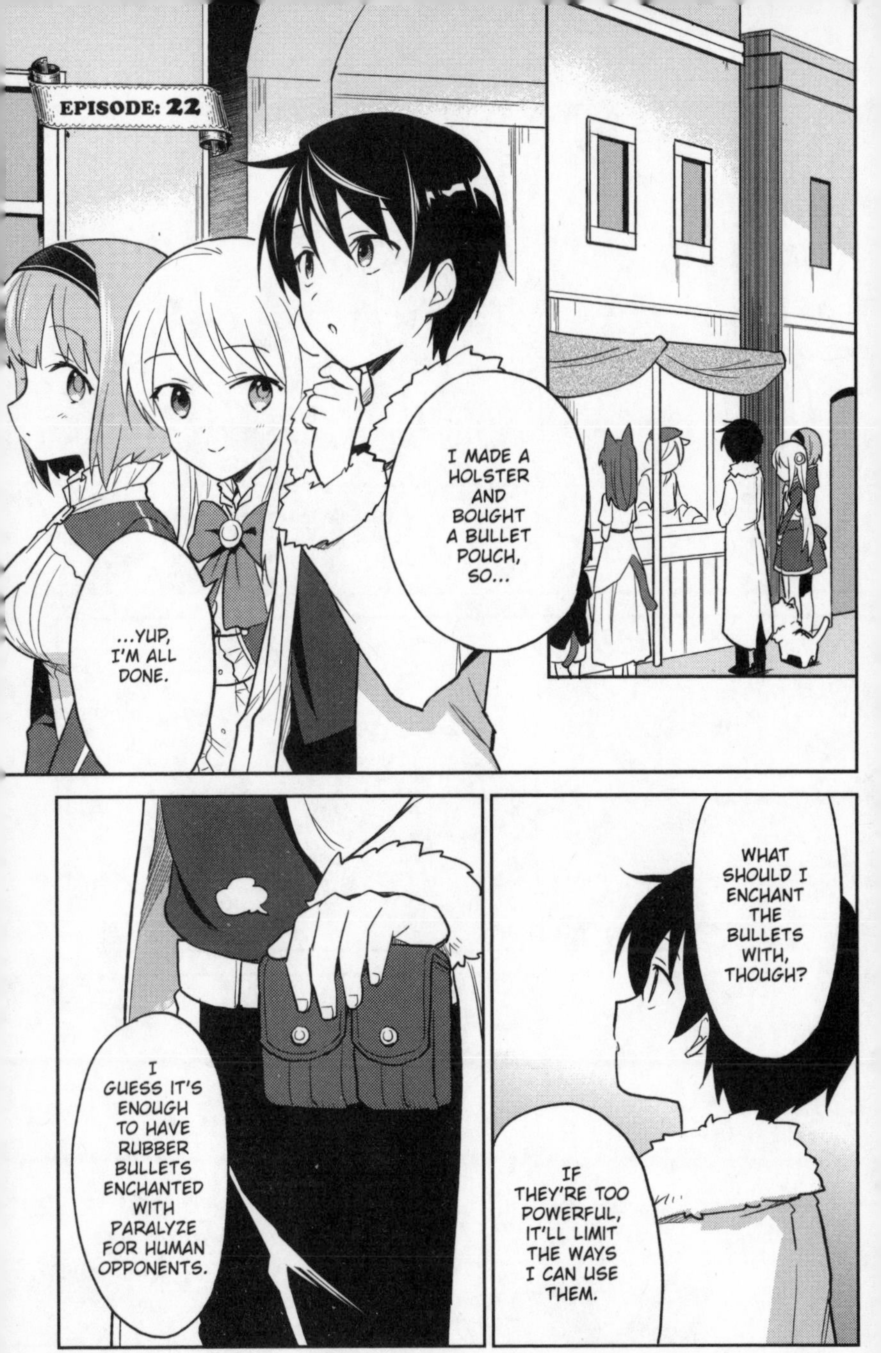
EPISODE: 22
I MADE A HOLSTER AND BOUGHT A BULLET POUCH, SO...
...YUP, I'M ALL DONE.
WHAT SHOULD I ENCHANT THE BULLETS WITH, THOUGH?
IF THEY'RE TOO POWERFUL, IT'LL LIMIT THE WAYS I CAN USE THEM.
I GUESS IT'S ENOUGH TO HAVE RUBBER BULLETS ENCHANTED WITH PARALYZE FOR HUMAN OPPONENTS.

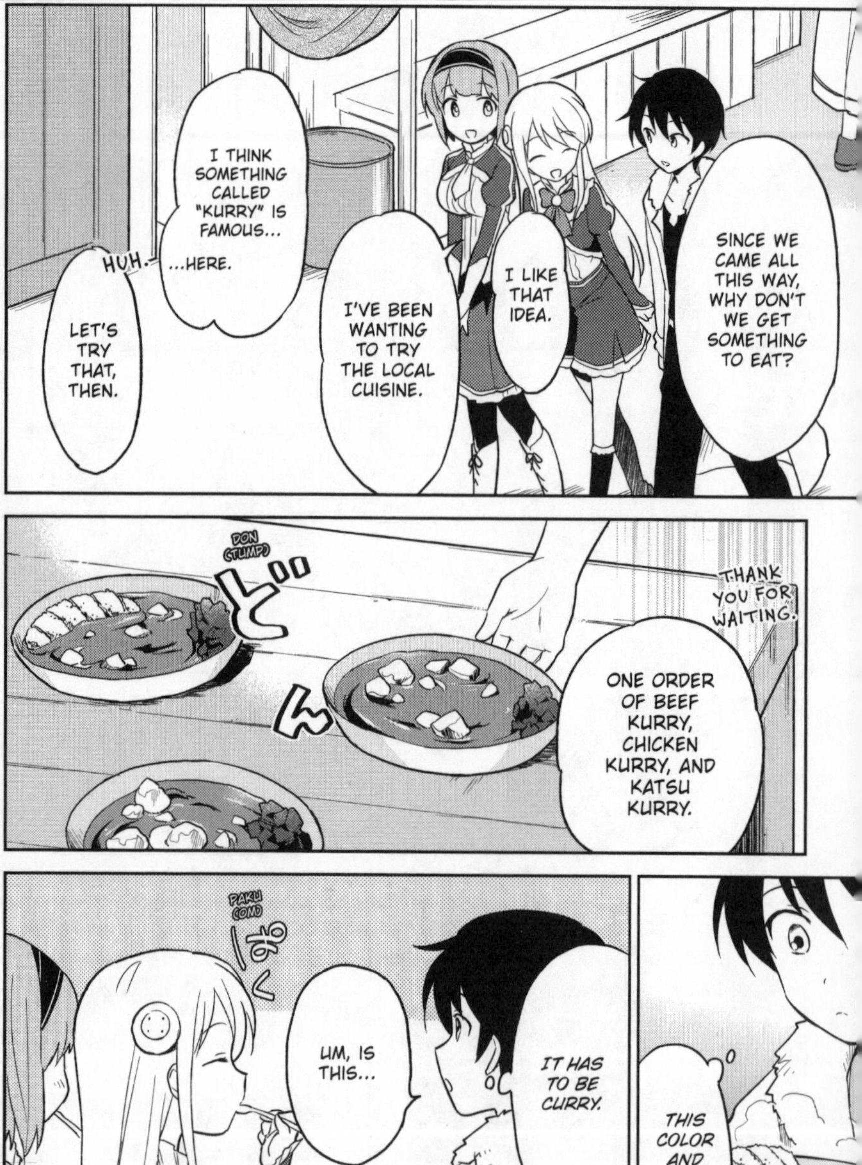
SINCE WE CAME ALL THIS WAY, WHY DON'T WE GET SOMETHING TO EAT?
I LIKE THAT IDEA.
I'VE BEEN WANTING TO TRY THE LOCAL CUISINE.
I THINK SOMETHING CALLED "KURRY" IS FAMOUS...
...HERE.
HUH.
LET'S TRY THAT, THEN.
THANK YOU FOR WAITING.
ONE ORDER OF BEEF KURRY, CHICKEN KURRY, AND KATSU KURRY.
DON (TUMP)
THIS COLOR AND SMELL...
IT HAS TO BE CURRY.
UM, IS THIS...
PAKU (COMD)

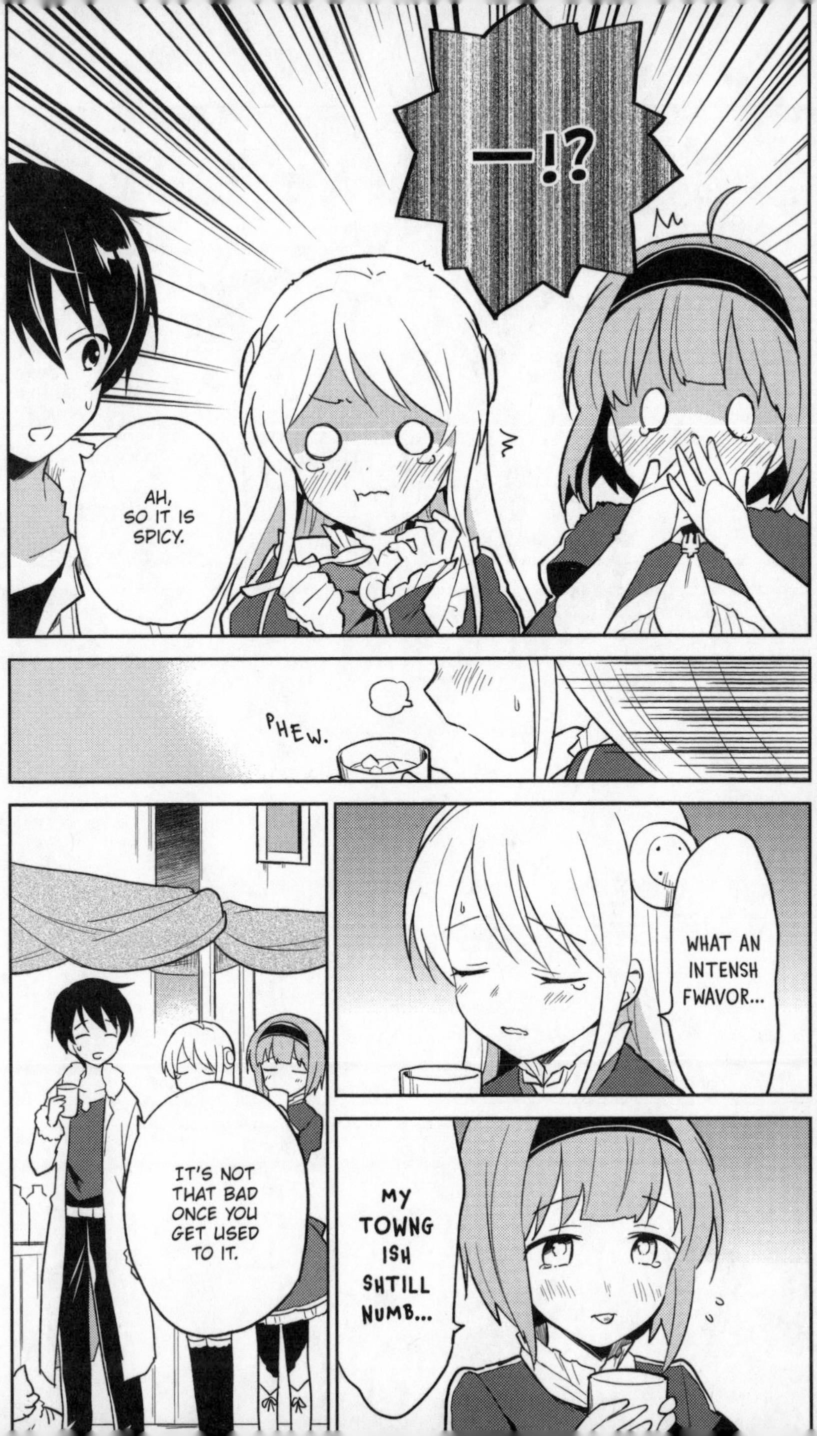
—!?
AH, SO IT IS SPICY.
PHEW.
WHAT AN INTENSH FWAVOR...
MY TOWNG ISH SHTILL NUMB...
IT'S NOT THAT BAD ONCE YOU GET USED TO IT.

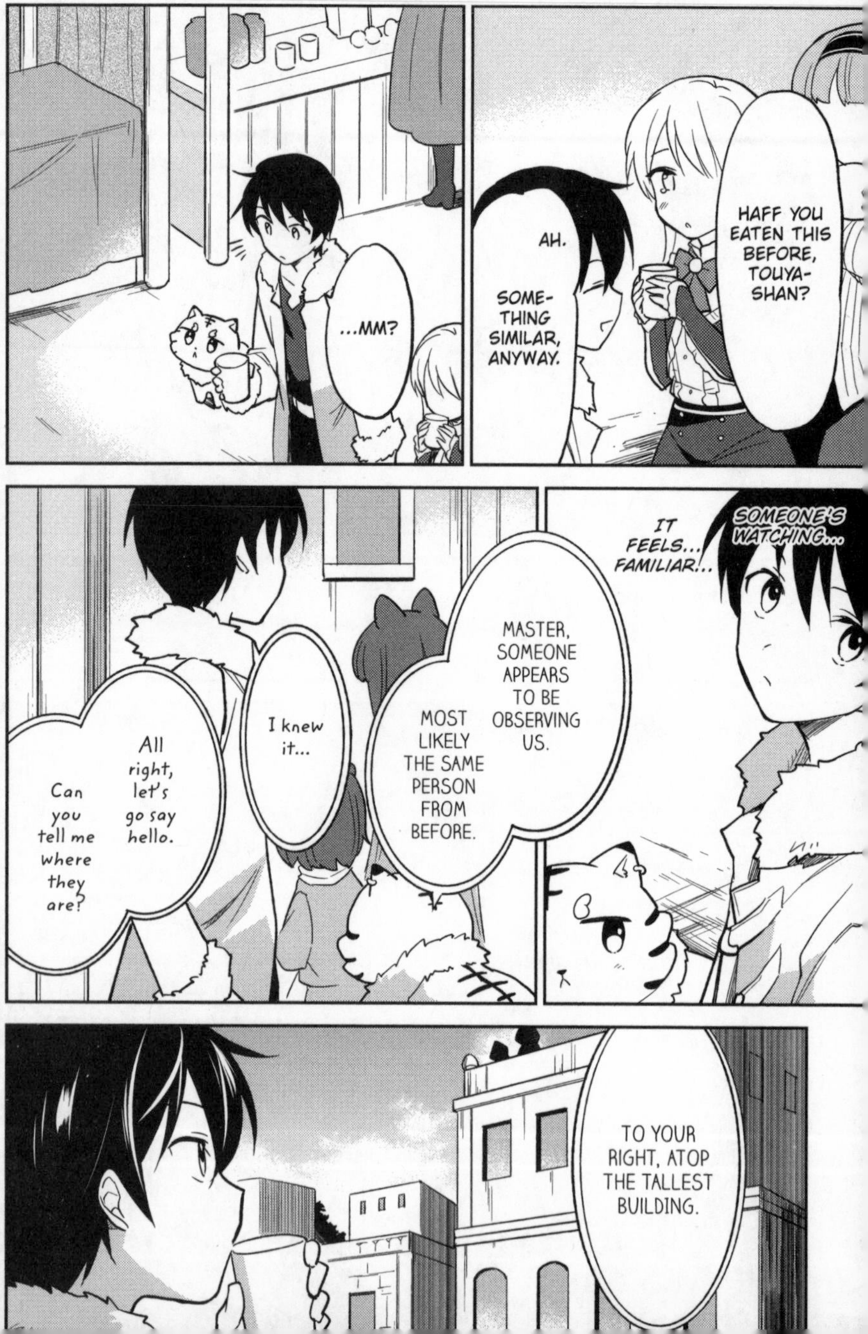
HAFF YOU EATEN THIS BEFORE, TOUYA-SHAN?
AH.
SOMETHING SIMILAR, ANYWAY.
...MM?
SOMEONE'S WATCHING...
IT FEELS... FAMILIAR...
MASTER, SOMEONE APPEARS TO BE OBSERVING US.
MOST LIKELY THE SAME PERSON FROM BEFORE.
I knew it...
All right, let's go say hello.
Can you tell me where they are?
TO YOUR RIGHT, ATOP THE TALLEST BUILDING.

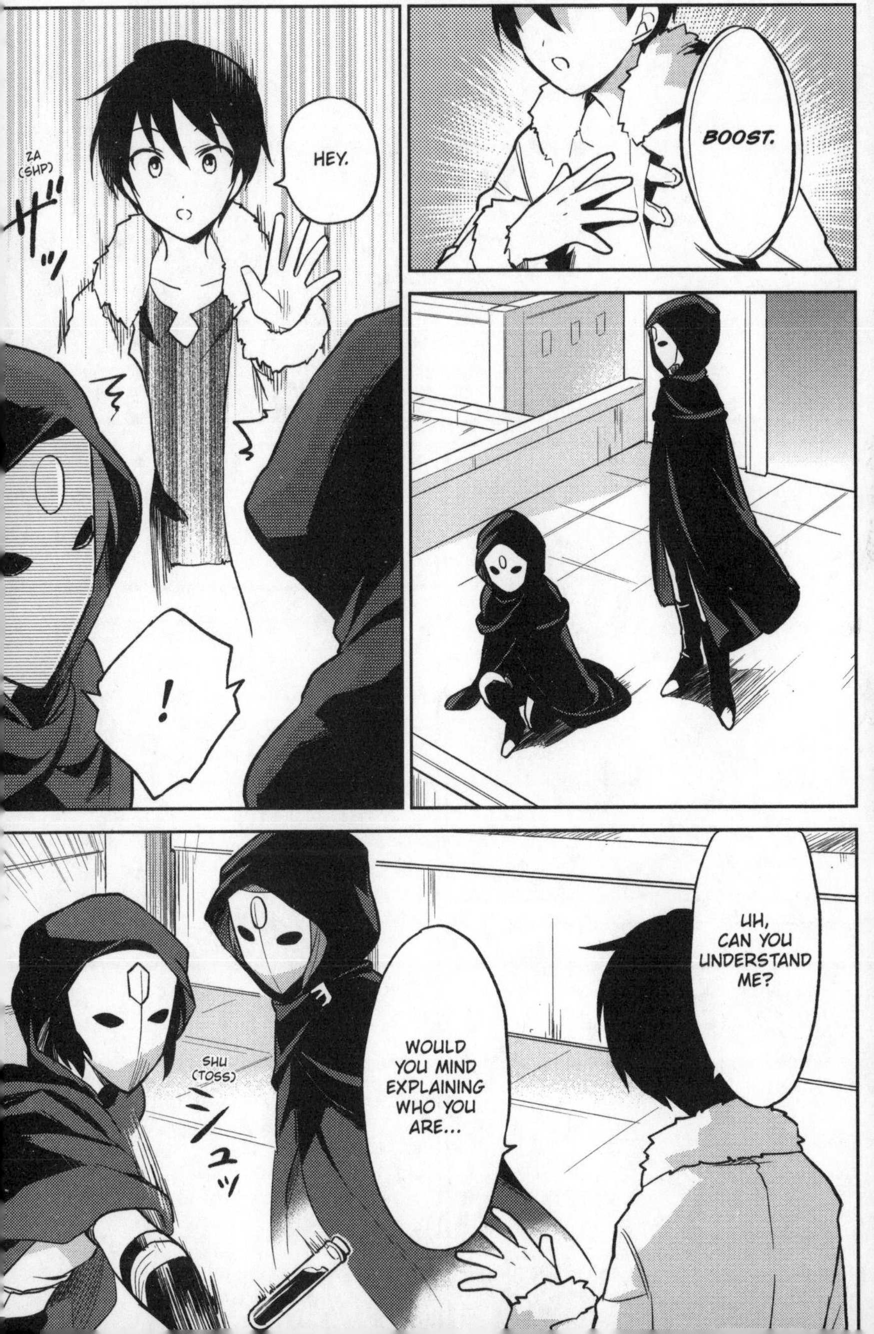
BOOST.
HEY.
ZA (SHP)
!
UH, CAN YOU UNDERSTAND ME?
WOULD YOU MIND EXPLAINING WHO YOU ARE...
SHU (TOSS)

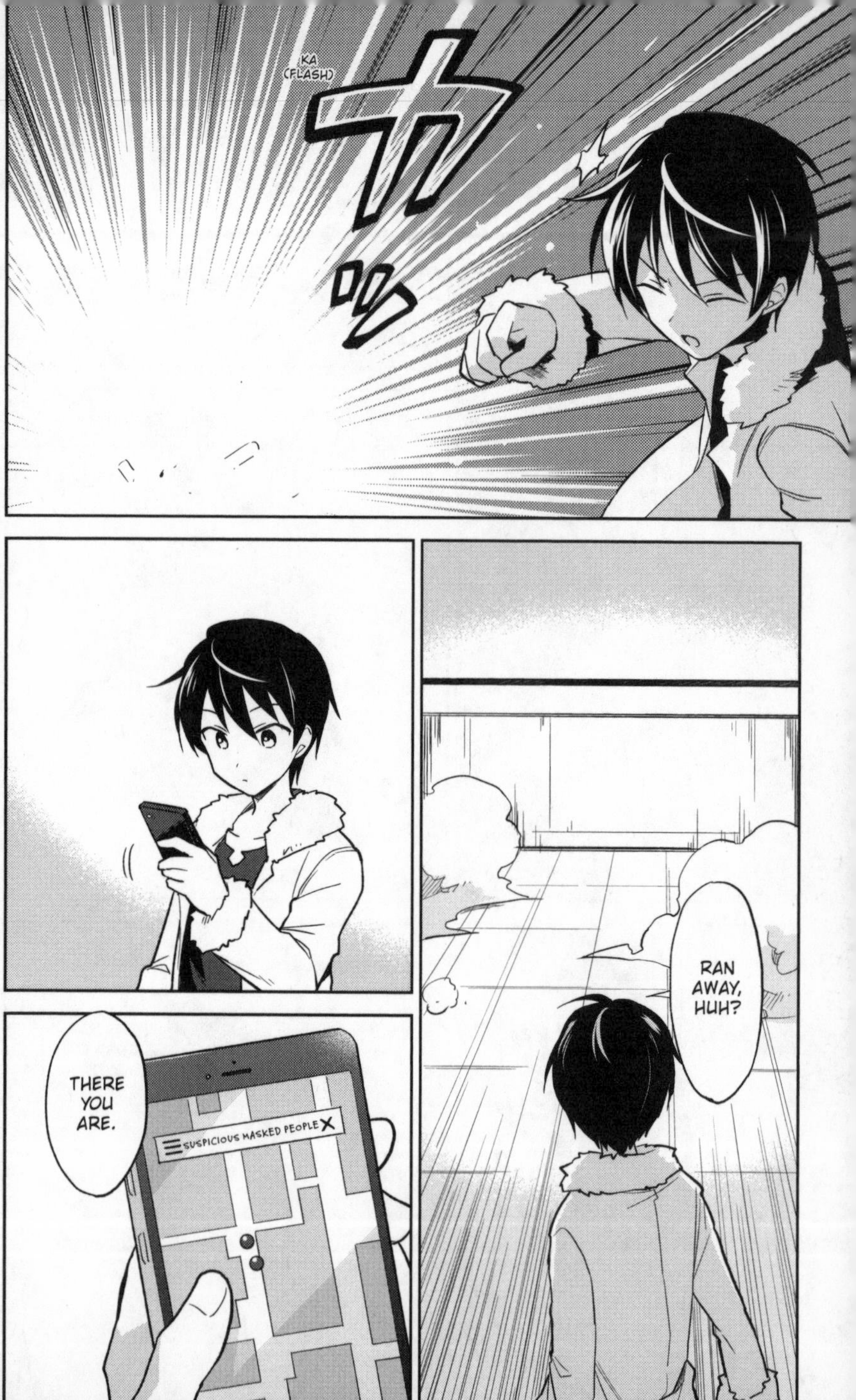
KA (FLASH)
RAN AWAY, HUH?
THERE YOU ARE.
SUSPICIOUS MASKED PEOPLE

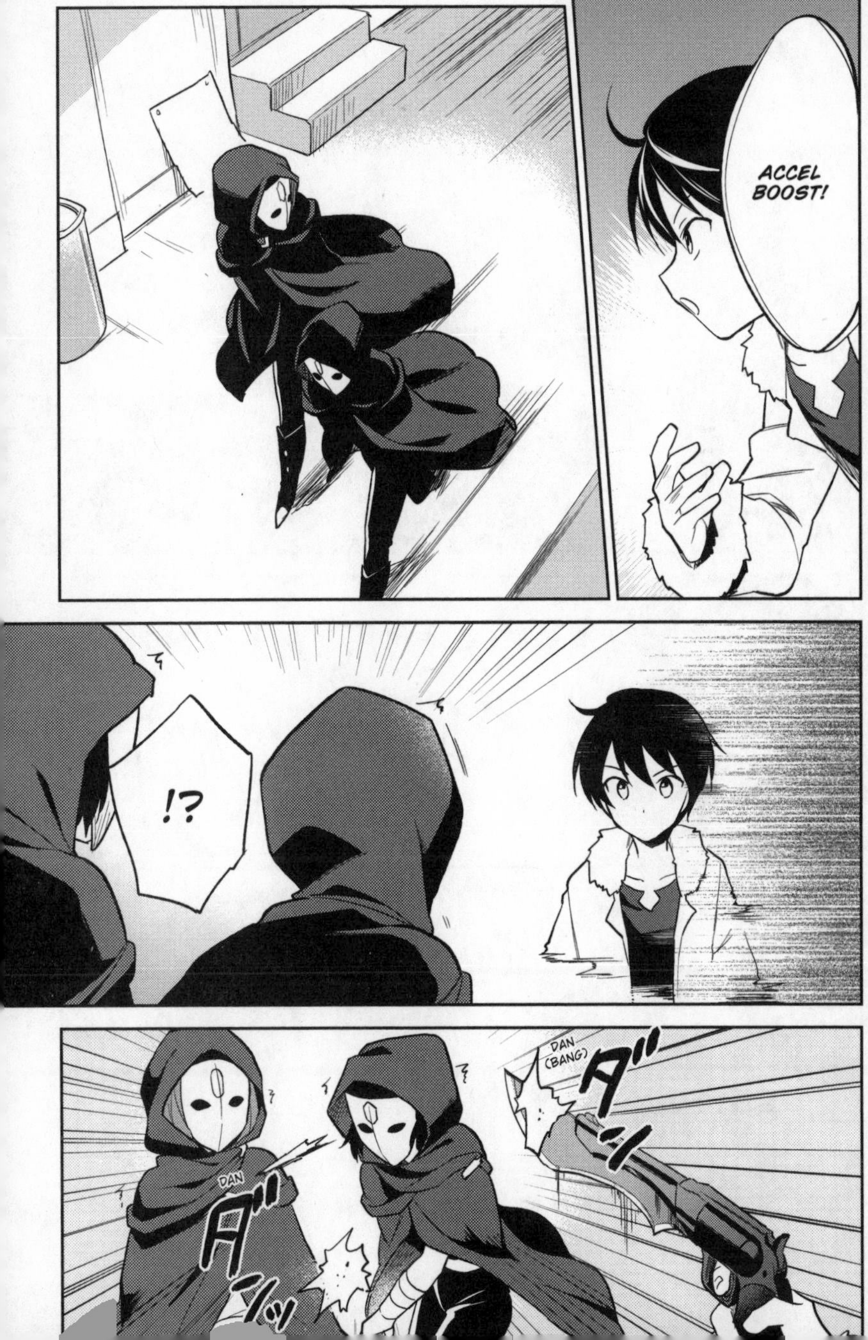
ACCEL BOOST!
!?
DAN (BANG)
DAN

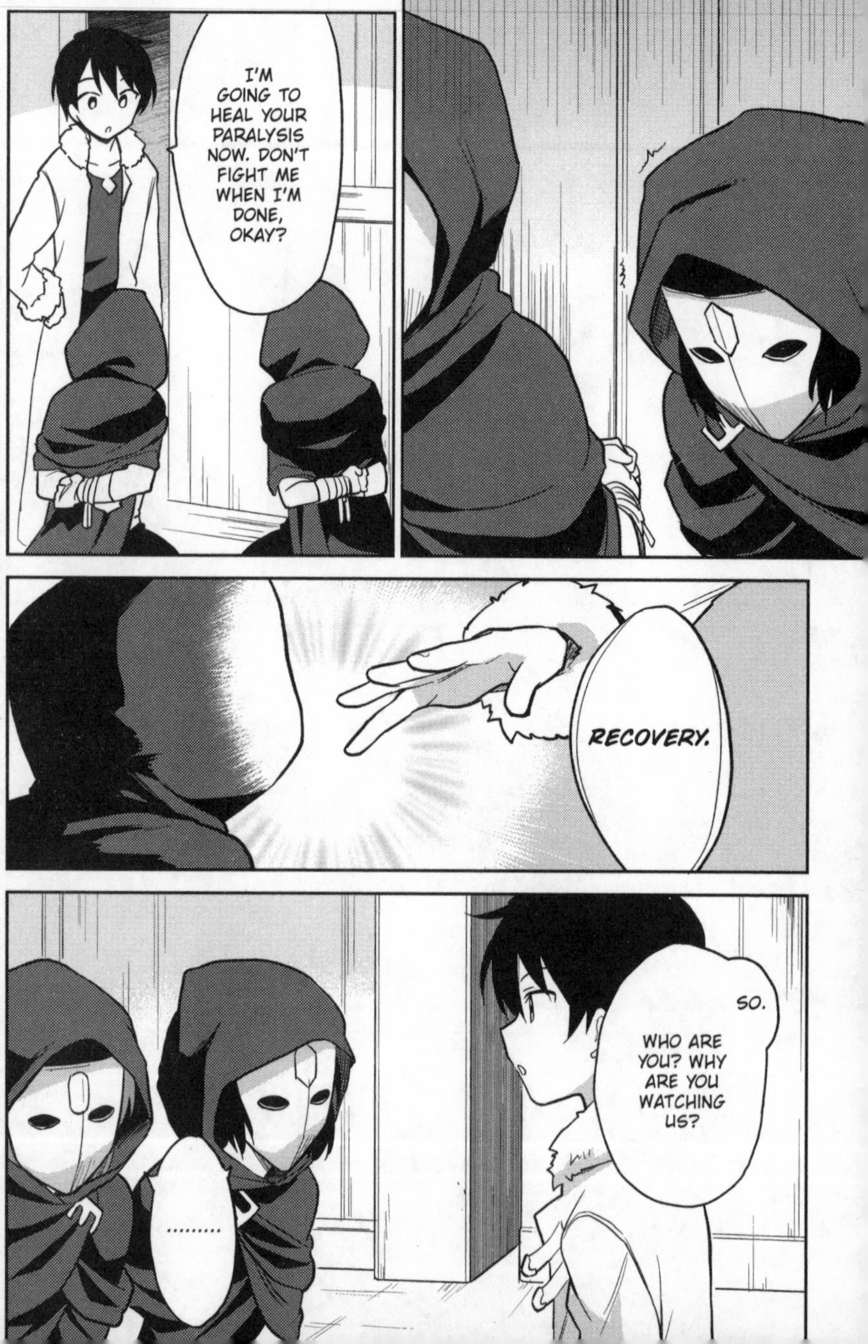
I'M GOING TO HEAL YOUR PARALYSIS NOW. DON'T FIGHT ME WHEN I'M DONE, OKAY?
RECOVERY.
SO.
WHO ARE YOU? WHY ARE YOU WATCHING US?
....

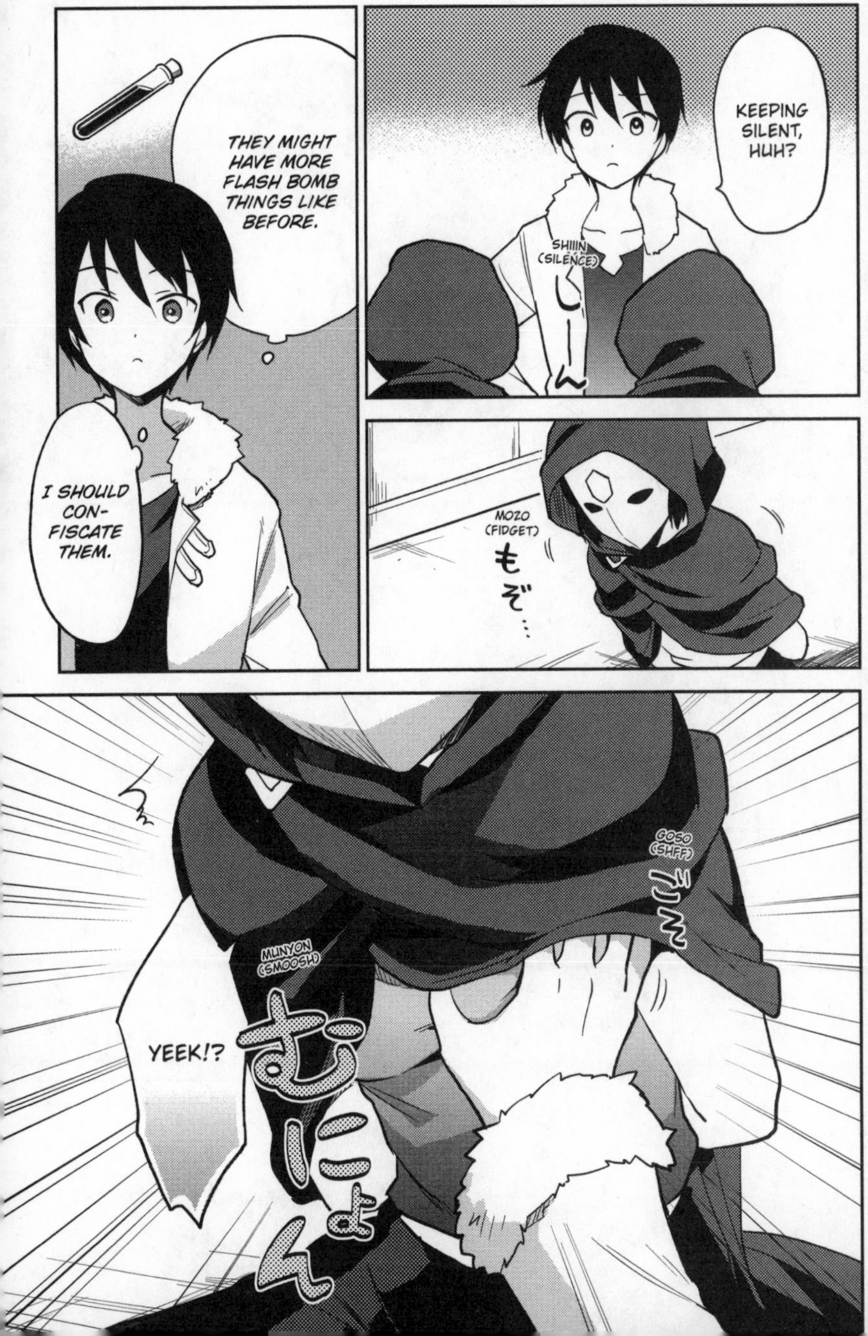
KEEPING SILENT, HUH?
SHIIIN (SILENCE)
しーん
MOZO (FIDGET)
もぞ…
THEY MIGHT HAVE MORE FLASH BOMB THINGS LIKE BEFORE.
I SHOULD CON-FISCATE THEM.
GOSO (SHFF)
ごそ
MUNYON (SMOOSH)
むにょん
YEEK!?

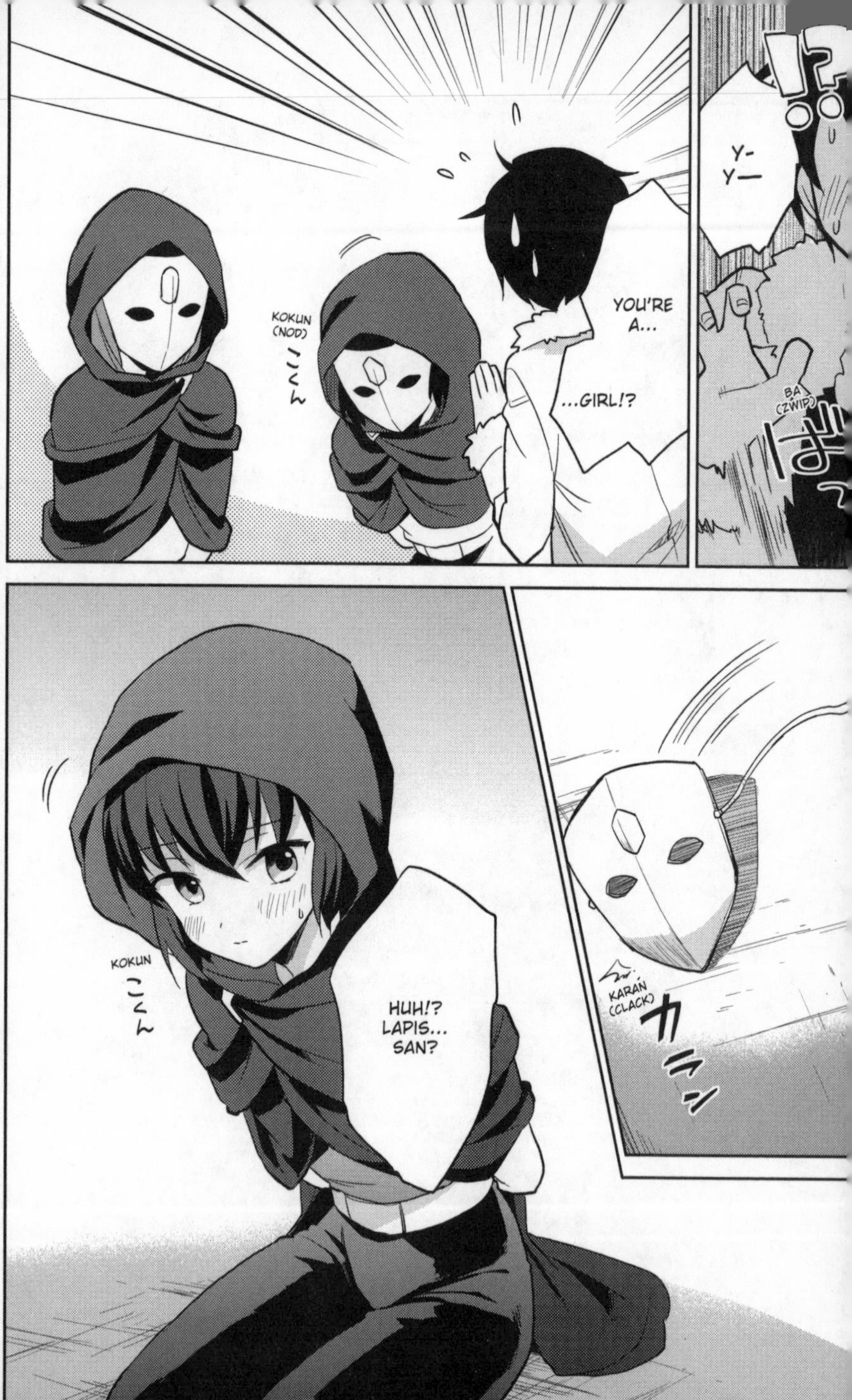

Y-
Y—
BA (ZWIP)
YOU'RE A...
...GIRL!?
KOKUN (NOD)
こくん
KARAN (CLACK)
カラッ
HUH!? LAPIS... SAN?
KOKUN
こくん

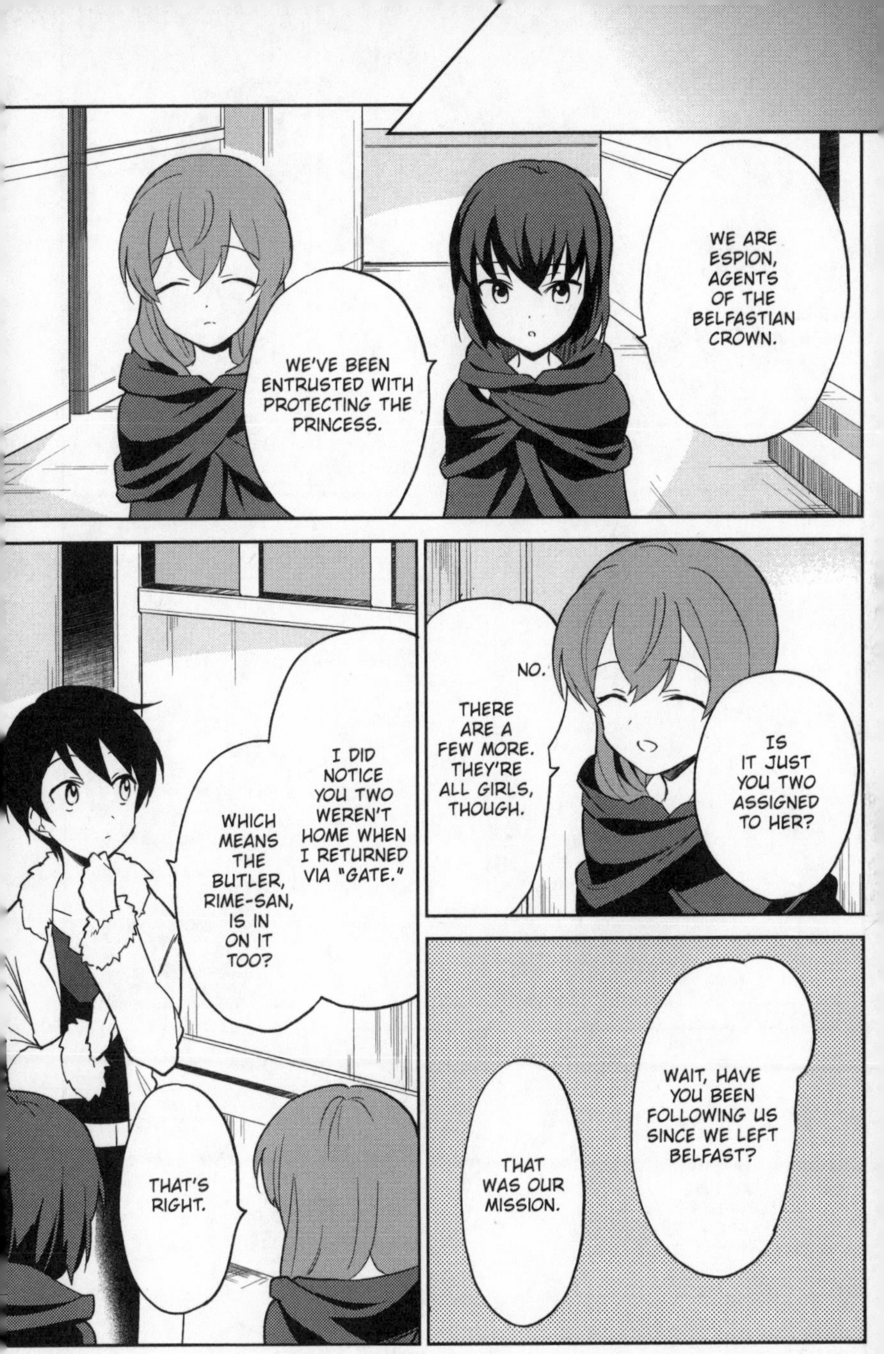
WE ARE ESPION, AGENTS OF THE BELFASTIAN CROWN.
WE'VE BEEN ENTRUSTED WITH PROTECTING THE PRINCESS.
IS IT JUST YOU TWO ASSIGNED TO HER?
NO.
THERE ARE A FEW MORE. THEY'RE ALL GIRLS, THOUGH.
WAIT, HAVE YOU BEEN FOLLOWING US SINCE WE LEFT BELFAST?
THAT WAS OUR MISSION.
I DID NOTICE YOU TWO WEREN'T HOME WHEN I RETURNED VIA "GATE."
WHICH MEANS THE BUTLER, RIME-SAN, IS IN ON IT TOO?
THAT'S RIGHT.

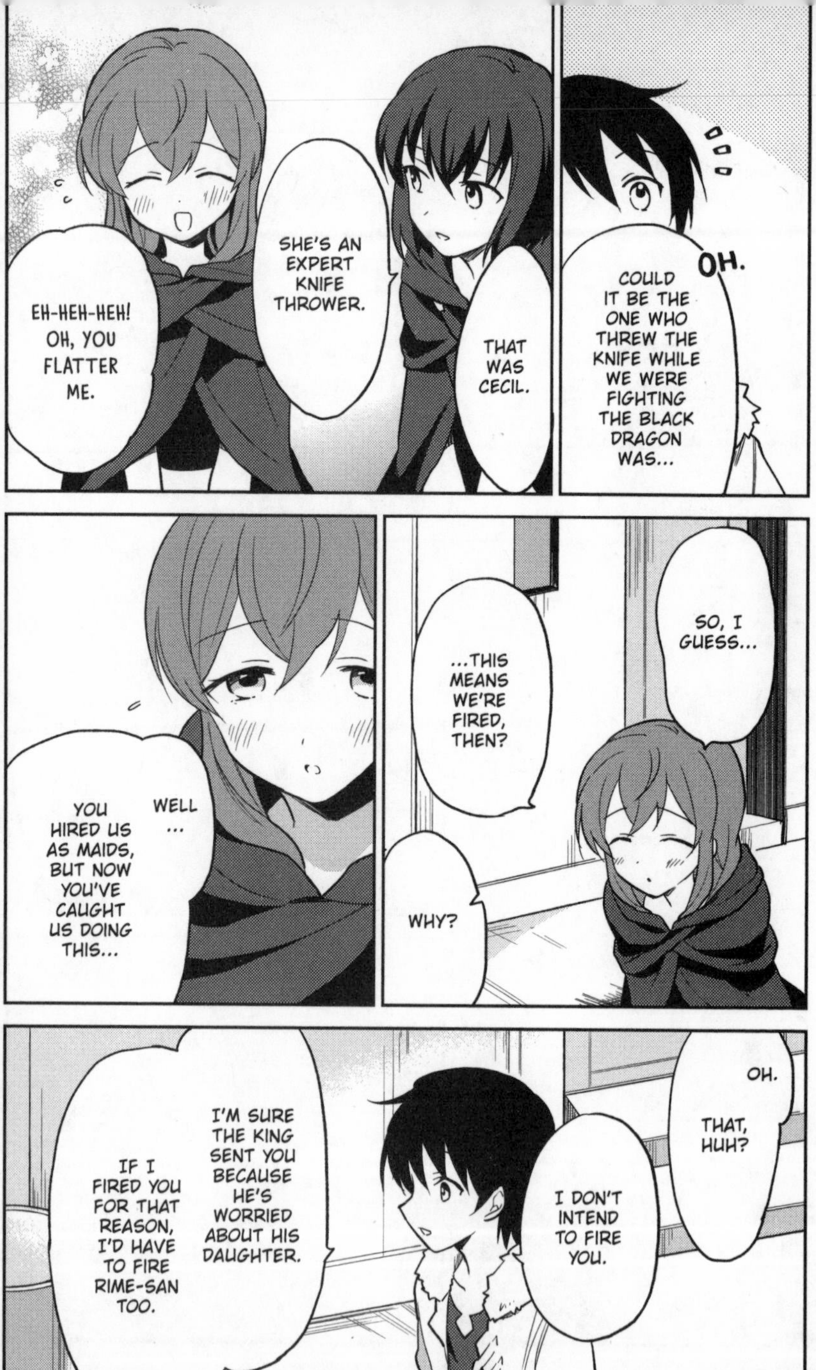
OH.
COULD IT BE THE ONE WHO THREW THE KNIFE WHILE WE WERE FIGHTING THE BLACK DRAGON WAS...
THAT WAS CECIL.
SHE'S AN EXPERT KNIFE THROWER.
EH-HEH-HEH! OH, YOU FLATTER ME.
SO, I GUESS...
...THIS MEANS WE'RE FIRED, THEN?
WHY?
WELL...
YOU HIRED US AS MAIDS, BUT NOW YOU'VE CAUGHT US DOING THIS...
OH.
THAT, HUH?
I DON'T INTEND TO FIRE YOU.
I'M SURE THE KING SENT YOU BECAUSE HE'S WORRIED ABOUT HIS DAUGHTER.
IF I FIRED YOU FOR THAT REASON, I'D HAVE TO FIRE RIME-SAN TOO.

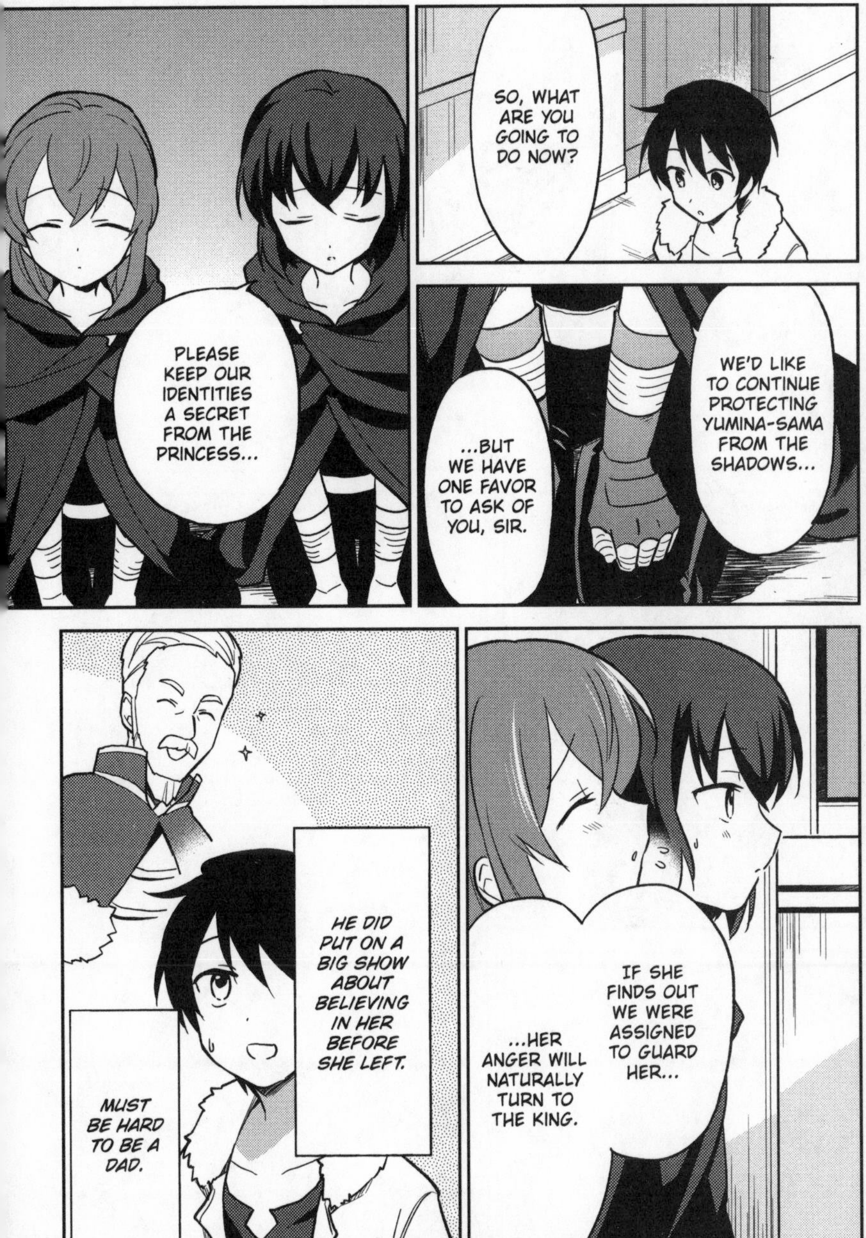
SO, WHAT ARE YOU GOING TO DO NOW?
WE'D LIKE TO CONTINUE PROTECTING YUMINA-SAMA FROM THE SHADOWS...
...BUT WE HAVE ONE FAVOR TO ASK OF YOU, SIR.
PLEASE KEEP OUR IDENTITIES A SECRET FROM THE PRINCESS...
IF SHE FINDS OUT WE WERE ASSIGNED TO GUARD HER...
...HER ANGER WILL NATURALLY TURN TO THE KING.
HE DID PUT ON A BIG SHOW ABOUT BELIEVING IN HER BEFORE SHE LEFT.
MUST BE HARD TO BE A DAD.

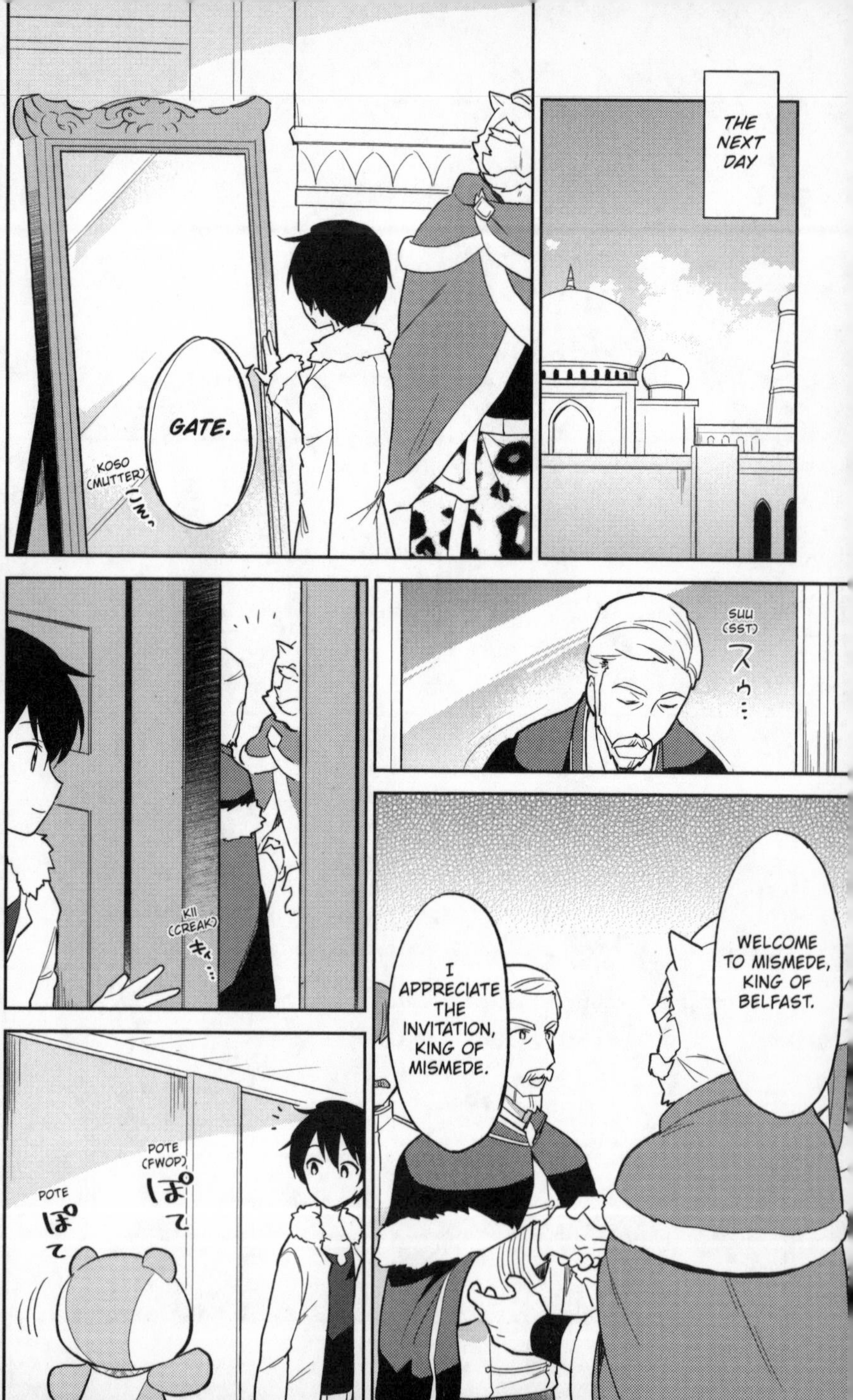
THE NEXT DAY
GATE.
KOSO (MUTTER)
こそ
SUU (SST)
スゥ…
KII (CREAK)
キィ…
WELCOME TO MISMEDE, KING OF BELFAST.
I APPRECIATE THE INVITATION, KING OF MISMEDE.
POTE (FWOP)
ぽて
POTE
ぽて

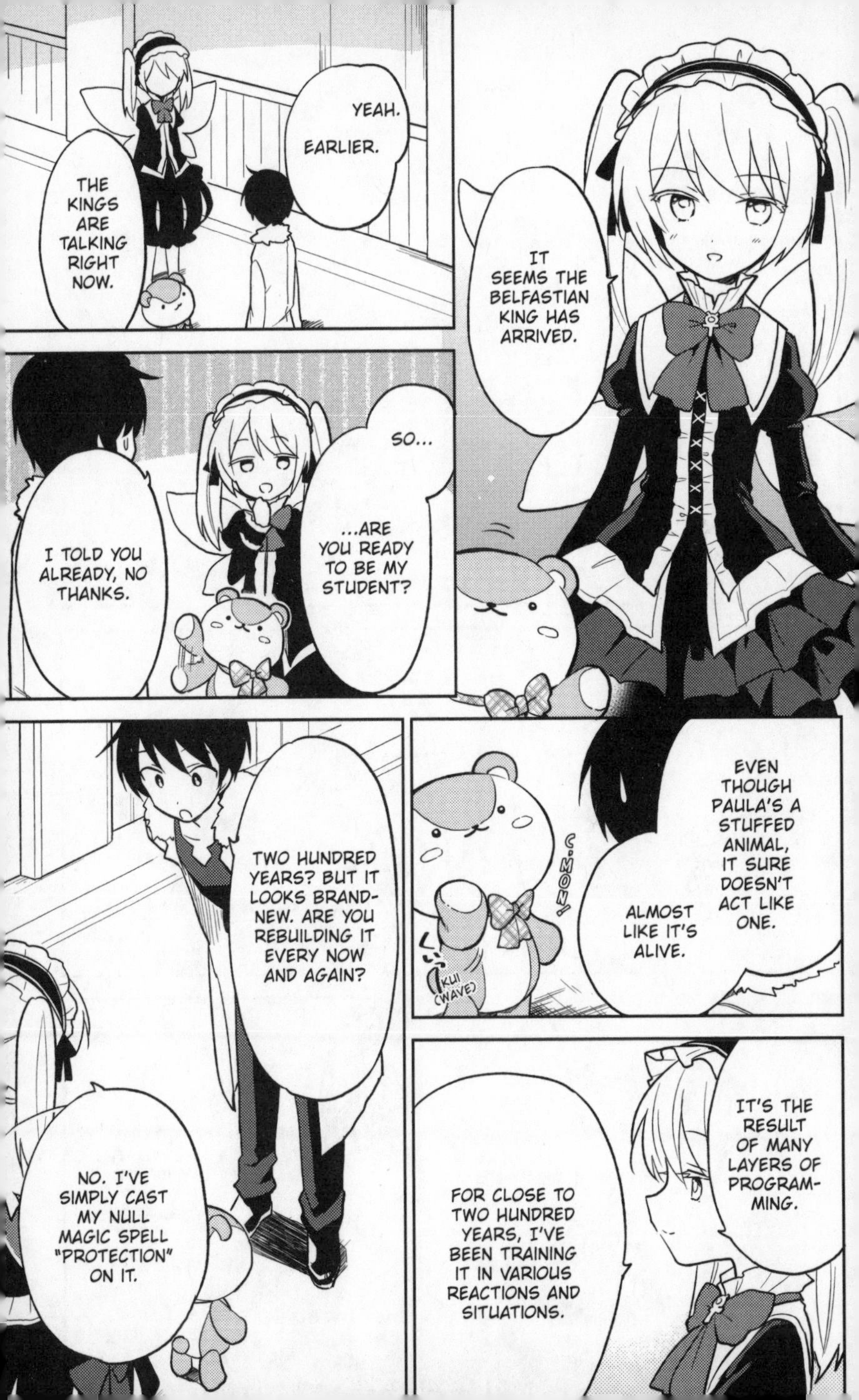
IT SEEMS THE BELFASTIAN KING HAS ARRIVED.
YEAH.
EARLIER.
THE KINGS ARE TALKING RIGHT NOW.
SO...
...ARE YOU READY TO BE MY STUDENT?
I TOLD YOU ALREADY, NO THANKS.
EVEN THOUGH PAULA'S A STUFFED ANIMAL, IT SURE DOESN'T ACT LIKE ONE.
ALMOST LIKE IT'S ALIVE.
C'MON!
KUI (WAVE)
IT'S THE RESULT OF MANY LAYERS OF PROGRAM-MING.
FOR CLOSE TO TWO HUNDRED YEARS, I'VE BEEN TRAINING IT IN VARIOUS REACTIONS AND SITUATIONS.
TWO HUNDRED YEARS? BUT IT LOOKS BRAND-NEW. ARE YOU REBUILDING IT EVERY NOW AND AGAIN?
NO. I'VE SIMPLY CAST MY NULL MAGIC SPELL "PROTECTION" ON IT.

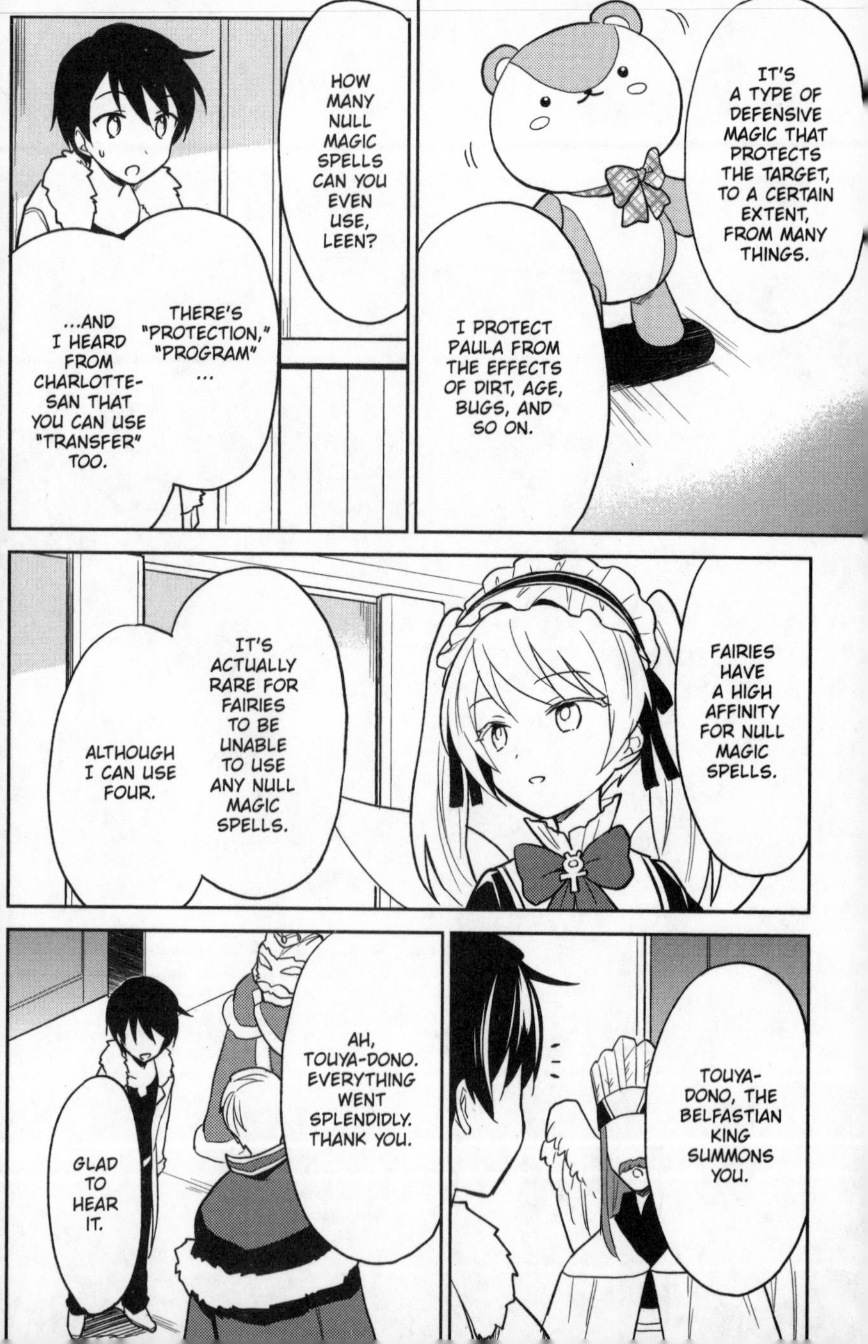
IT'S A TYPE OF DEFENSIVE MAGIC THAT PROTECTS THE TARGET, TO A CERTAIN EXTENT, FROM MANY THINGS.
I PROTECT PAULA FROM THE EFFECTS OF DIRT, AGE, BUGS, AND SO ON.
HOW MANY NULL MAGIC SPELLS CAN YOU EVEN USE, LEEN?
THERE'S "PROTECTION," "PROGRAM" ...
...AND I HEARD FROM CHARLOTTE-SAN THAT YOU CAN USE "TRANSFER" TOO.
FAIRIES HAVE A HIGH AFFINITY FOR NULL MAGIC SPELLS.
IT'S ACTUALLY RARE FOR FAIRIES TO BE UNABLE TO USE ANY NULL MAGIC SPELLS.
ALTHOUGH I CAN USE FOUR.
TOUYA-DONO, THE BELFASTIAN KING SUMMONS YOU.
AH, TOUYA-DONO. EVERYTHING WENT SPLENDIDLY. THANK YOU.
GLAD TO HEAR IT.

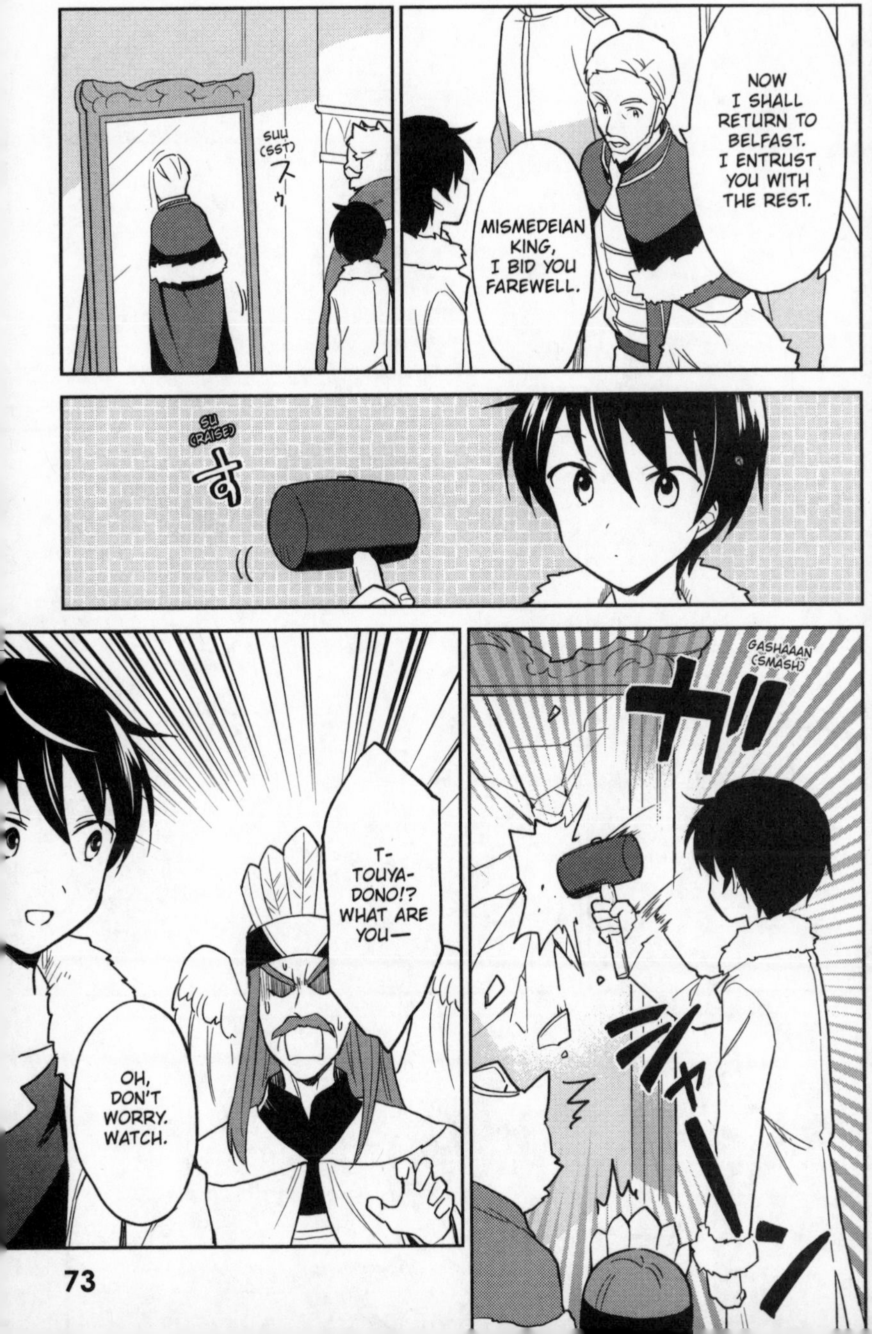
NOW I SHALL RETURN TO BELFAST. I ENTRUST YOU WITH THE REST.
MISMEDEIAN KING, I BID YOU FAREWELL.
SUU (SST)
スゥ
SU (RAISED)
す
GASHAAAN (SMASH)
ガシャーン
T-TOUYA-DONO!? WHAT ARE YOU—
OH, DON'T WORRY. WATCH.

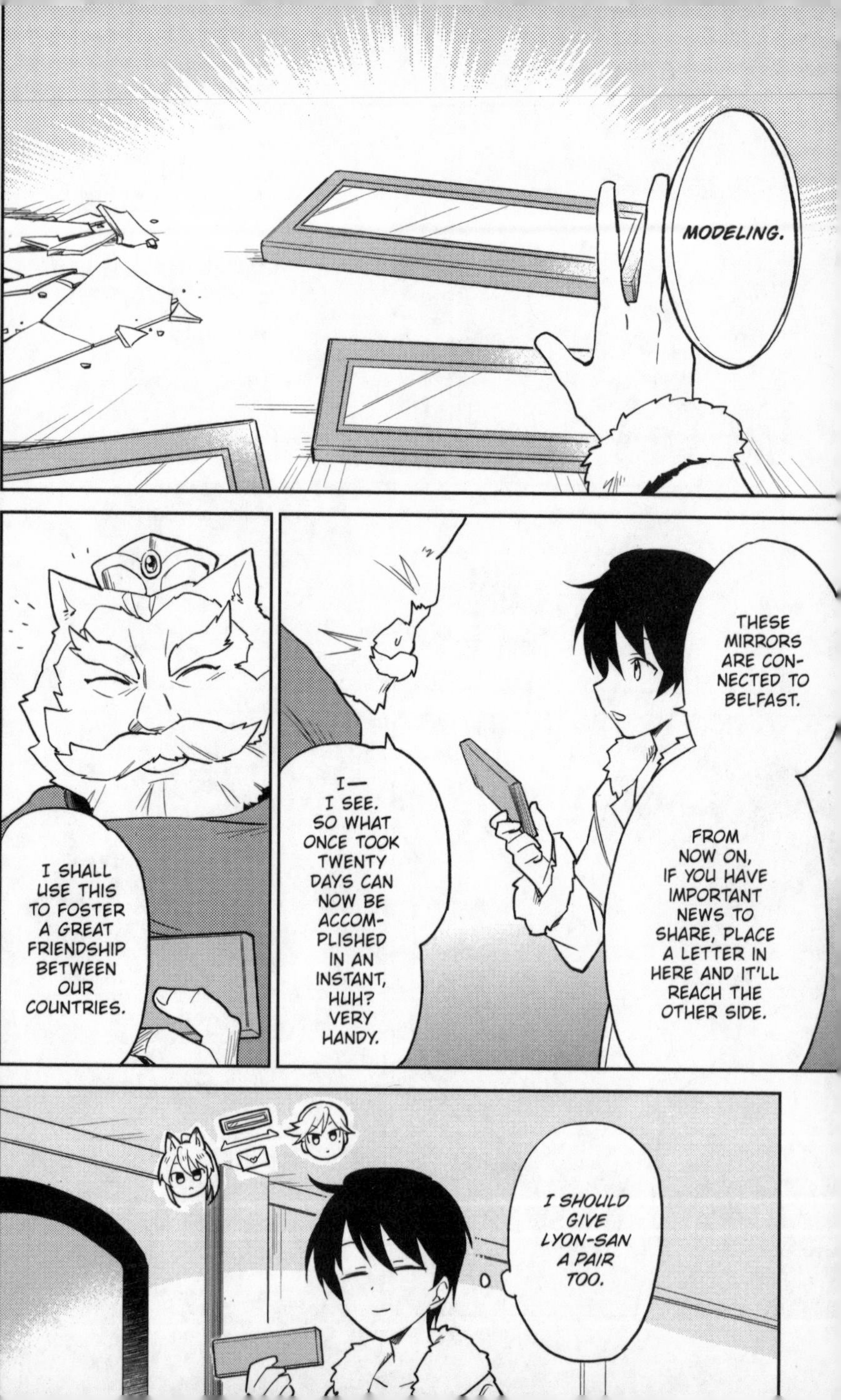
MODELING.
THESE MIRRORS ARE CONNECTED TO BELFAST.
FROM NOW ON, IF YOU HAVE IMPORTANT NEWS TO SHARE, PLACE A LETTER IN HERE AND IT'LL REACH THE OTHER SIDE.
I— I SEE. SO WHAT ONCE TOOK TWENTY DAYS CAN NOW BE ACCOMPLISHED IN AN INSTANT, HUH? VERY HANDY.
I SHALL USE THIS TO FOSTER A GREAT FRIENDSHIP BETWEEN OUR COUNTRIES.
I SHOULD GIVE LYON-SAN A PAIR TOO.

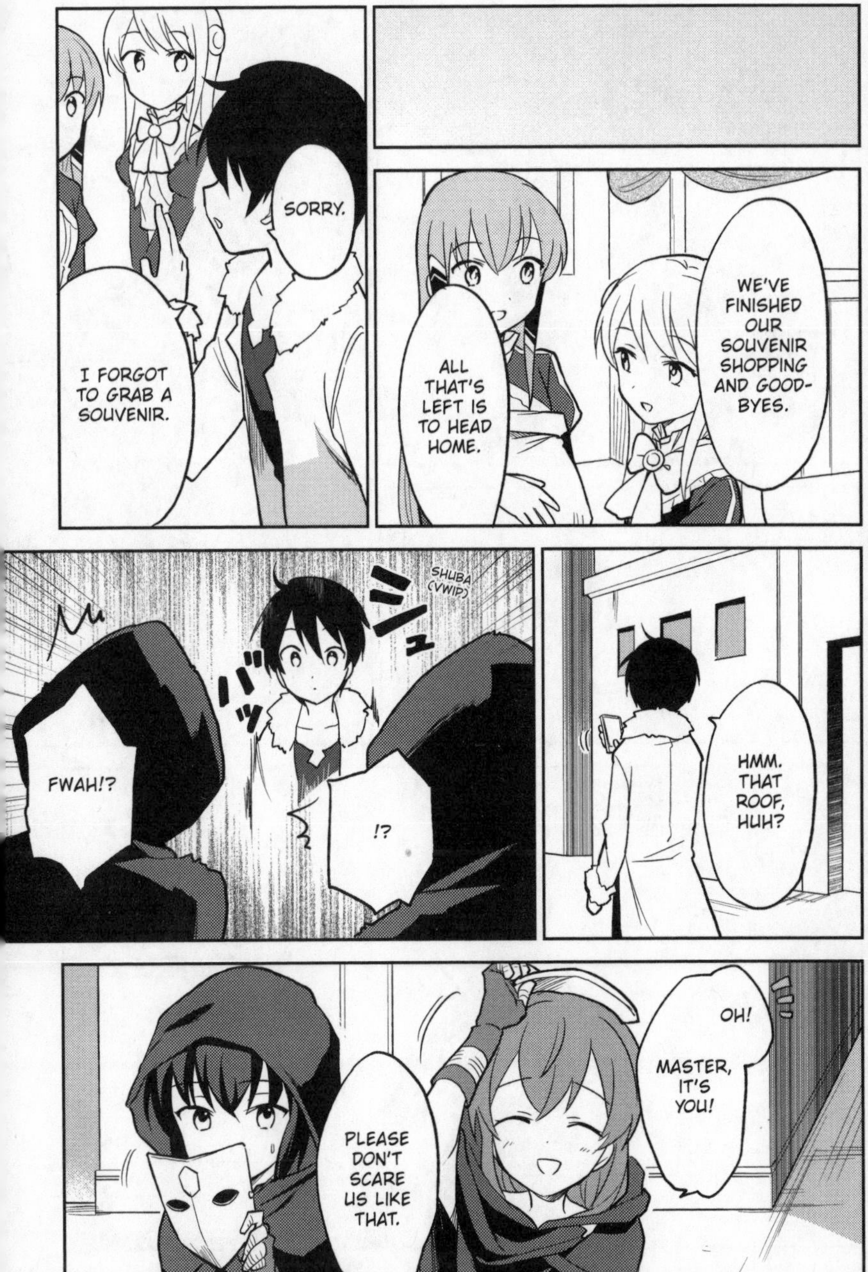
WE'VE FINISHED OUR SOUVENIR SHOPPING AND GOOD-BYES.
ALL THAT'S LEFT IS TO HEAD HOME.
SORRY.
I FORGOT TO GRAB A SOUVENIR.
HMM. THAT ROOF, HUH?
SHUBA (VWIP)
!?
FWAH!?
OH!
MASTER, IT'S YOU!
PLEASE DON'T SCARE US LIKE THAT.

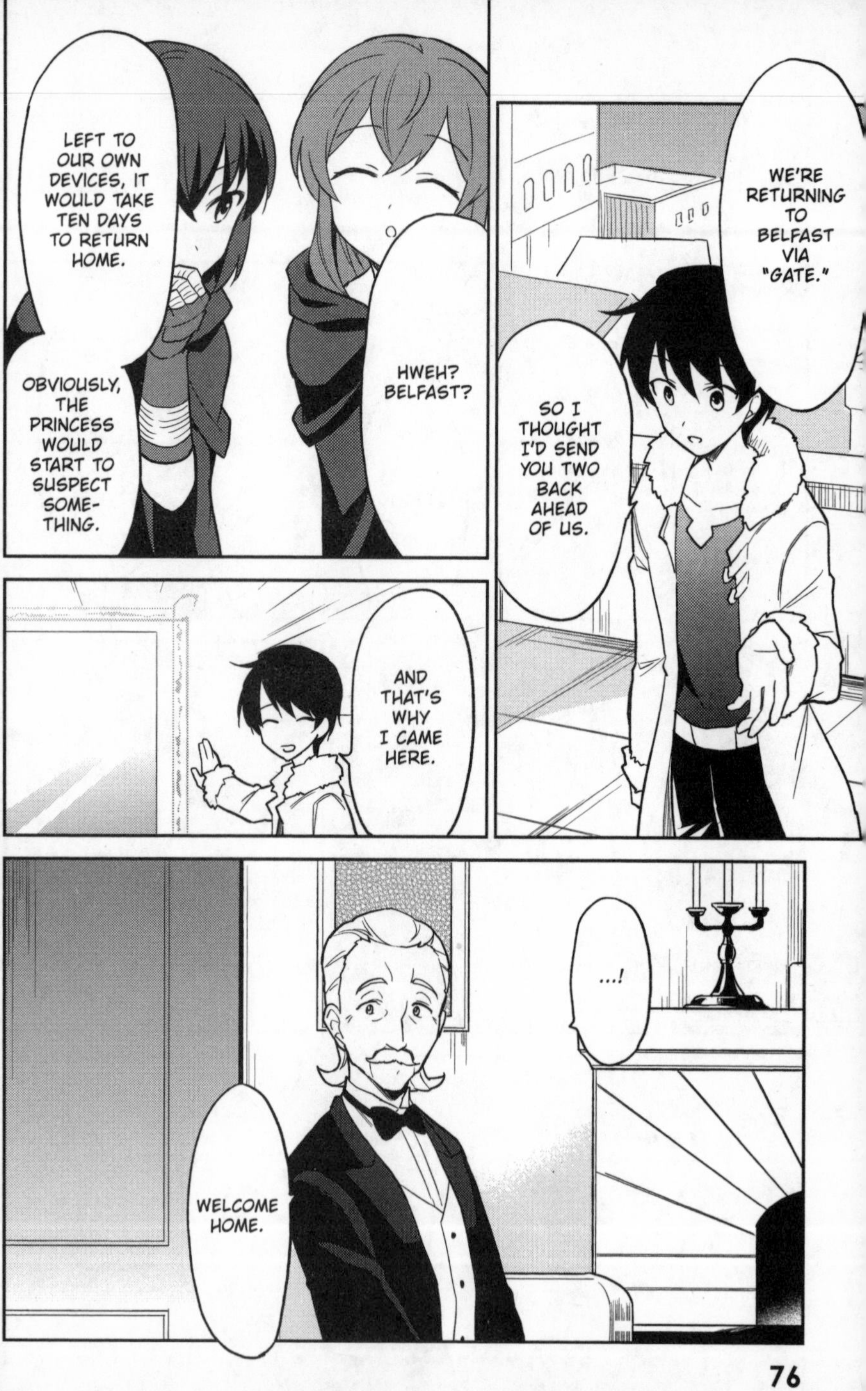
WE'RE RETURNING TO BELFAST VIA "GATE."
SO I THOUGHT I'D SEND YOU TWO BACK AHEAD OF US.
HWEH? BELFAST?
LEFT TO OUR OWN DEVICES, IT WOULD TAKE TEN DAYS TO RETURN HOME.
OBVIOUSLY, THE PRINCESS WOULD START TO SUSPECT SOME-THING.
AND THAT'S WHY I CAME HERE.
...!
WELCOME HOME.

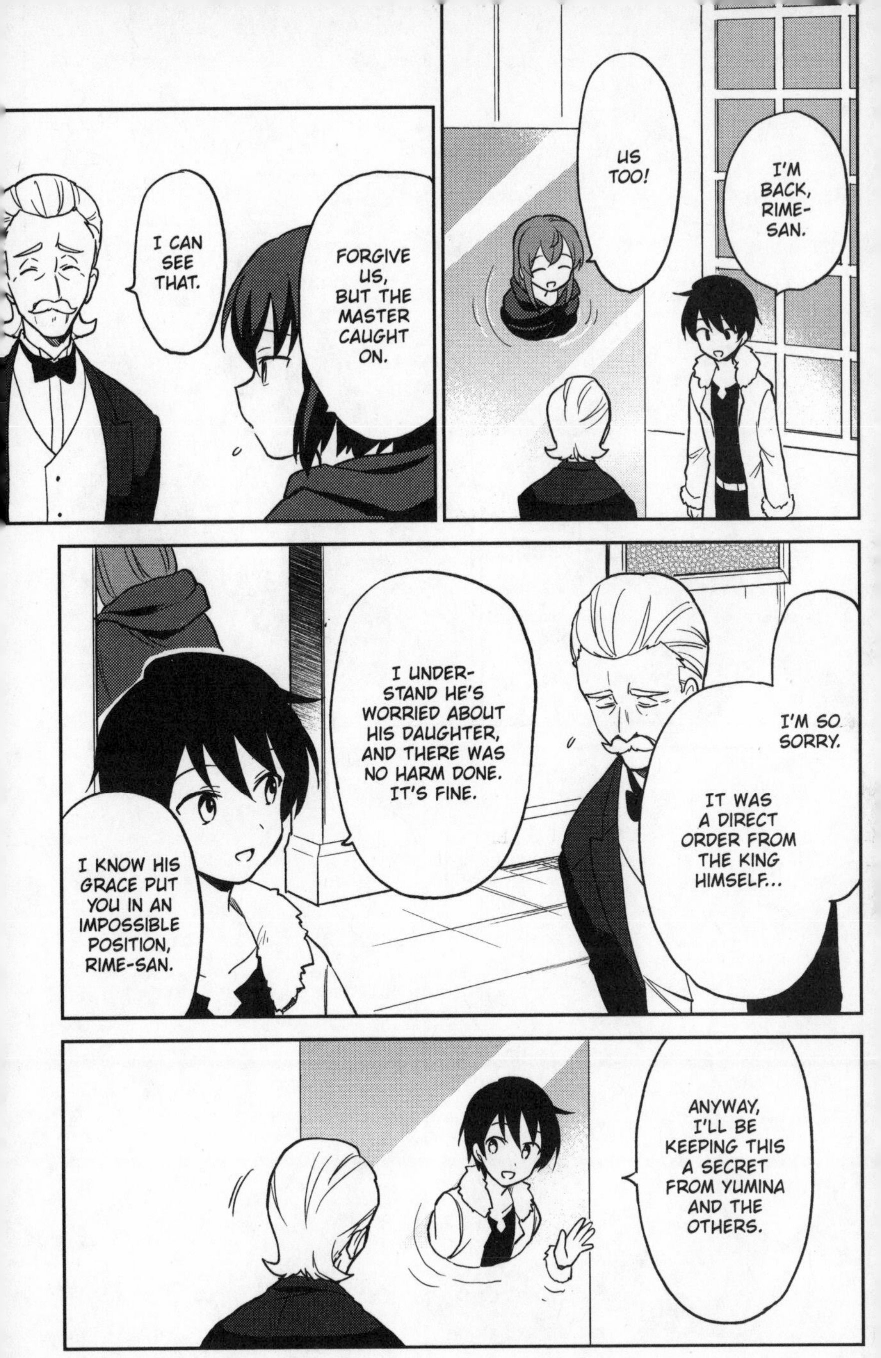
I'M BACK, RIME-SAN.
US TOO!
FORGIVE US, BUT THE MASTER CAUGHT ON.
I CAN SEE THAT.
I'M SO SORRY.
IT WAS A DIRECT ORDER FROM THE KING HIMSELF...
I UNDER-STAND HE'S WORRIED ABOUT HIS DAUGHTER, AND THERE WAS NO HARM DONE. IT'S FINE.
I KNOW HIS GRACE PUT YOU IN AN IMPOSSIBLE POSITION, RIME-SAN.
ANYWAY, I'LL BE KEEPING THIS A SECRET FROM YUMINA AND THE OTHERS.

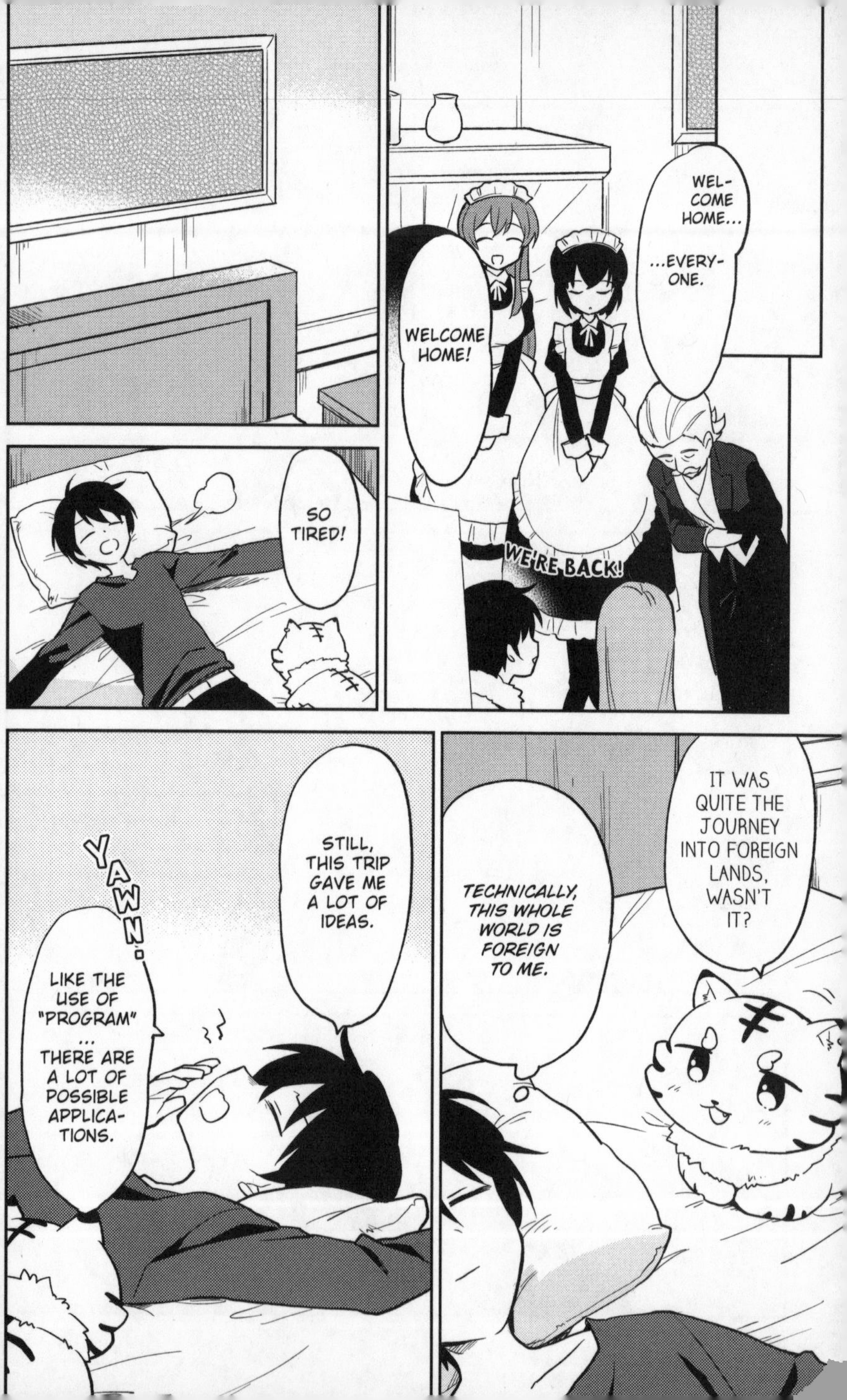
WELCOME HOME... ...EVERYONE.
WELCOME HOME!
WE'RE BACK!
SO TIRED!
IT WAS QUITE THE JOURNEY INTO FOREIGN LANDS, WASN'T IT?
TECHNICALLY, THIS WHOLE WORLD IS FOREIGN TO ME.
STILL, THIS TRIP GAVE ME A LOT OF IDEAS.
YAWN.
LIKE THE USE OF "PROGRAM"... THERE ARE A LOT OF POSSIBLE APPLICATIONS.

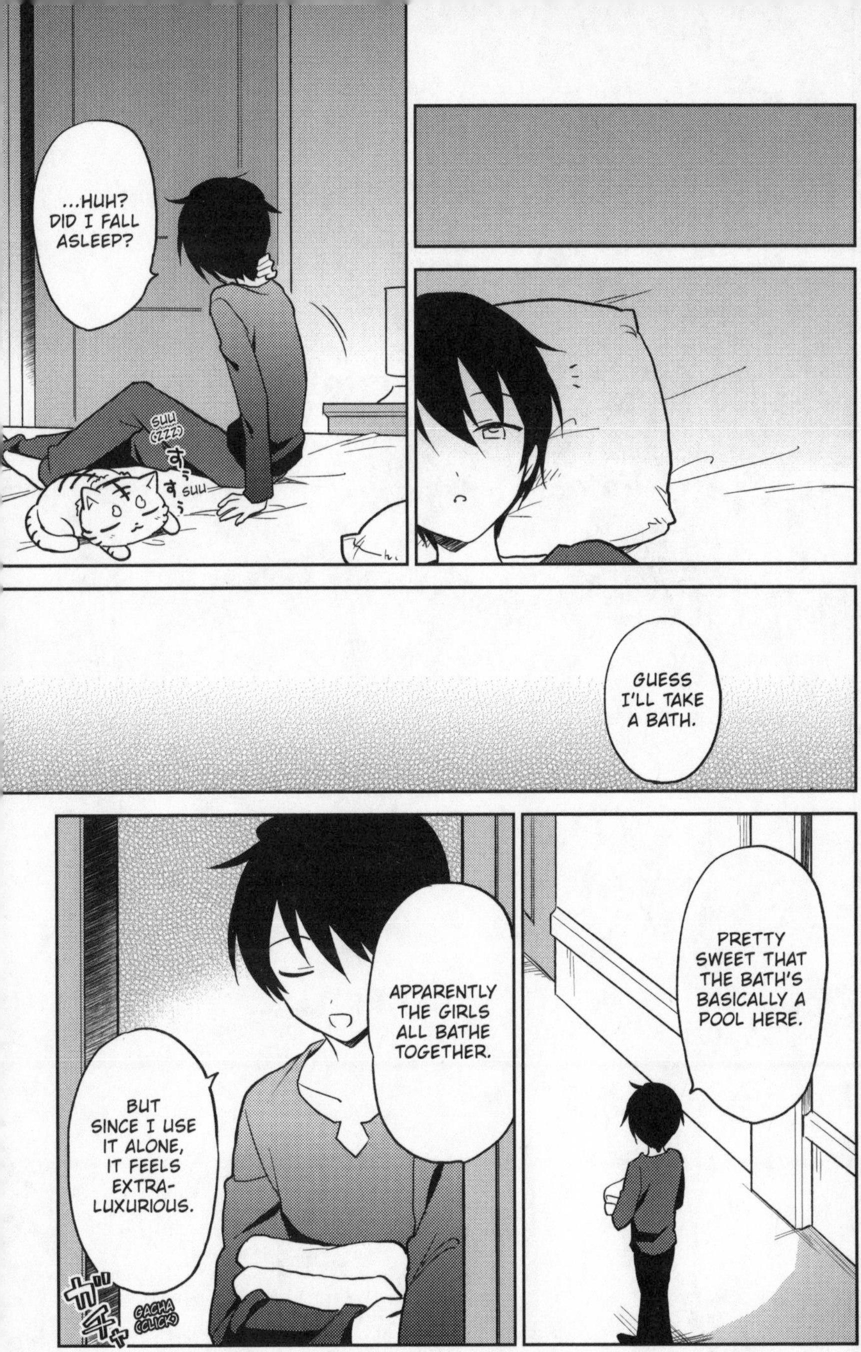
...HUH? DID I FALL ASLEEP?
SUU (ZZZ)
SUU
GUESS I'LL TAKE A BATH.
PRETTY SWEET THAT THE BATH'S BASICALLY A POOL HERE.
APPARENTLY THE GIRLS ALL BATHE TOGETHER.
BUT SINCE I USE IT ALONE, IT FEELS EXTRA-LUXURIOUS.
GACHA (CLICK)

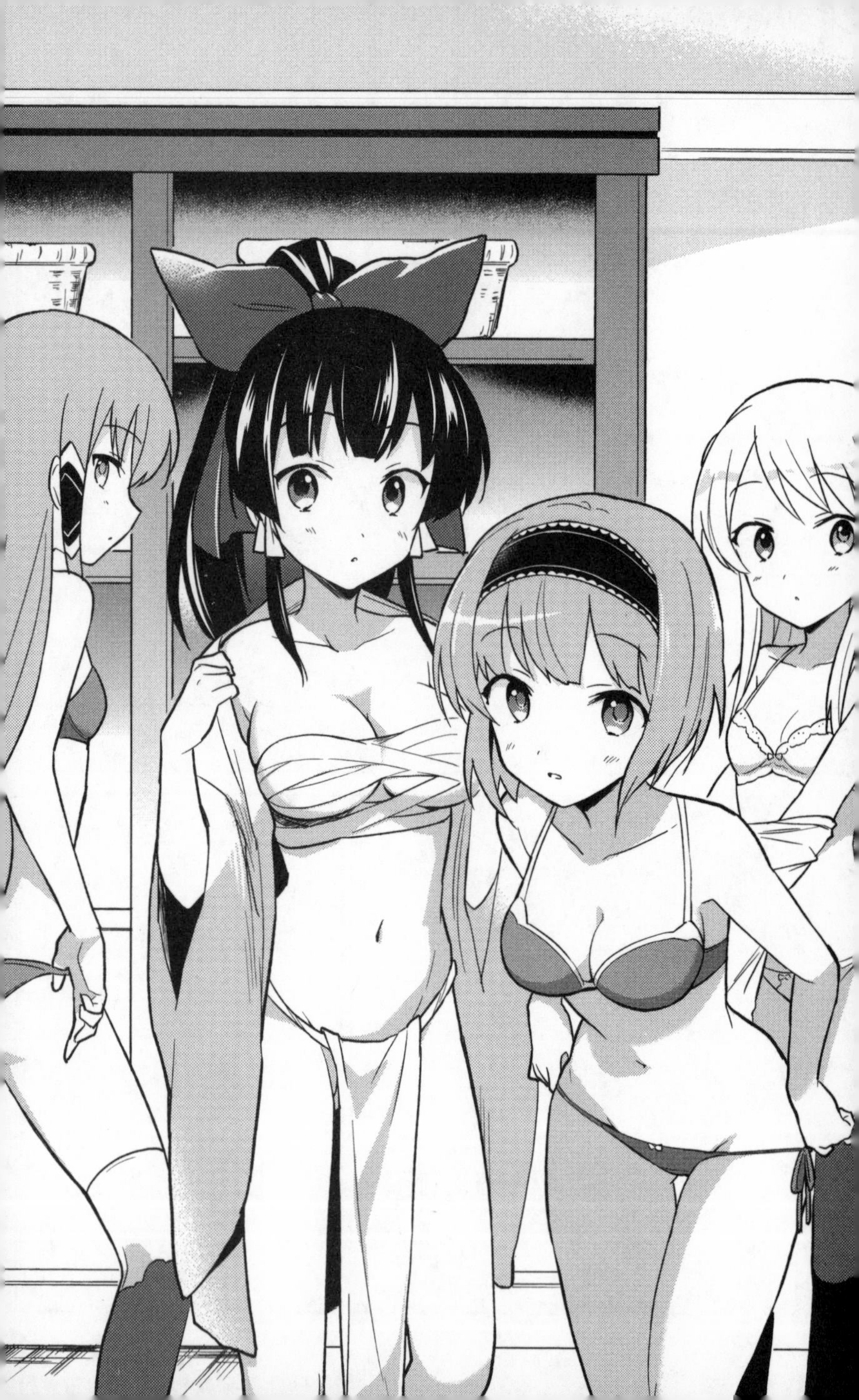

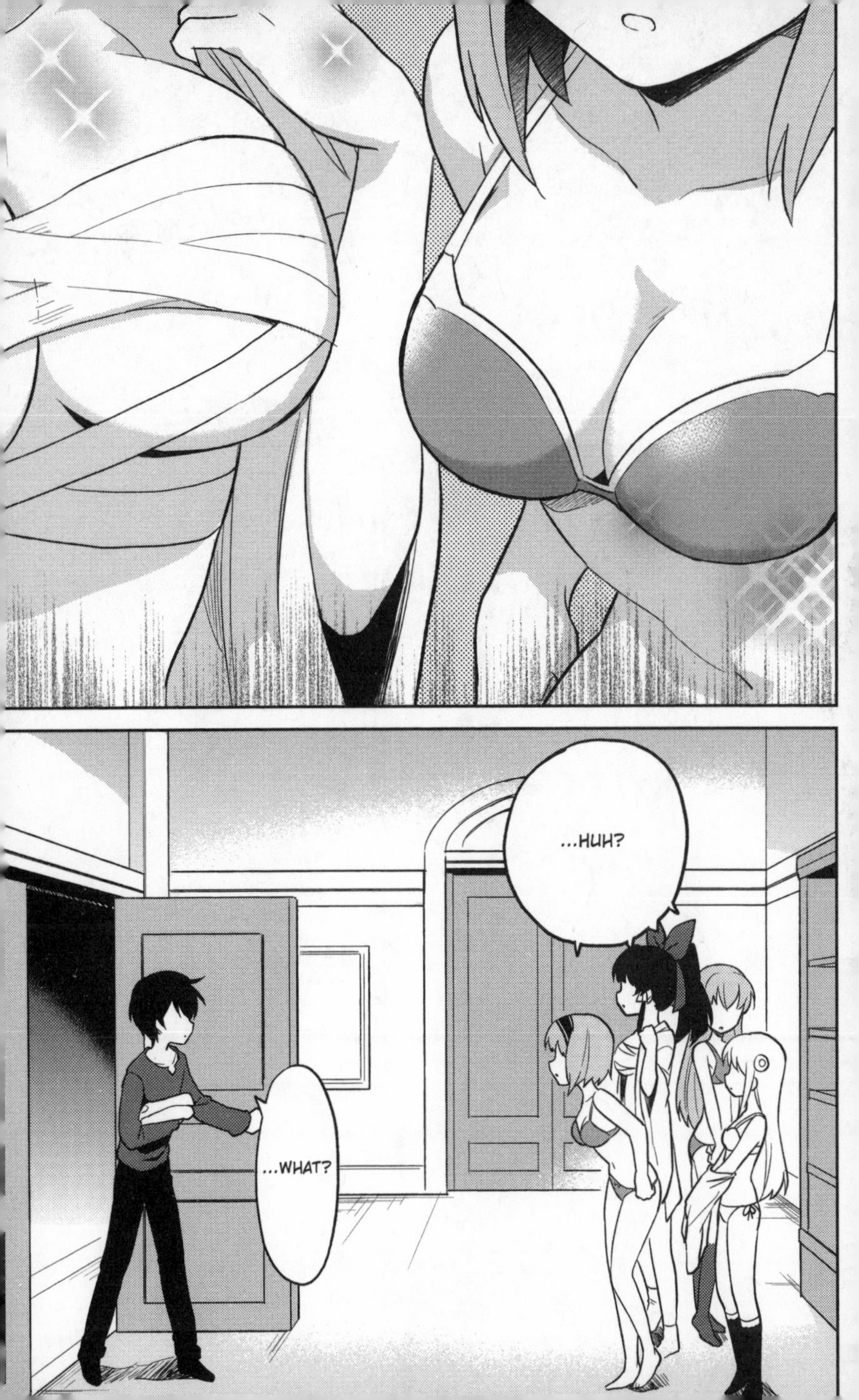
...HUH?
...WHAT?

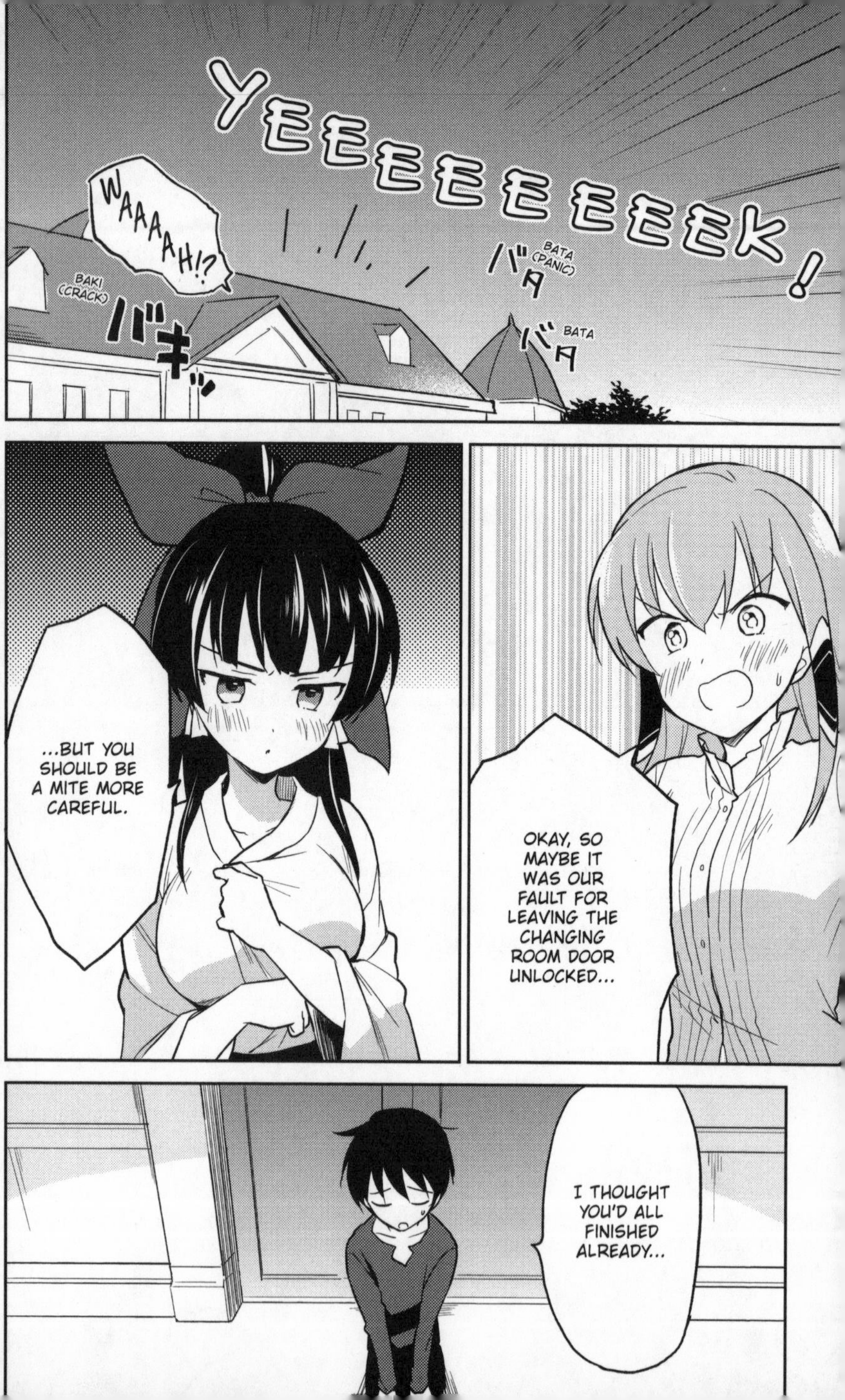
YEEEEEEEEK!
BATA (PANIC)
BATA
WAAAAAH!?
BAKI (CRACK)
OKAY, SO MAYBE IT WAS OUR FAULT FOR LEAVING THE CHANGING ROOM DOOR UNLOCKED...
...BUT YOU SHOULD BE A MITE MORE CAREFUL.
I THOUGHT YOU'D ALL FINISHED ALREADY...

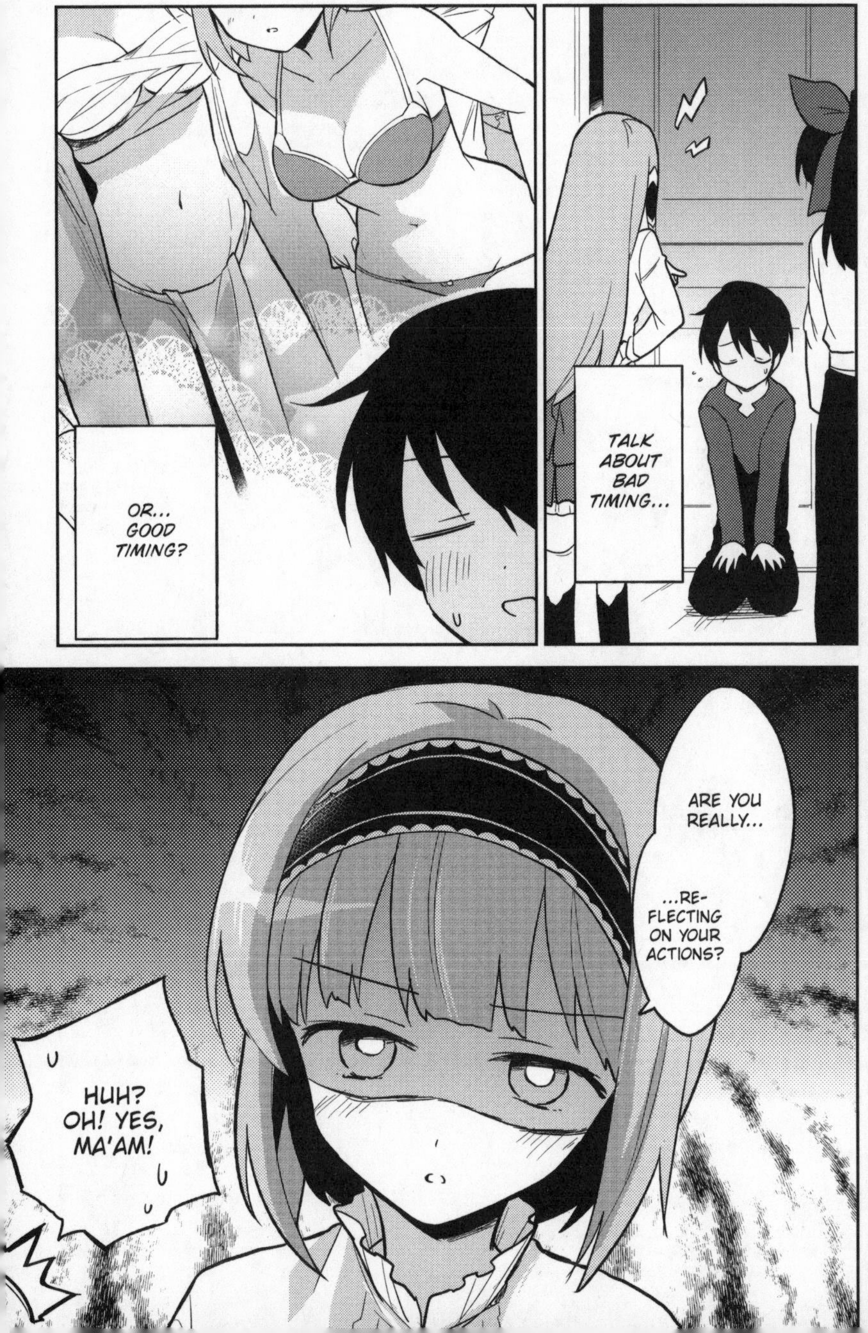
TALK ABOUT BAD TIMING...
OR... GOOD TIMING?
ARE YOU REALLY...
...RE-FLECTING ON YOUR ACTIONS?
HUH? OH! YES, MA'AM!

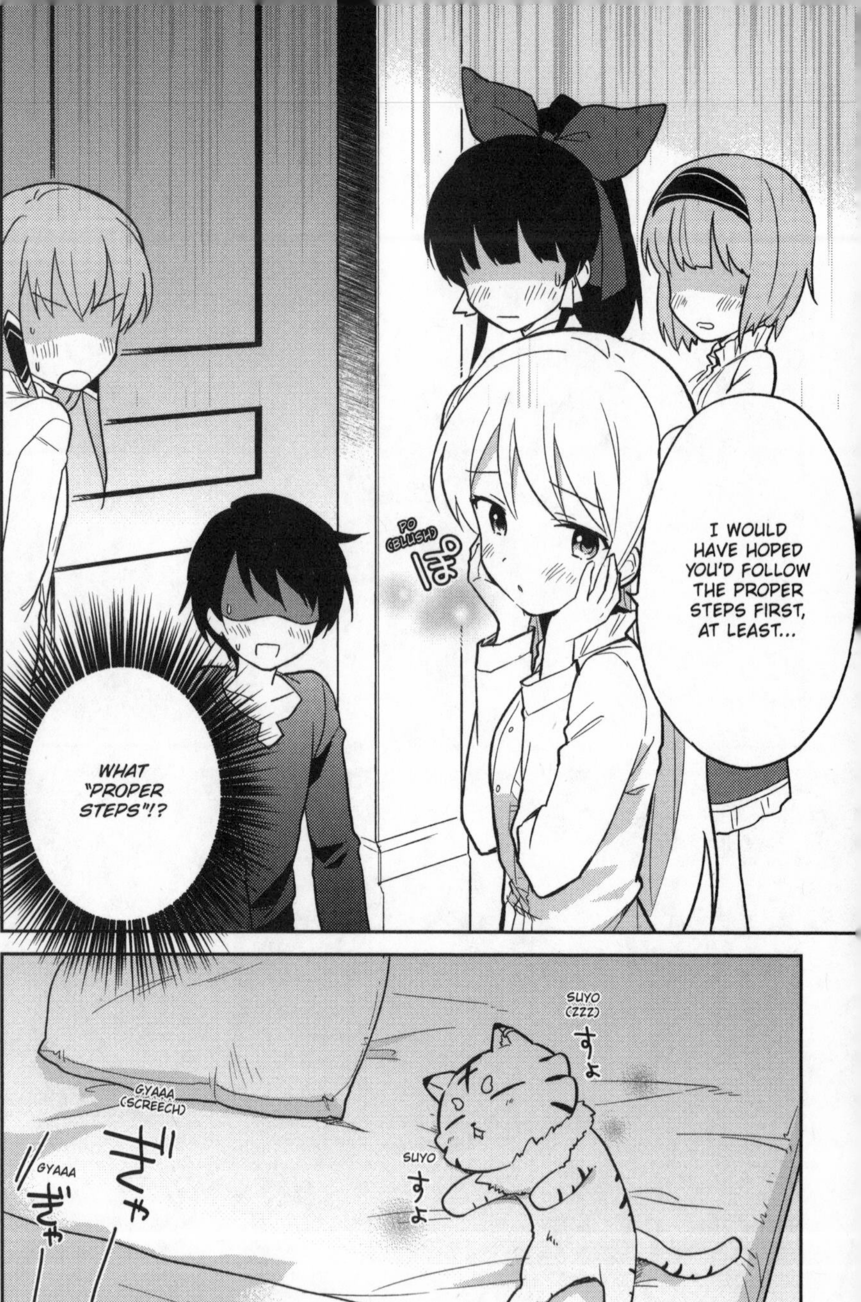

I WOULD HAVE HOPED YOU'D FOLLOW THE PROPER STEPS FIRST, AT LEAST...
PO (BLUSH)
ぽ
WHAT "PROPER STEPS"!?
SUYO (ZZZ)
すよ
SUYO
すよ
GYAAA (SCREECH)
ギャー
GYAAA
ギャー

EPISODE: 22 » END

In Another World with
My Smartphone

In Another World with my Smartphone

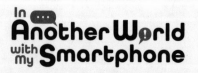

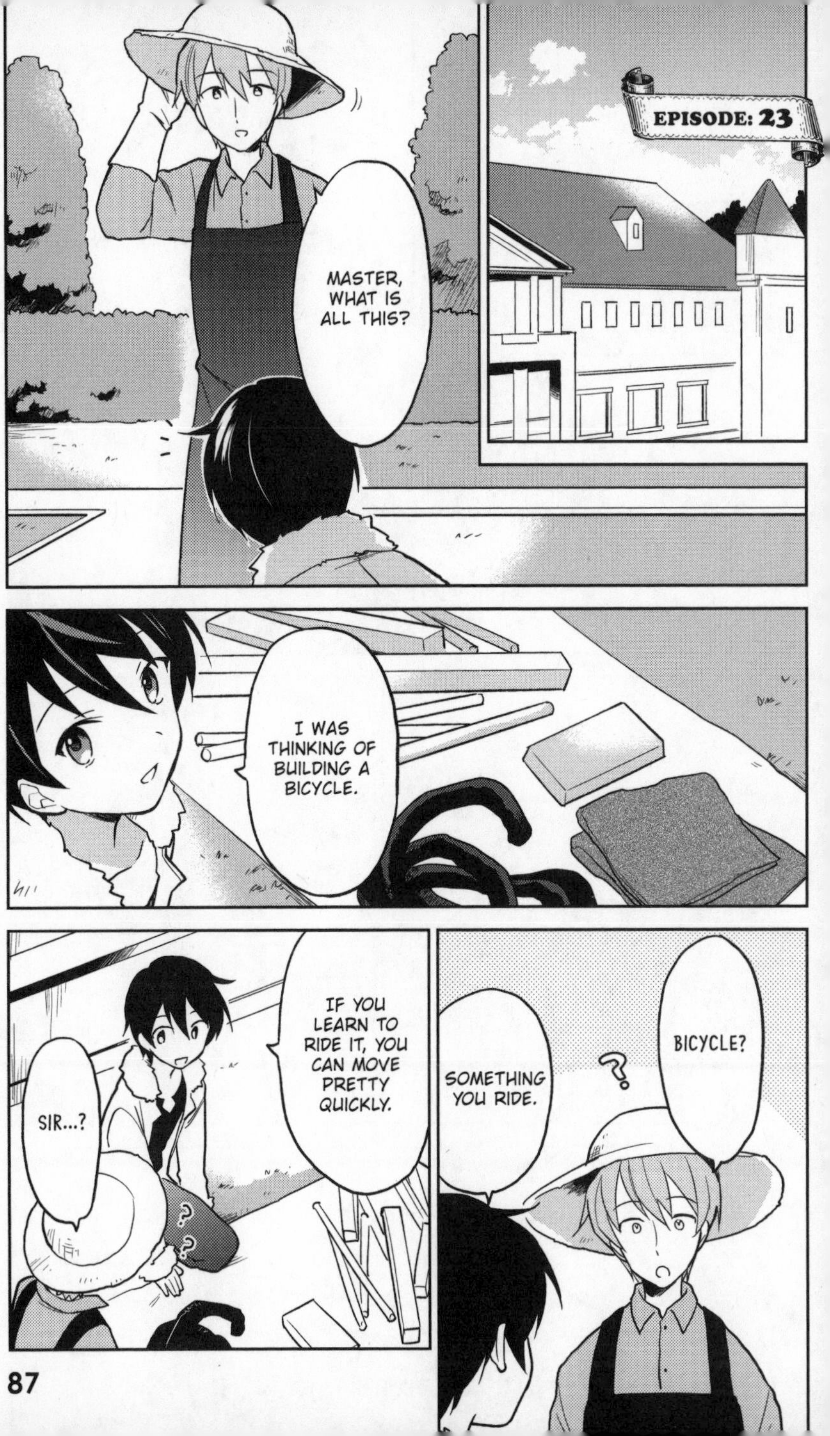

EPISODE: 23
MASTER, WHAT IS ALL THIS?
I WAS THINKING OF BUILDING A BICYCLE.
BICYCLE?
SOMETHING YOU RIDE.
IF YOU LEARN TO RIDE IT, YOU CAN MOVE PRETTY QUICKLY.
SIR...?

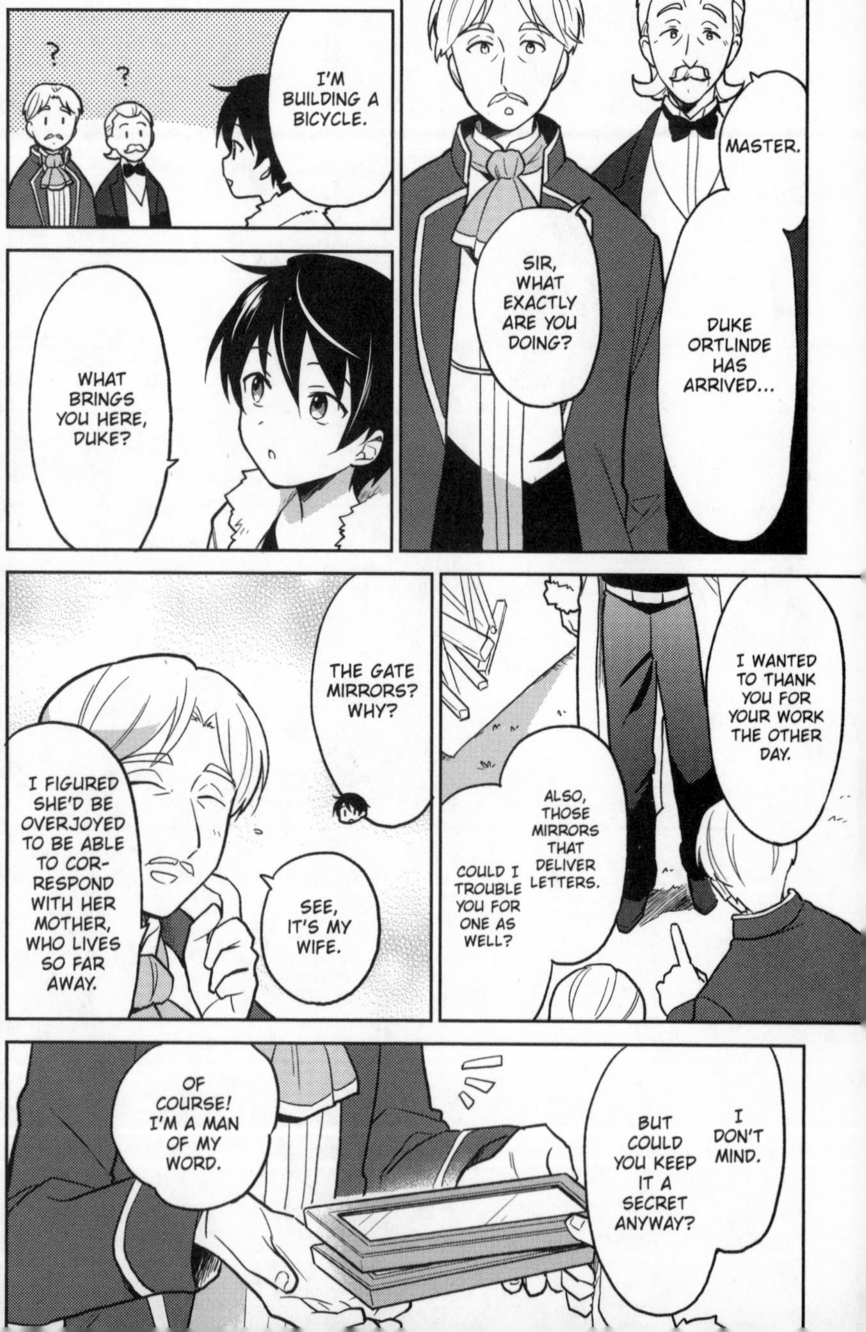
MASTER.
DUKE ORTLINDE HAS ARRIVED...
SIR, WHAT EXACTLY ARE YOU DOING?
I'M BUILDING A BICYCLE.
WHAT BRINGS YOU HERE, DUKE?
I WANTED TO THANK YOU FOR YOUR WORK THE OTHER DAY.
ALSO, THOSE MIRRORS THAT DELIVER LETTERS.
COULD I TROUBLE YOU FOR ONE AS WELL?
THE GATE MIRRORS? WHY?
SEE, IT'S MY WIFE.
I FIGURED SHE'D BE OVERJOYED TO BE ABLE TO CORRESPOND WITH HER MOTHER, WHO LIVES SO FAR AWAY.
I DON'T MIND.
BUT COULD YOU KEEP IT A SECRET ANYWAY?
OF COURSE! I'M A MAN OF MY WORD.

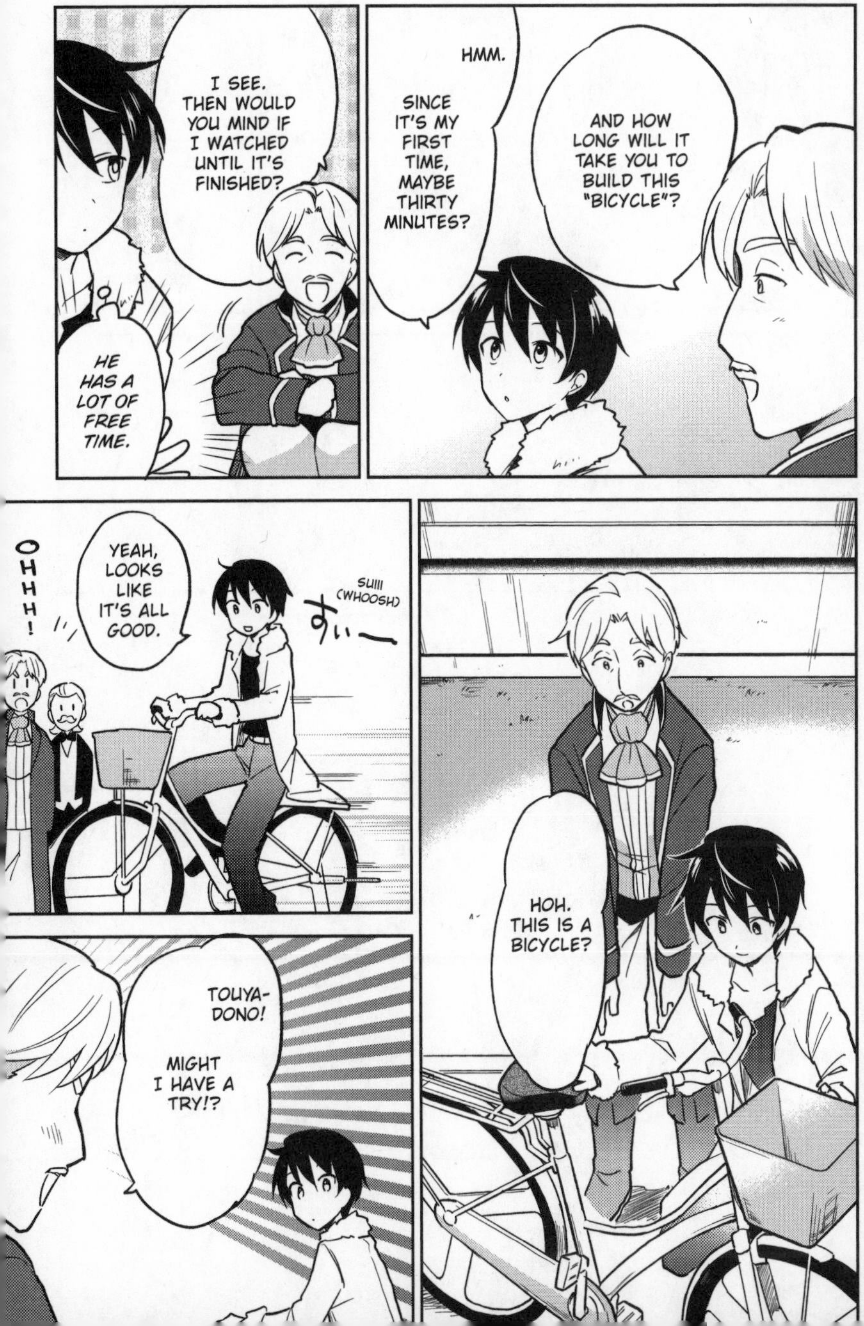
AND HOW LONG WILL IT TAKE YOU TO BUILD THIS "BICYCLE"?
HMM.
SINCE IT'S MY FIRST TIME, MAYBE THIRTY MINUTES?
I SEE. THEN WOULD YOU MIND IF I WATCHED UNTIL IT'S FINISHED?
HE HAS A LOT OF FREE TIME.
HOH. THIS IS A BICYCLE?
SUIII (WHOOSH)
すい～
YEAH, LOOKS LIKE IT'S ALL GOOD.
OHHH!
TOUYA-DONO!
MIGHT I HAVE A TRY!?

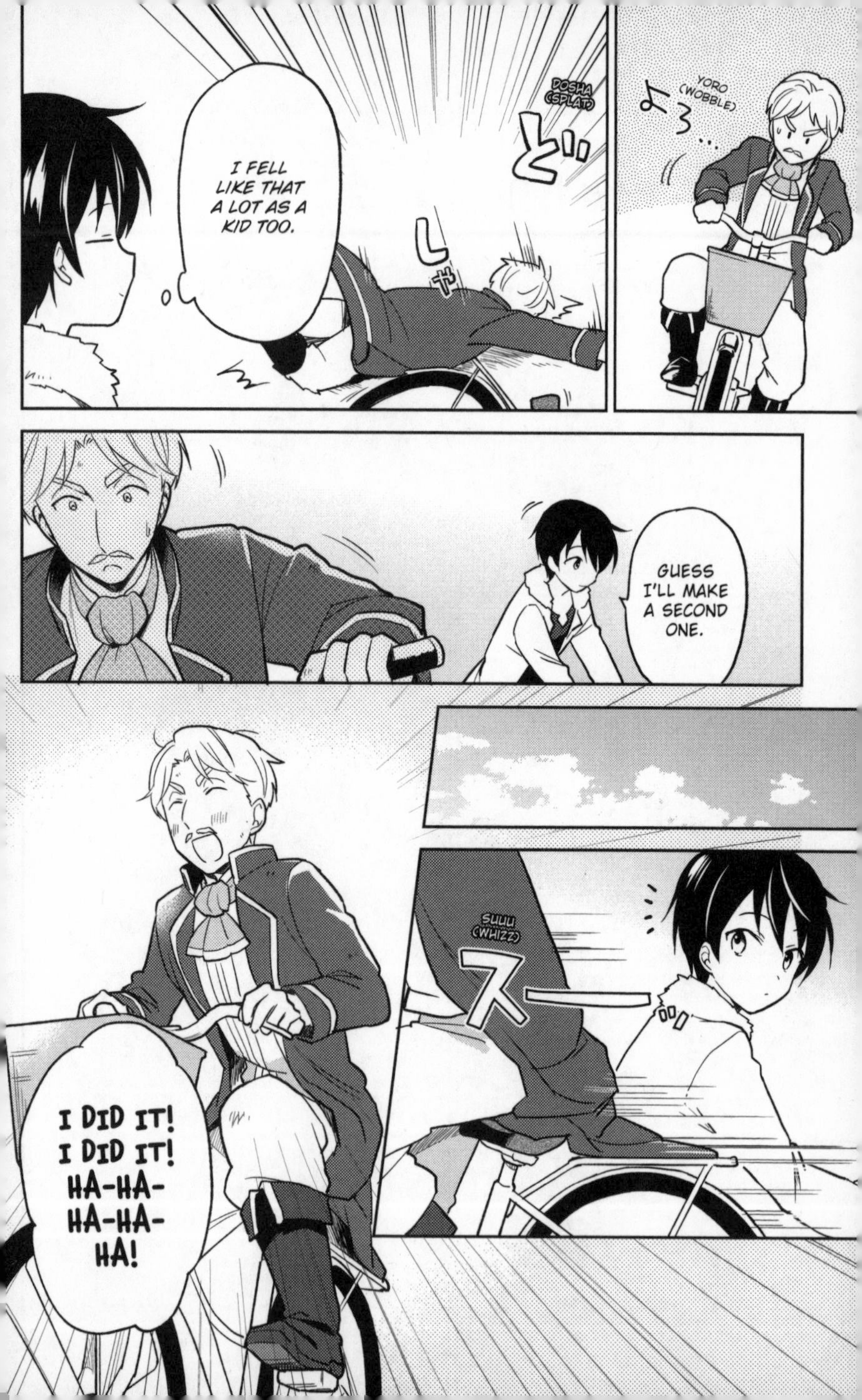
YORO (WOBBLE)
DOSHA (SPLAT)
I FELL LIKE THAT A LOT AS A KID TOO.
GUESS I'LL MAKE A SECOND ONE.
SUUU (WHIZZ)
I DID IT! I DID IT! HA-HA-HA-HA-HA!

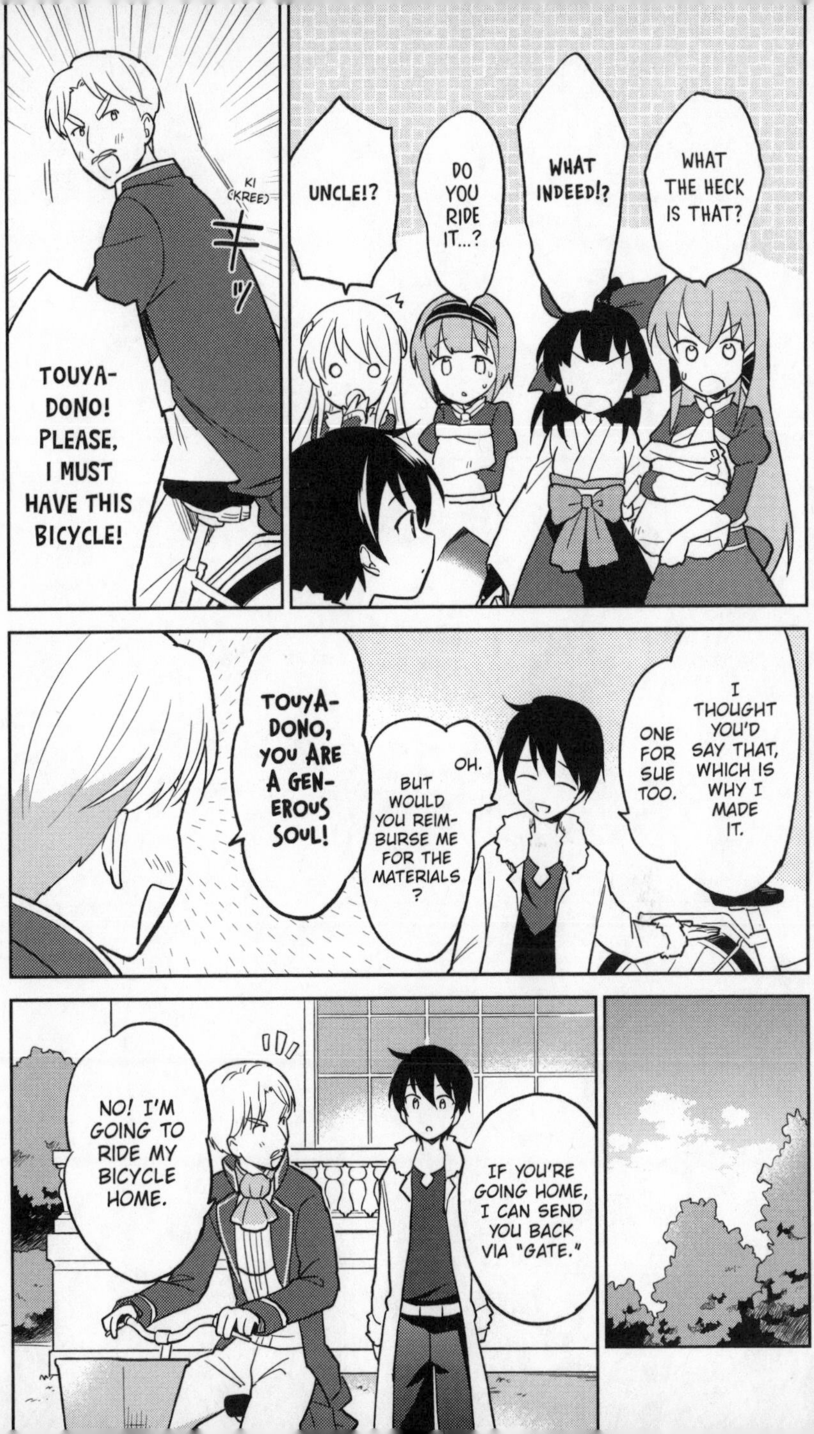
WHAT THE HECK IS THAT?
WHAT INDEED!?
DO YOU RIDE IT...?
UNCLE!?
キッ
KI (KREE)
TOUYA-DONO! PLEASE, I MUST HAVE THIS BICYCLE!
I THOUGHT YOU'D SAY THAT, WHICH IS WHY I MADE IT.
ONE FOR SUE TOO.
OH.
BUT WOULD YOU REIMBURSE ME FOR THE MATERIALS?
TOUYA-DONO, YOU ARE A GEN-EROUS SOUL!
IF YOU'RE GOING HOME, I CAN SEND YOU BACK VIA "GATE."
NO! I'M GOING TO RIDE MY BICYCLE HOME.

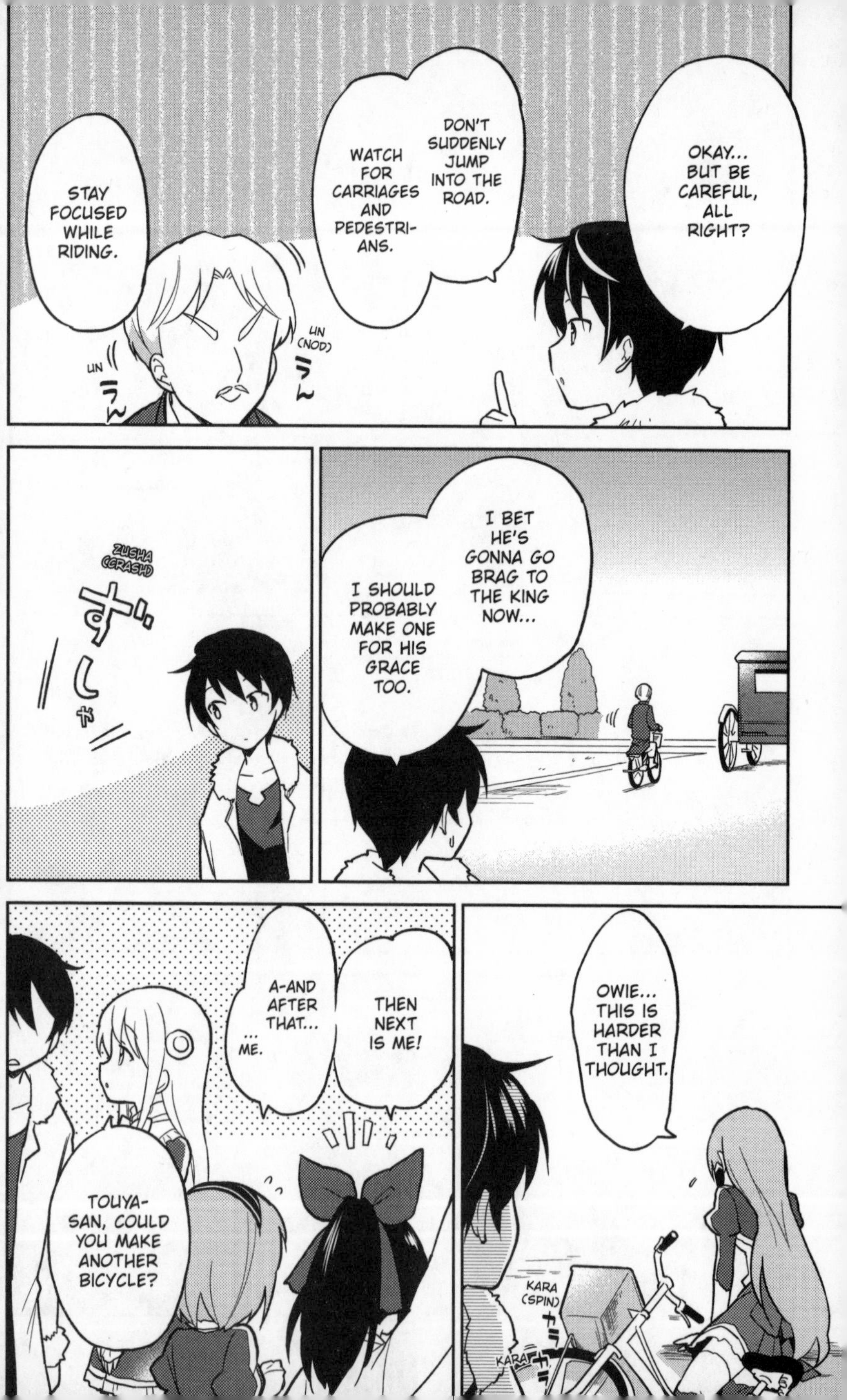
OKAY... BUT BE CAREFUL, ALL RIGHT?
DON'T SUDDENLY JUMP INTO THE ROAD.
WATCH FOR CARRIAGES AND PEDESTRIANS.
UN (NOD)
STAY FOCUSED WHILE RIDING.
UN
I BET HE'S GONNA GO BRAG TO THE KING NOW...
I SHOULD PROBABLY MAKE ONE FOR HIS GRACE TOO.
ZUSHA (CRASH)
OWIE... THIS IS HARDER THAN I THOUGHT.
KARA (SPIN)
KARA
THEN NEXT IS ME!
A-AND AFTER THAT...
... ME.
TOUYA-SAN, COULD YOU MAKE ANOTHER BICYCLE?

I JUST WANTED TO MAKE LIFE EASIER FOR HULIO-SAN AND THE MAIDS WHEN THEY GO SHOPPING...

OH WELL.

STORAGE: IN.

STORAGE: OUT.

BYON (POP)

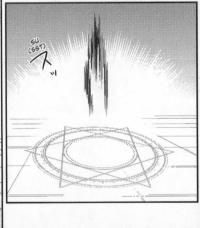

SU (SST)

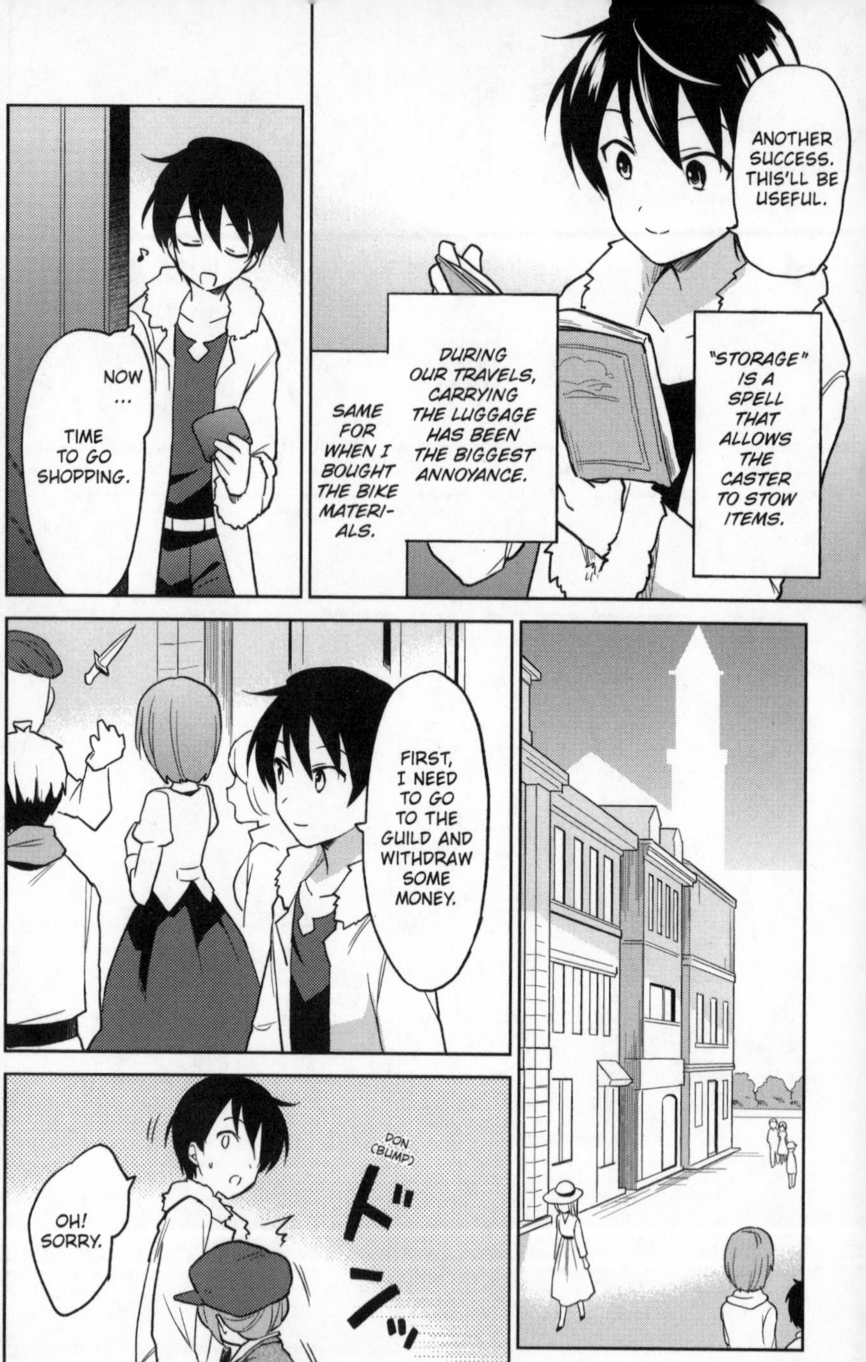
ANOTHER SUCCESS. THIS'LL BE USEFUL.
"STORAGE" IS A SPELL THAT ALLOWS THE CASTER TO STOW ITEMS.
DURING OUR TRAVELS, CARRYING THE LUGGAGE HAS BEEN THE BIGGEST ANNOYANCE.
SAME FOR WHEN I BOUGHT THE BIKE MATERI-ALS.
NOW ... TIME TO GO SHOPPING.
FIRST, I NEED TO GO TO THE GUILD AND WITHDRAW SOME MONEY.
DON (BUMP)
OH! SORRY.

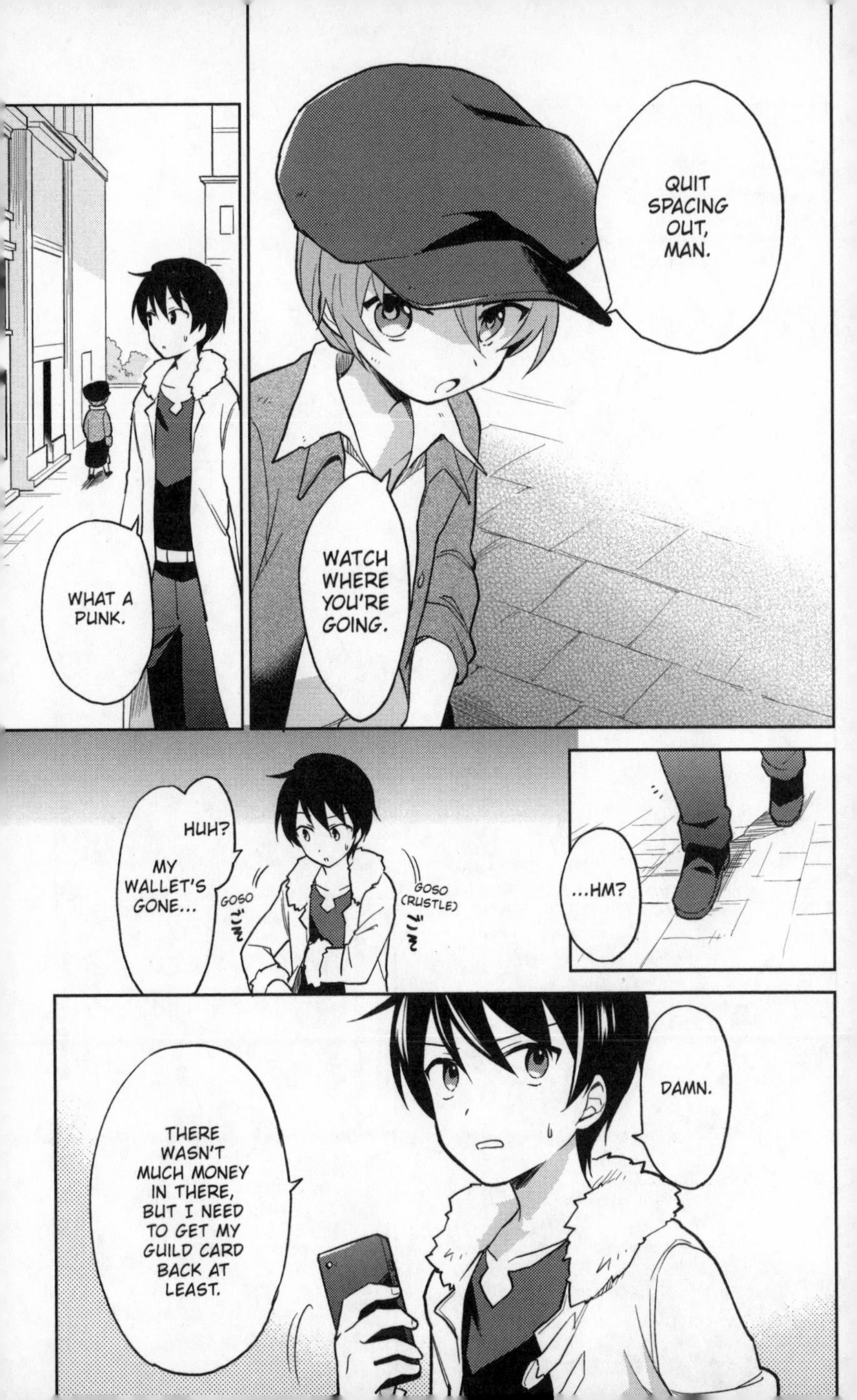
QUIT SPACING OUT, MAN.
WATCH WHERE YOU'RE GOING.
WHAT A PUNK.
...HM?
HUH?
MY WALLET'S GONE...
GOSO (RUSTLE)
GOSO
DAMN.
THERE WASN'T MUCH MONEY IN THERE, BUT I NEED TO GET MY GUILD CARD BACK AT LEAST.

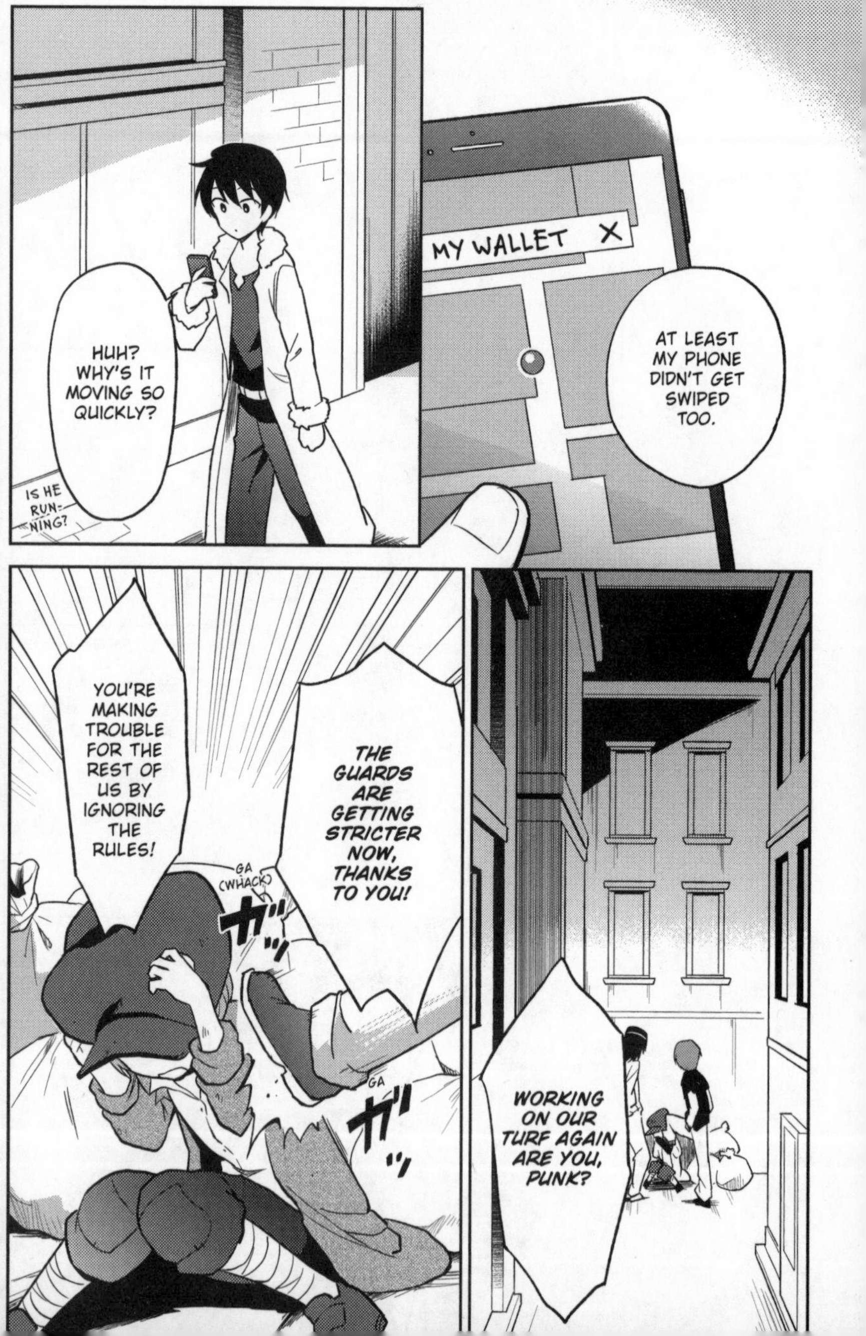
MY WALLET
AT LEAST MY PHONE DIDN'T GET SWIPED TOO.
HUH? WHY'S IT MOVING SO QUICKLY?
IS HE RUN-NING?
WORKING ON OUR TURF AGAIN ARE YOU, PUNK?
THE GUARDS ARE GETTING STRICTER NOW, THANKS TO YOU!
YOU'RE MAKING TROUBLE FOR THE REST OF US BY IGNORING THE RULES!
GA (WHACK)
GA

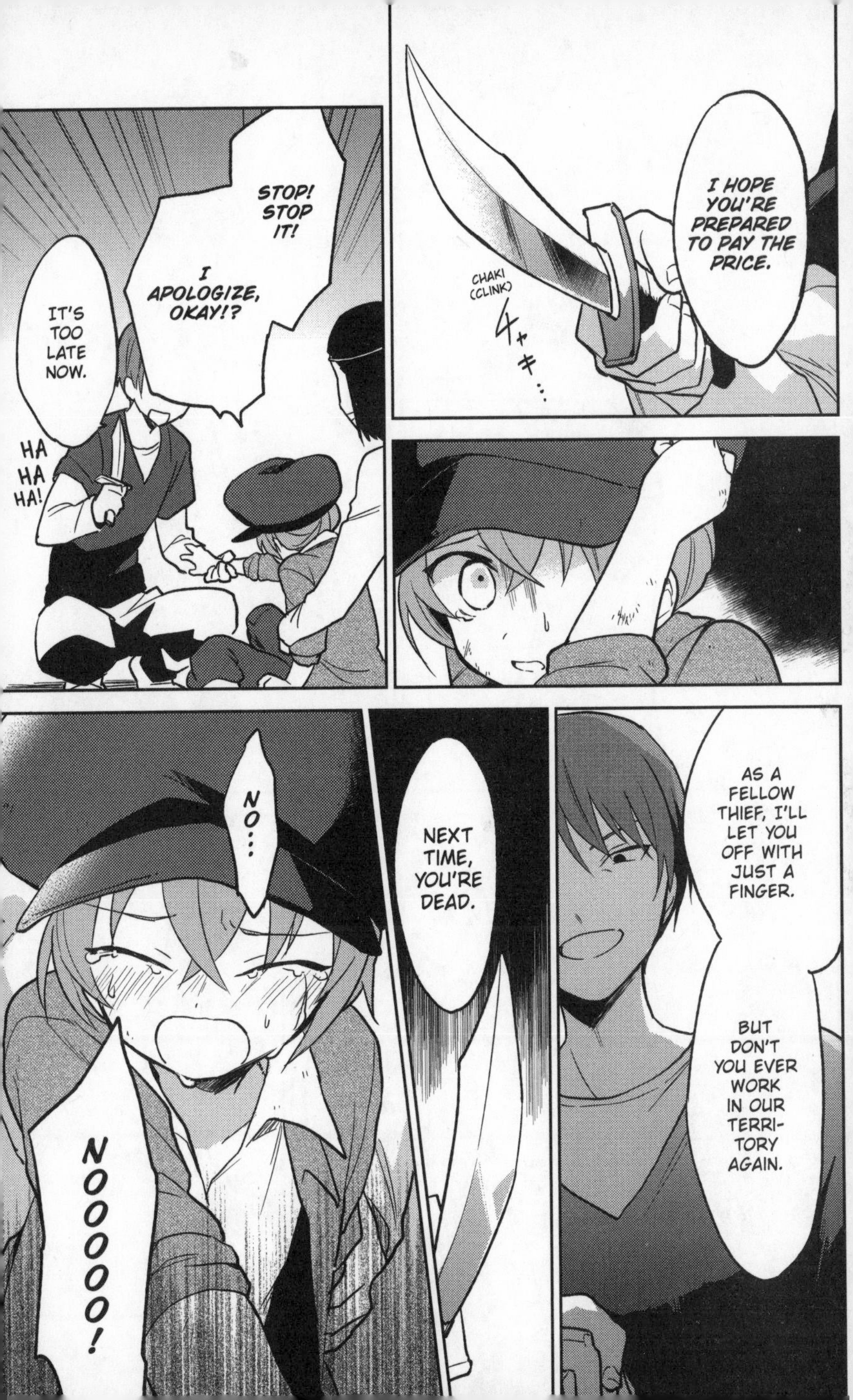
I HOPE YOU'RE PREPARED TO PAY THE PRICE.
CHAKI (CLINK)
チャキ…
STOP! STOP IT!
I APOLOGIZE, OKAY!?
IT'S TOO LATE NOW.
HA HA HA!
AS A FELLOW THIEF, I'LL LET YOU OFF WITH JUST A FINGER.
BUT DON'T YOU EVER WORK IN OUR TERRI-TORY AGAIN.
NEXT TIME, YOU'RE DEAD.
NO...
NOOOOOO!

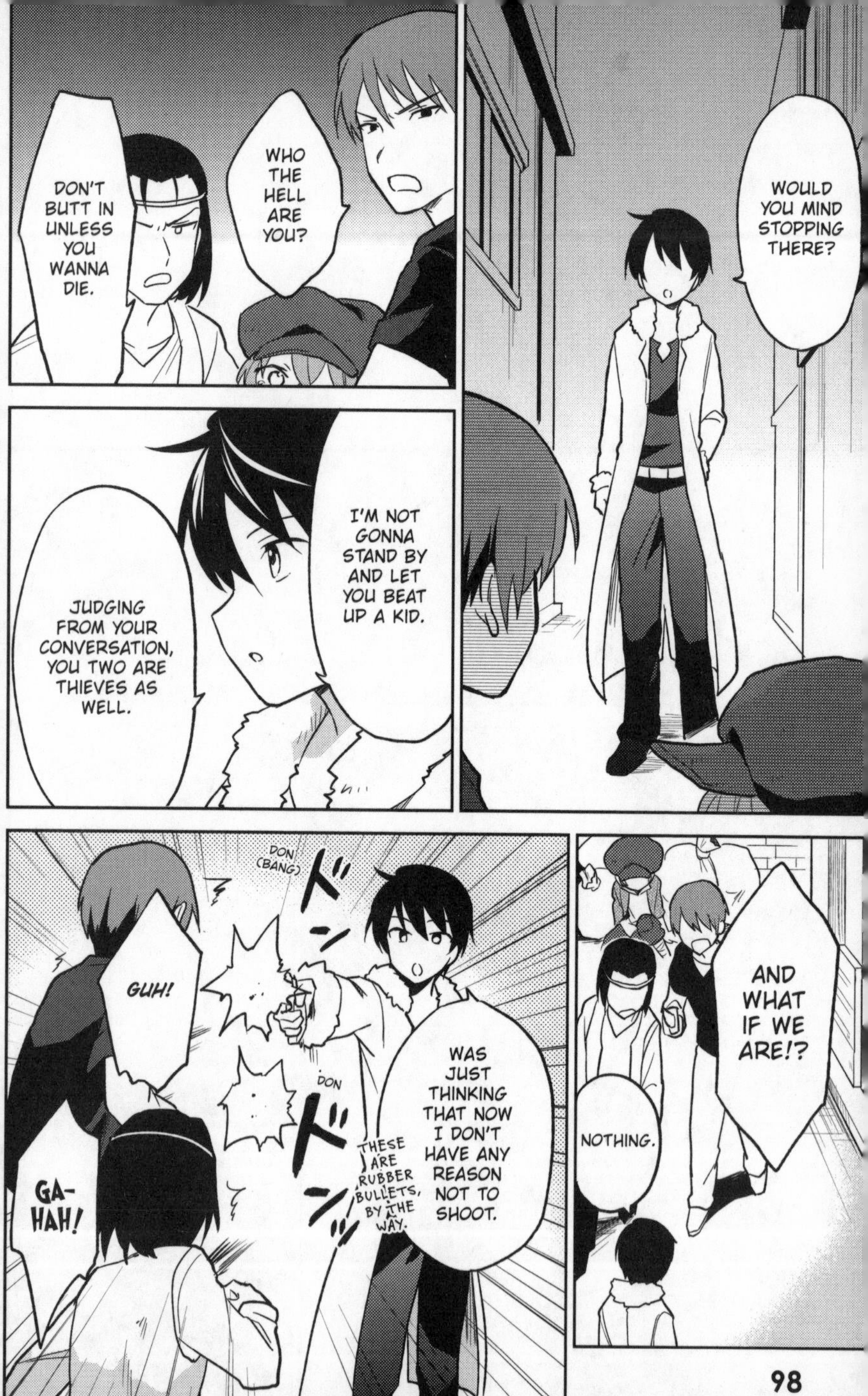
WOULD YOU MIND STOPPING THERE?
WHO THE HELL ARE YOU?
DON'T BUTT IN UNLESS YOU WANNA DIE.
I'M NOT GONNA STAND BY AND LET YOU BEAT UP A KID.
JUDGING FROM YOUR CONVERSATION, YOU TWO ARE THIEVES AS WELL.
AND WHAT IF WE ARE!?
NOTHING.
DON (BANG)
ド
WAS JUST THINKING THAT NOW I DON'T HAVE ANY REASON NOT TO SHOOT.
GUH!
THESE ARE RUBBER BULLETS, BY THE WAY.
DON
ド
GA-HAH!

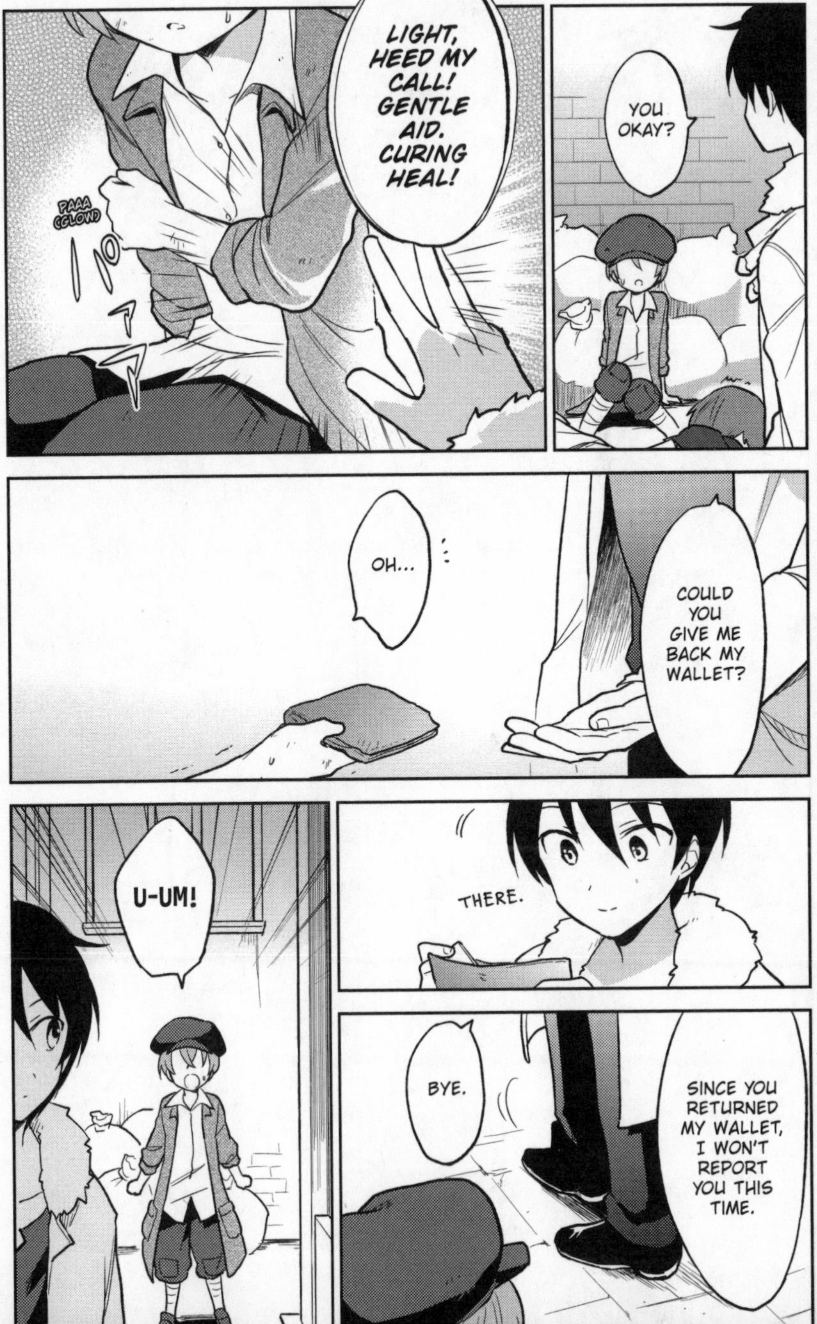
YOU OKAY?
LIGHT, HEED MY CALL! GENTLE AID. CURING HEAL!
PAAA (GLOW)
COULD YOU GIVE ME BACK MY WALLET?
OH...
THERE.
SINCE YOU RETURNED MY WALLET, I WON'T REPORT YOU THIS TIME.
BYE.
U-UM!

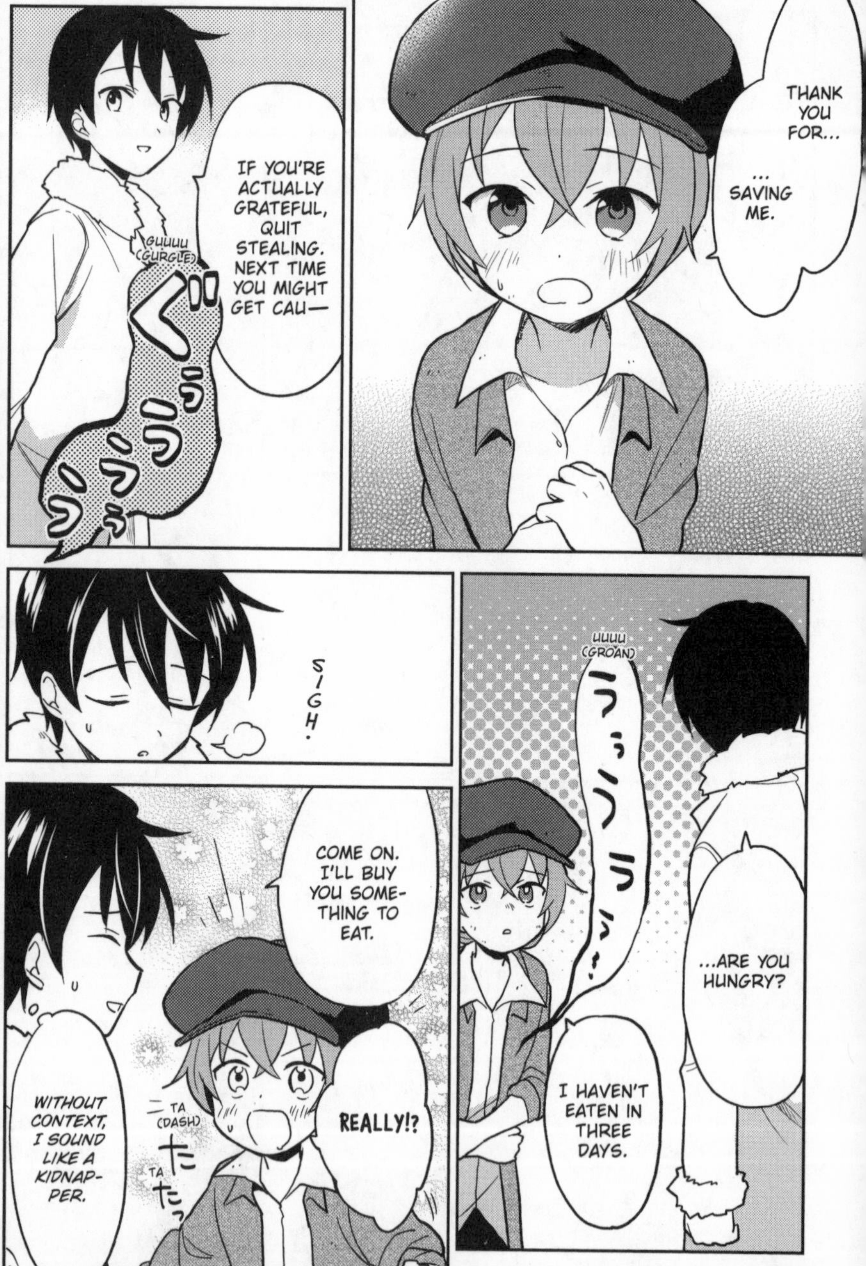
THANK YOU FOR...
...SAVING ME.
IF YOU'RE ACTUALLY GRATEFUL, QUIT STEALING. NEXT TIME YOU MIGHT GET CAU—
GUUUU (GURGLE)
UUUU (GROAN)
...ARE YOU HUNGRY?
I HAVEN'T EATEN IN THREE DAYS.
SIGH.
COME ON. I'LL BUY YOU SOMETHING TO EAT.
REALLY!?
TA TA (DASH)
WITHOUT CONTEXT, I SOUND LIKE A KIDNAPPER.

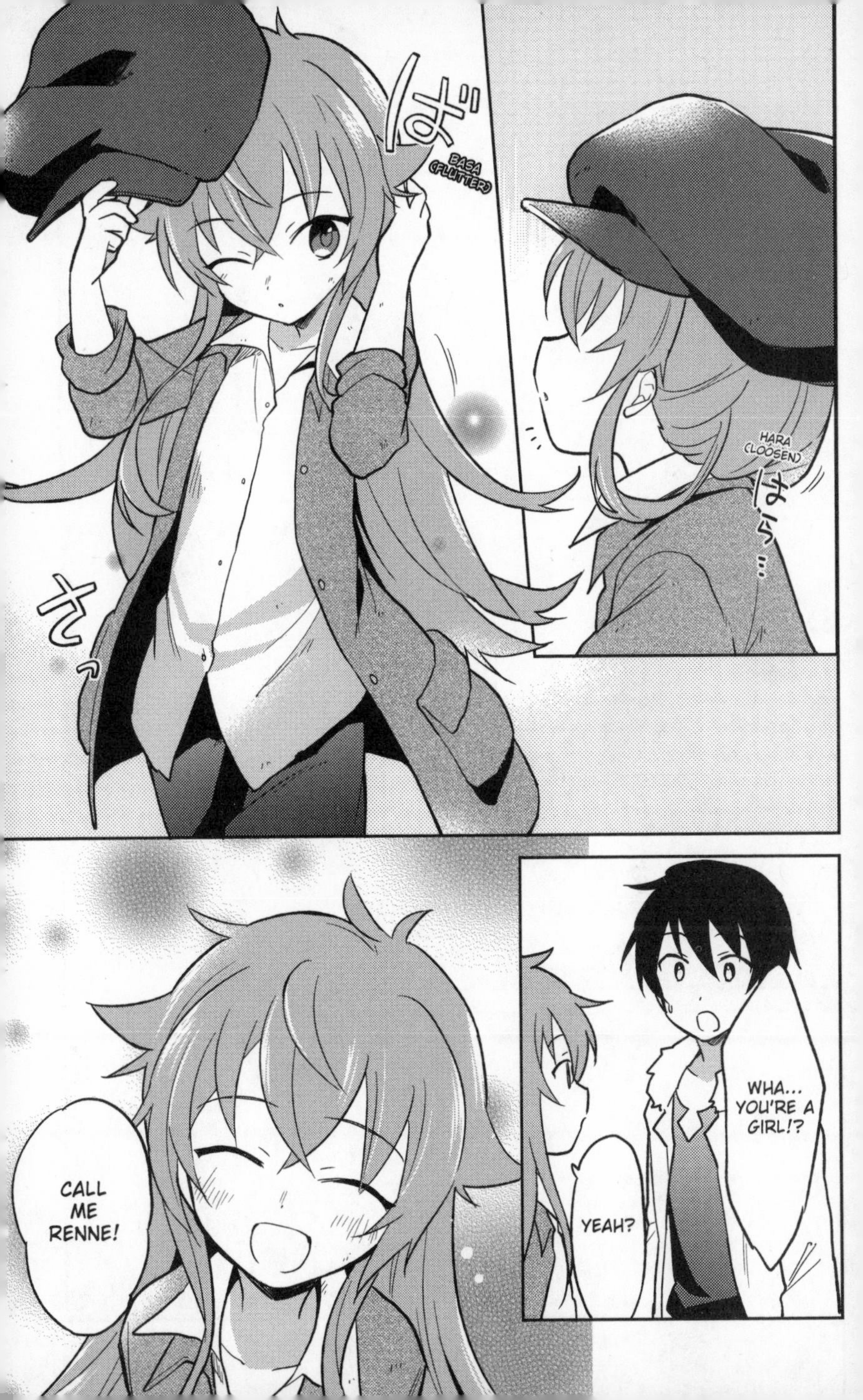
HARA (LOOSEN)
はら…
BASA (FLUTTER)
ば
さっ
WHA... YOU'RE A GIRL!?
YEAH?
CALL ME RENNE!

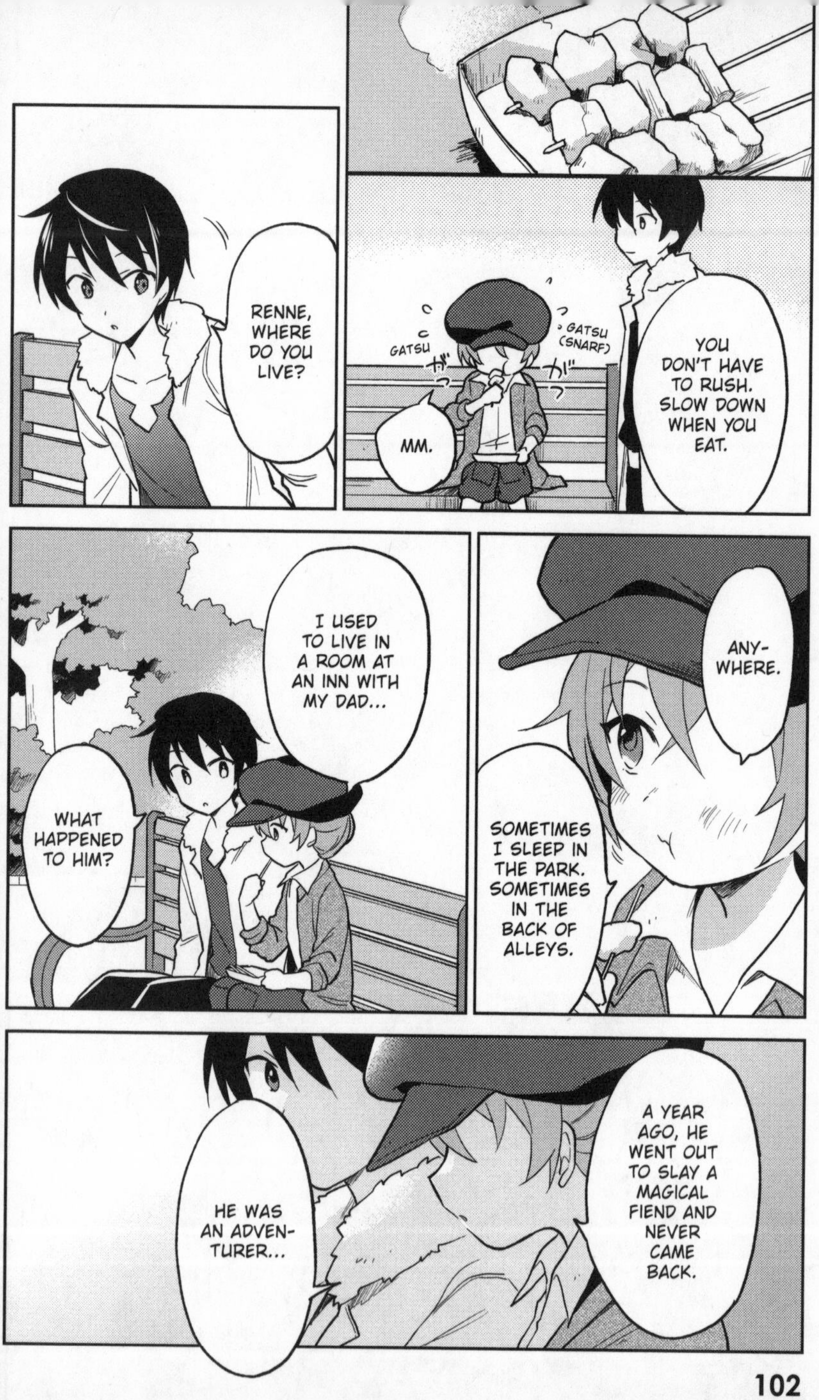

YOU DON'T HAVE TO RUSH. SLOW DOWN WHEN YOU EAT.
GATSU (SNARF)
GATSU
MM.
RENNE, WHERE DO YOU LIVE?
ANY-WHERE.
SOMETIMES I SLEEP IN THE PARK. SOMETIMES IN THE BACK OF ALLEYS.
I USED TO LIVE IN A ROOM AT AN INN WITH MY DAD...
WHAT HAPPENED TO HIM?
A YEAR AGO, HE WENT OUT TO SLAY A MAGICAL FIEND AND NEVER CAME BACK.
HE WAS AN ADVEN-TURER...

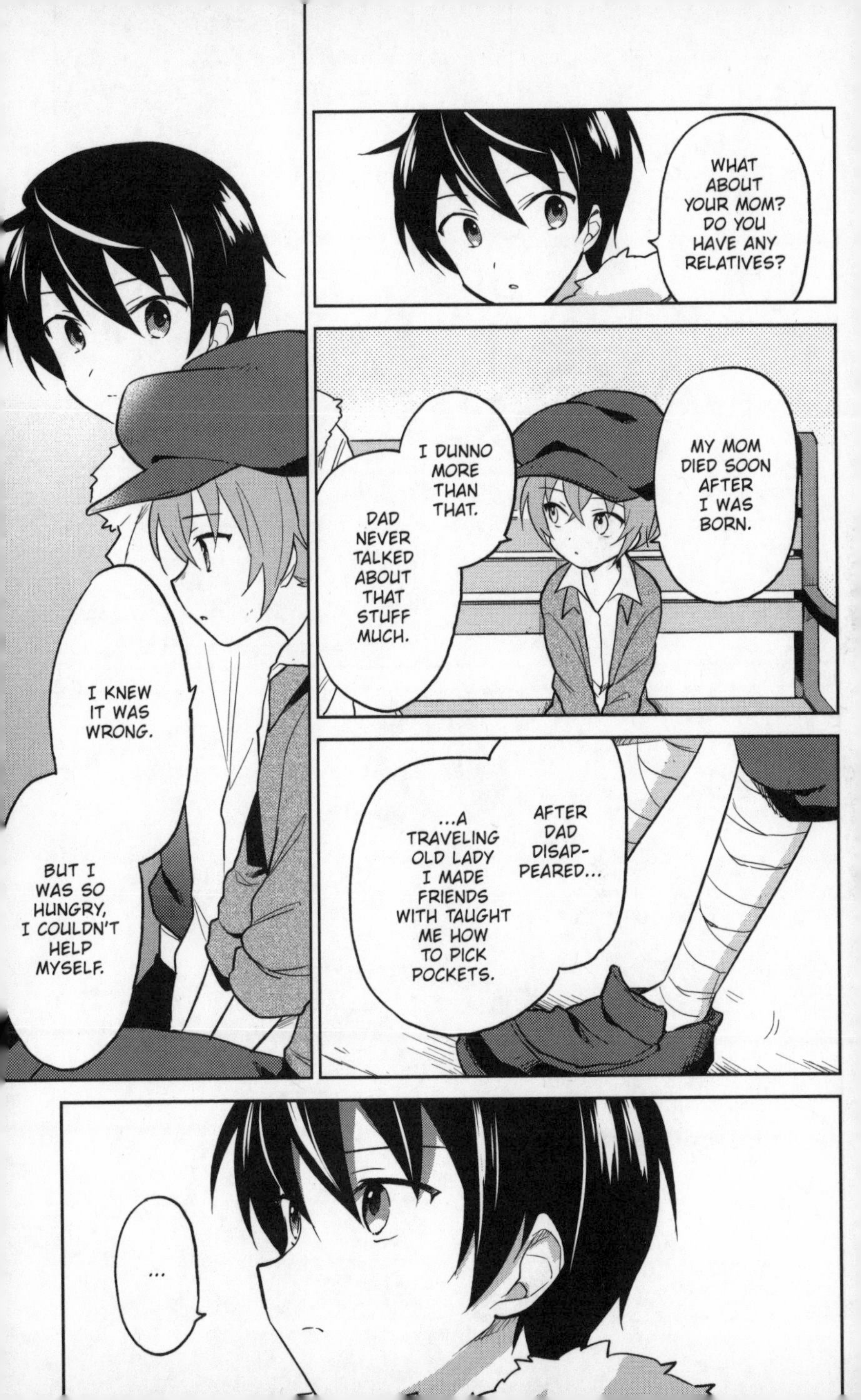
WHAT ABOUT YOUR MOM? DO YOU HAVE ANY RELATIVES?
MY MOM DIED SOON AFTER I WAS BORN.
I DUNNO MORE THAN THAT.
DAD NEVER TALKED ABOUT THAT STUFF MUCH.
AFTER DAD DISAP-PEARED...
...A TRAVELING OLD LADY I MADE FRIENDS WITH TAUGHT ME HOW TO PICK POCKETS.
I KNEW IT WAS WRONG.
BUT I WAS SO HUNGRY, I COULDN'T HELP MYSELF.
...

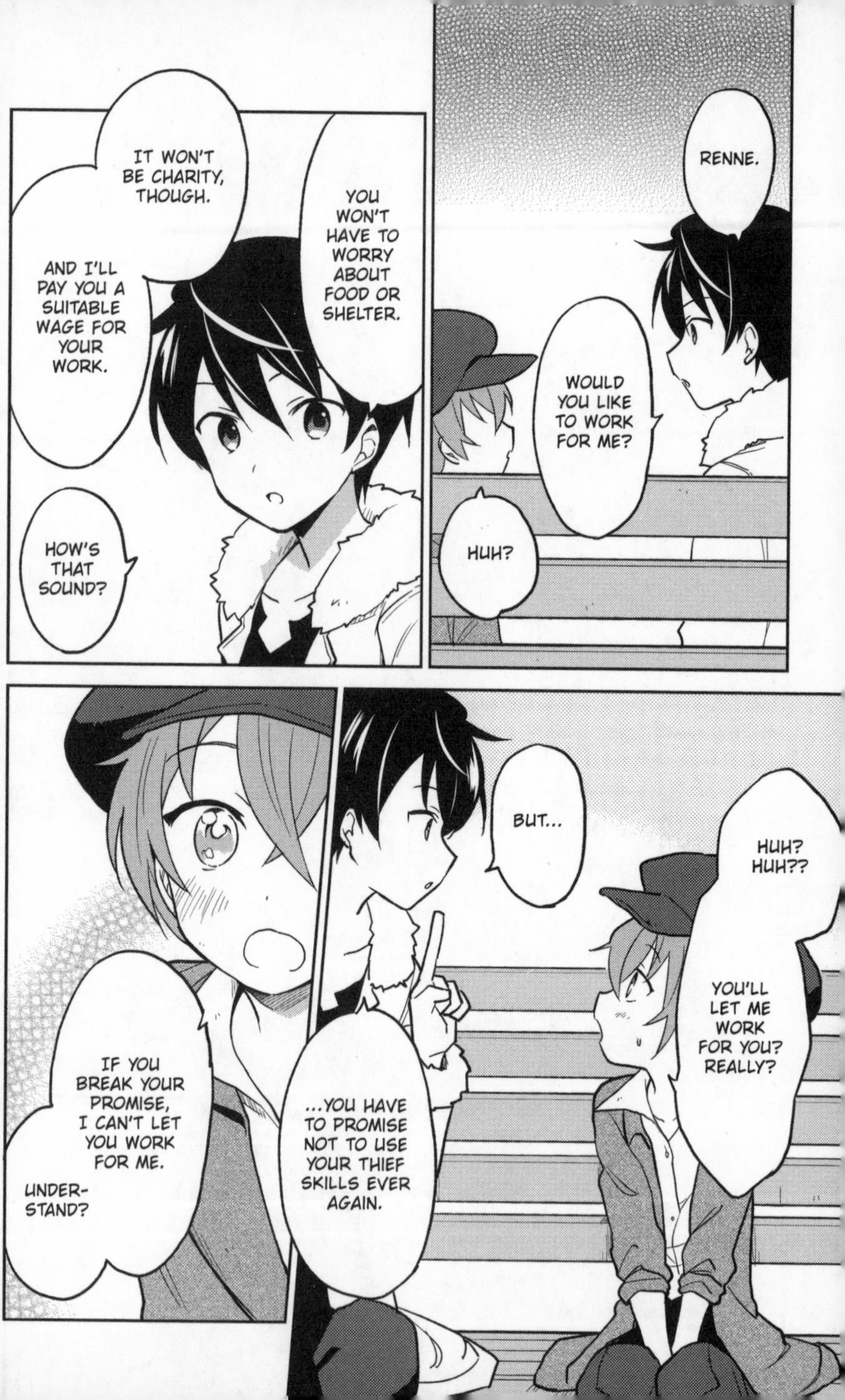
RENNE.
WOULD YOU LIKE TO WORK FOR ME?
HUH?
YOU WON'T HAVE TO WORRY ABOUT FOOD OR SHELTER.
IT WON'T BE CHARITY, THOUGH.
AND I'LL PAY YOU A SUITABLE WAGE FOR YOUR WORK.
HOW'S THAT SOUND?
HUH? HUH??
YOU'LL LET ME WORK FOR YOU? REALLY?
BUT...
...YOU HAVE TO PROMISE NOT TO USE YOUR THIEF SKILLS EVER AGAIN.
IF YOU BREAK YOUR PROMISE, I CAN'T LET YOU WORK FOR ME.
UNDER-STAND?

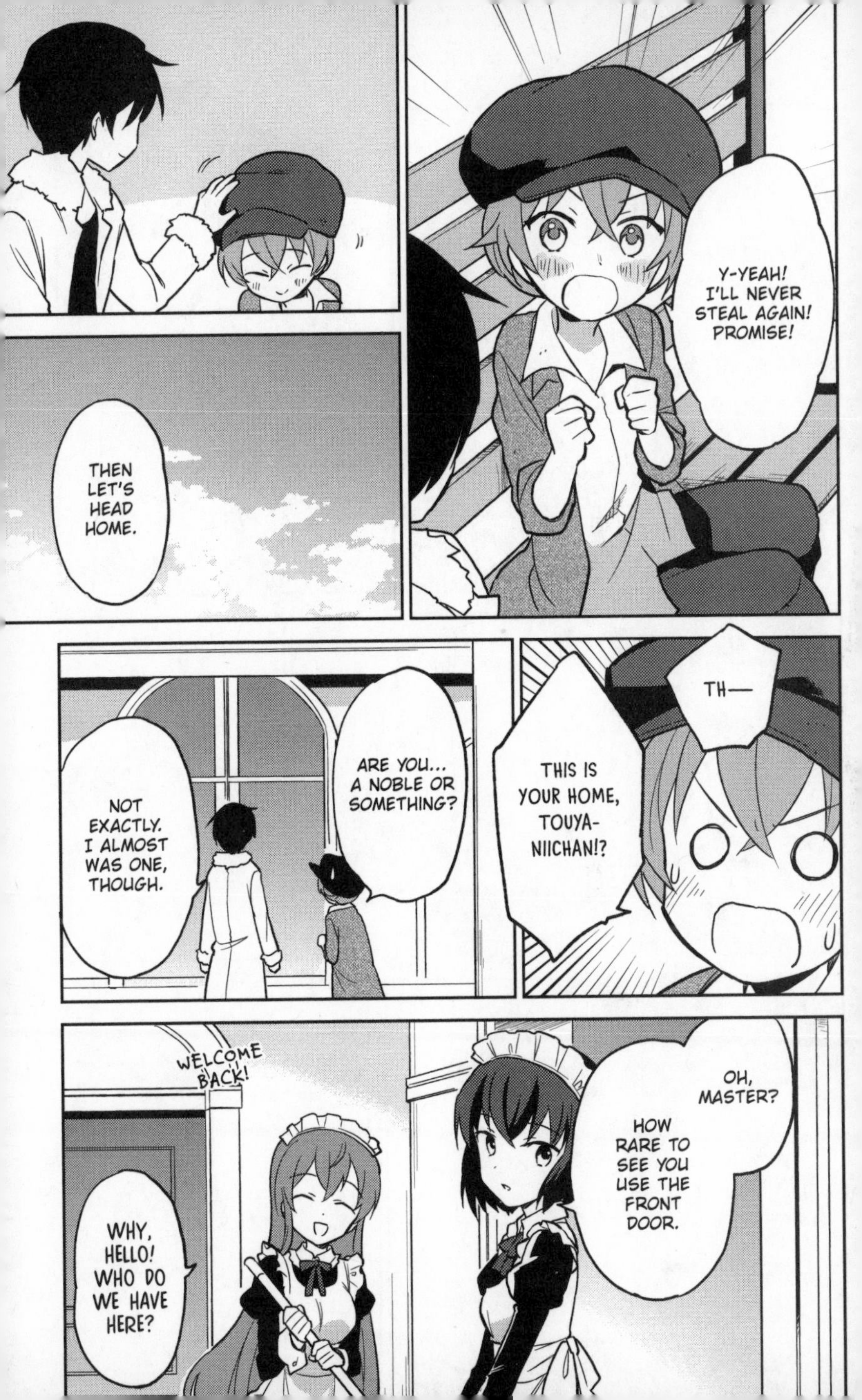

Y-YEAH! I'LL NEVER STEAL AGAIN! PROMISE!
THEN LET'S HEAD HOME.
TH—
THIS IS YOUR HOME, TOUYA-NIICHAN!?
ARE YOU... A NOBLE OR SOMETHING?
NOT EXACTLY. I ALMOST WAS ONE, THOUGH.
OH, MASTER?
HOW RARE TO SEE YOU USE THE FRONT DOOR.
WELCOME BACK!
WHY, HELLO! WHO DO WE HAVE HERE?

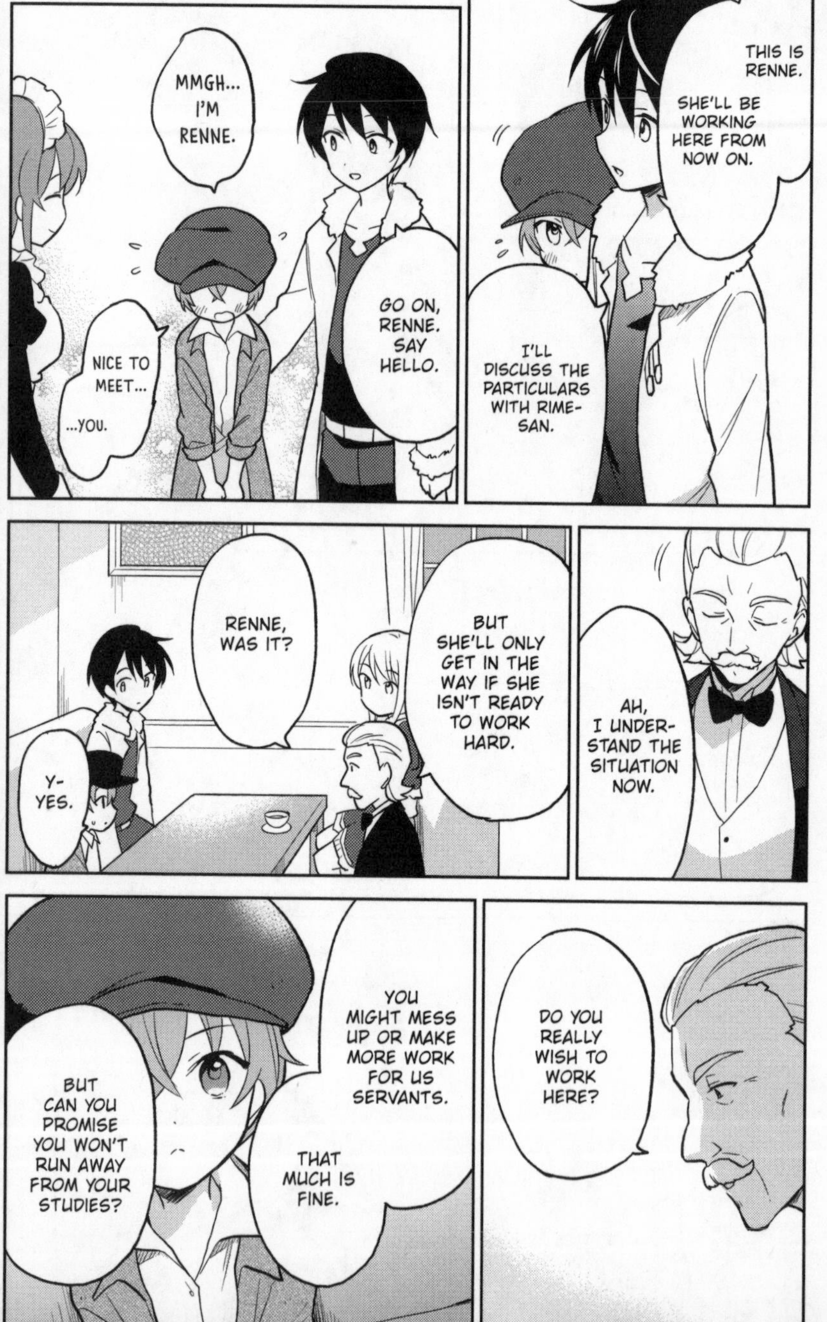
THIS IS RENNE.
SHE'LL BE WORKING HERE FROM NOW ON.
I'LL DISCUSS THE PARTICULARS WITH RIME-SAN.
GO ON, RENNE. SAY HELLO.
MMGH... I'M RENNE.
NICE TO MEET... ...YOU.
AH, I UNDERSTAND THE SITUATION NOW.
BUT SHE'LL ONLY GET IN THE WAY IF SHE ISN'T READY TO WORK HARD.
RENNE, WAS IT?
Y-YES.
DO YOU REALLY WISH TO WORK HERE?
YOU MIGHT MESS UP OR MAKE MORE WORK FOR US SERVANTS.
THAT MUCH IS FINE.
BUT CAN YOU PROMISE YOU WON'T RUN AWAY FROM YOUR STUDIES?

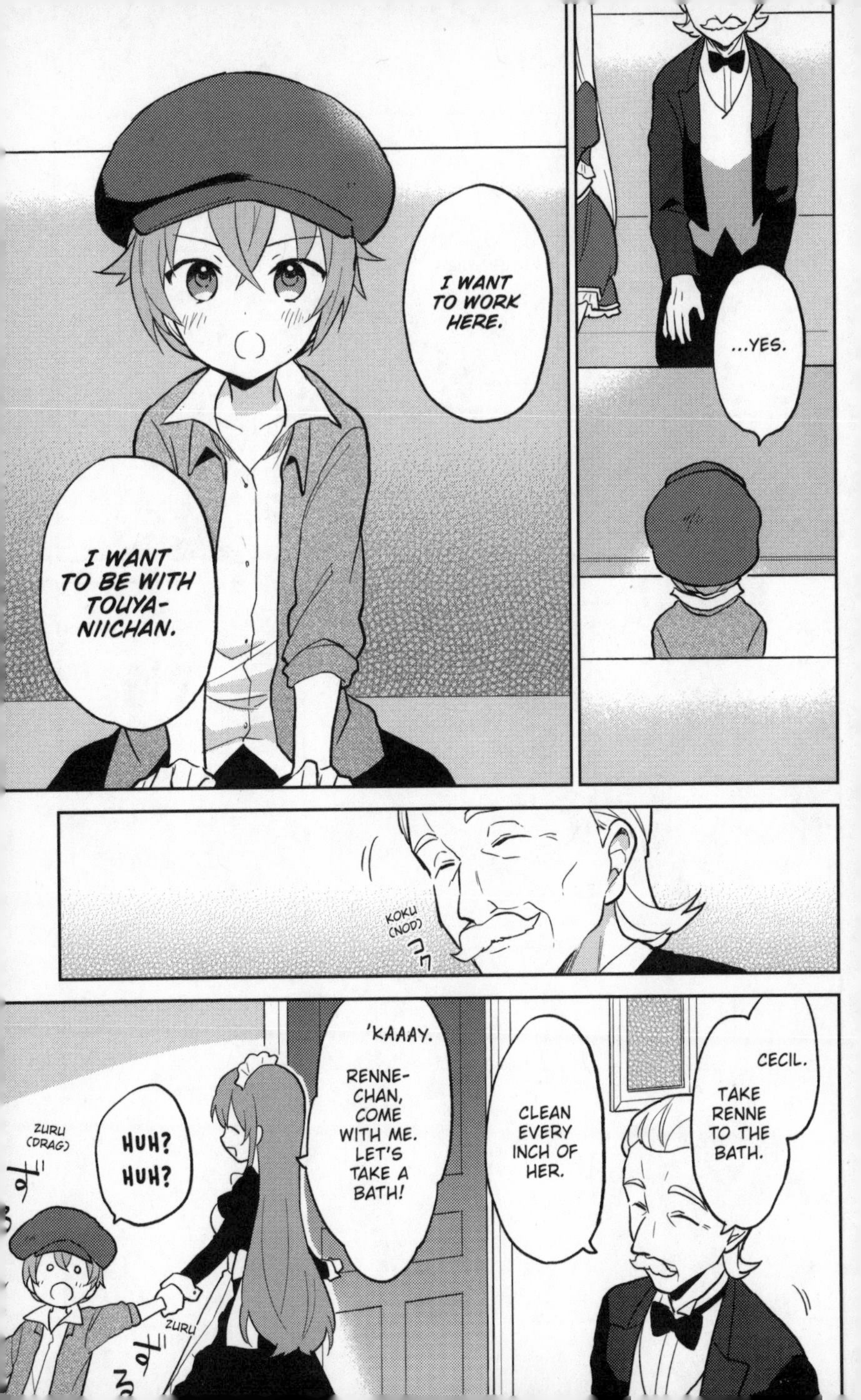
...YES.
I WANT TO WORK HERE.
I WANT TO BE WITH TOUYA-NIICHAN.
KOKU (NOD)
CECIL.
TAKE RENNE TO THE BATH.
CLEAN EVERY INCH OF HER.
'KAAAY.
RENNE-CHAN, COME WITH ME. LET'S TAKE A BATH!
HUH? HUH?
ZURU (DRAG)
ZURU

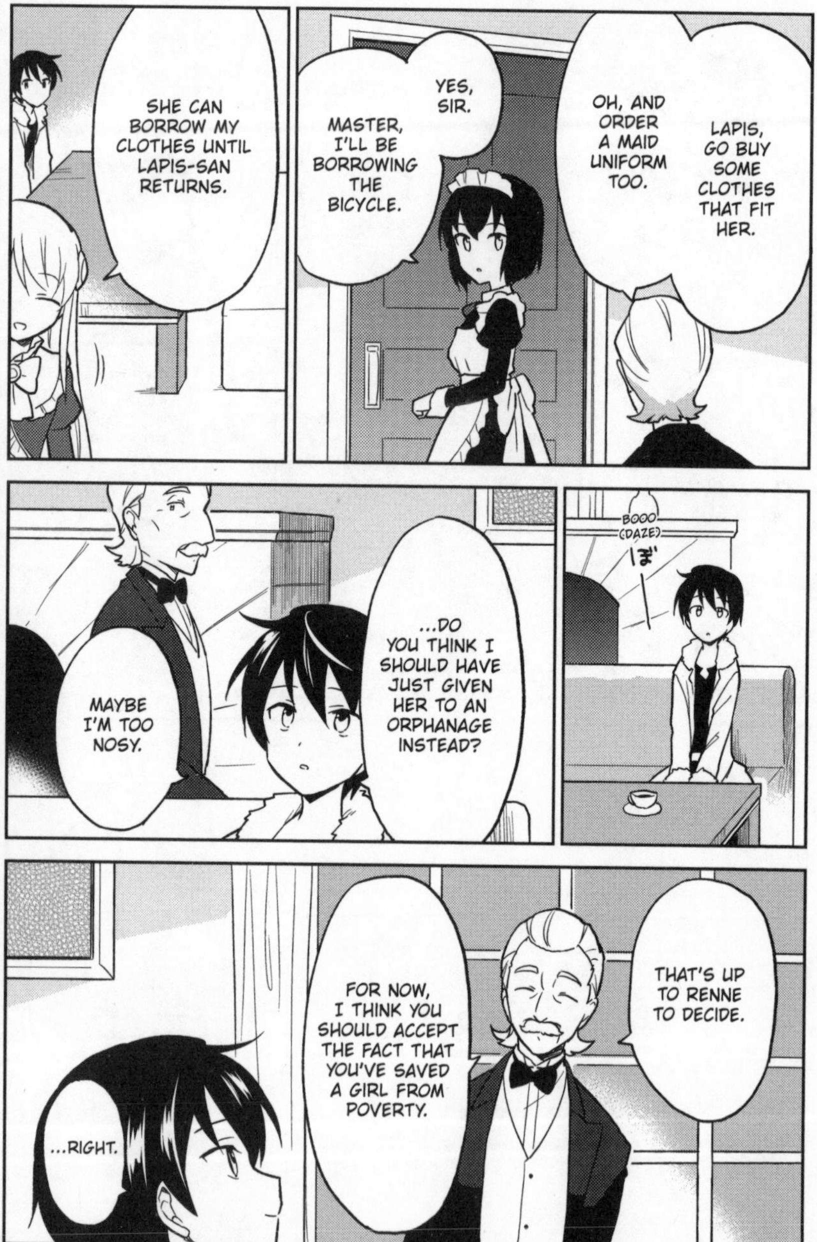
LAPIS, GO BUY SOME CLOTHES THAT FIT HER.
OH, AND ORDER A MAID UNIFORM TOO.
YES, SIR.
MASTER, I'LL BE BORROWING THE BICYCLE.
SHE CAN BORROW MY CLOTHES UNTIL LAPIS-SAN RETURNS.
BOOO (DAZE)
ぼー
...DO YOU THINK I SHOULD HAVE JUST GIVEN HER TO AN ORPHANAGE INSTEAD?
MAYBE I'M TOO NOSY.
THAT'S UP TO RENNE TO DECIDE.
FOR NOW, I THINK YOU SHOULD ACCEPT THE FACT THAT YOU'VE SAVED A GIRL FROM POVERTY.
...RIGHT.

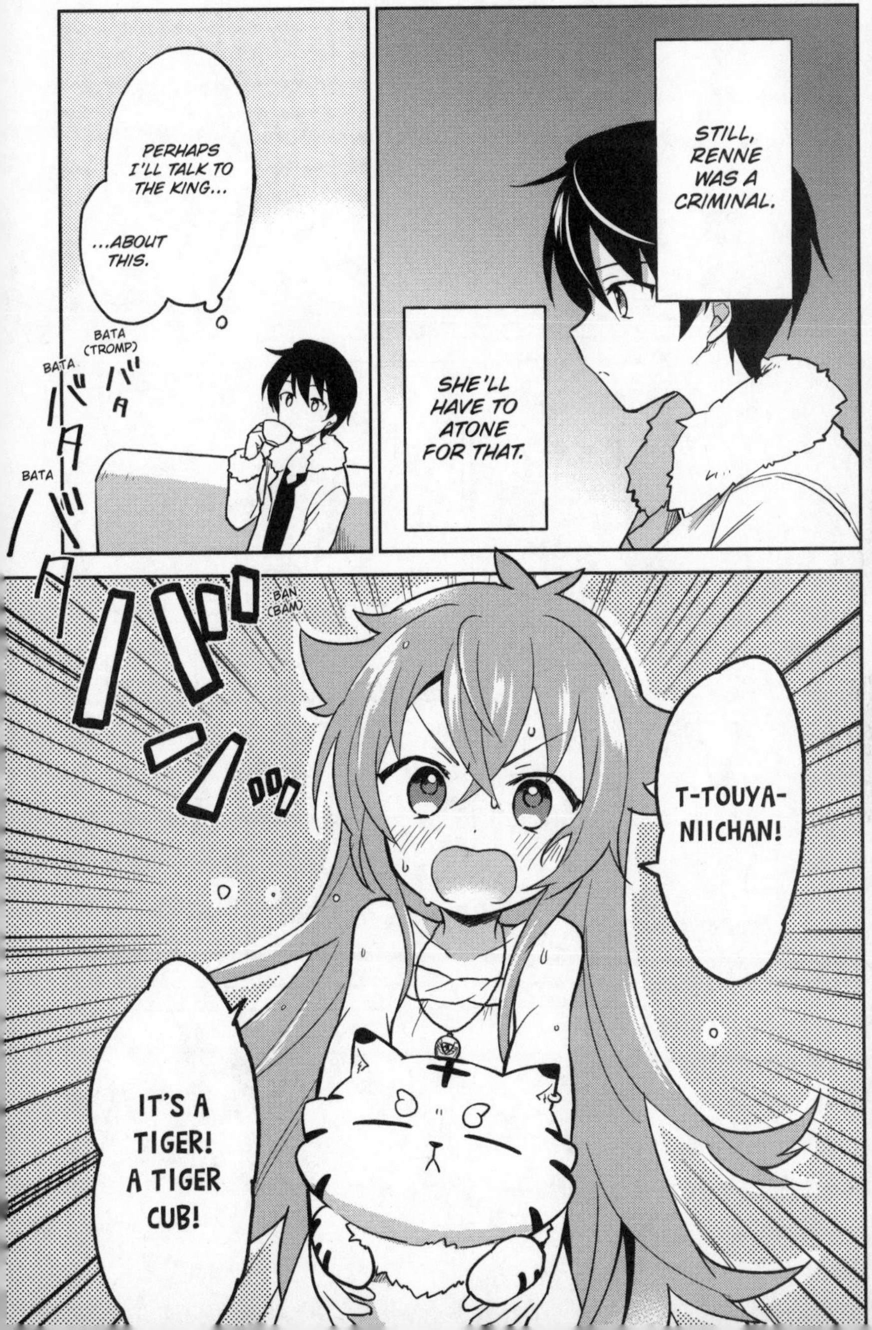
STILL, RENNE WAS A CRIMINAL.
SHE'LL HAVE TO ATONE FOR THAT.
PERHAPS I'LL TALK TO THE KING...
...ABOUT THIS.
BATA (TROMP)
BATA
BATA
BAN (BAM)
T-TOUYA-NIICHAN!
IT'S A TIGER! A TIGER CUB!

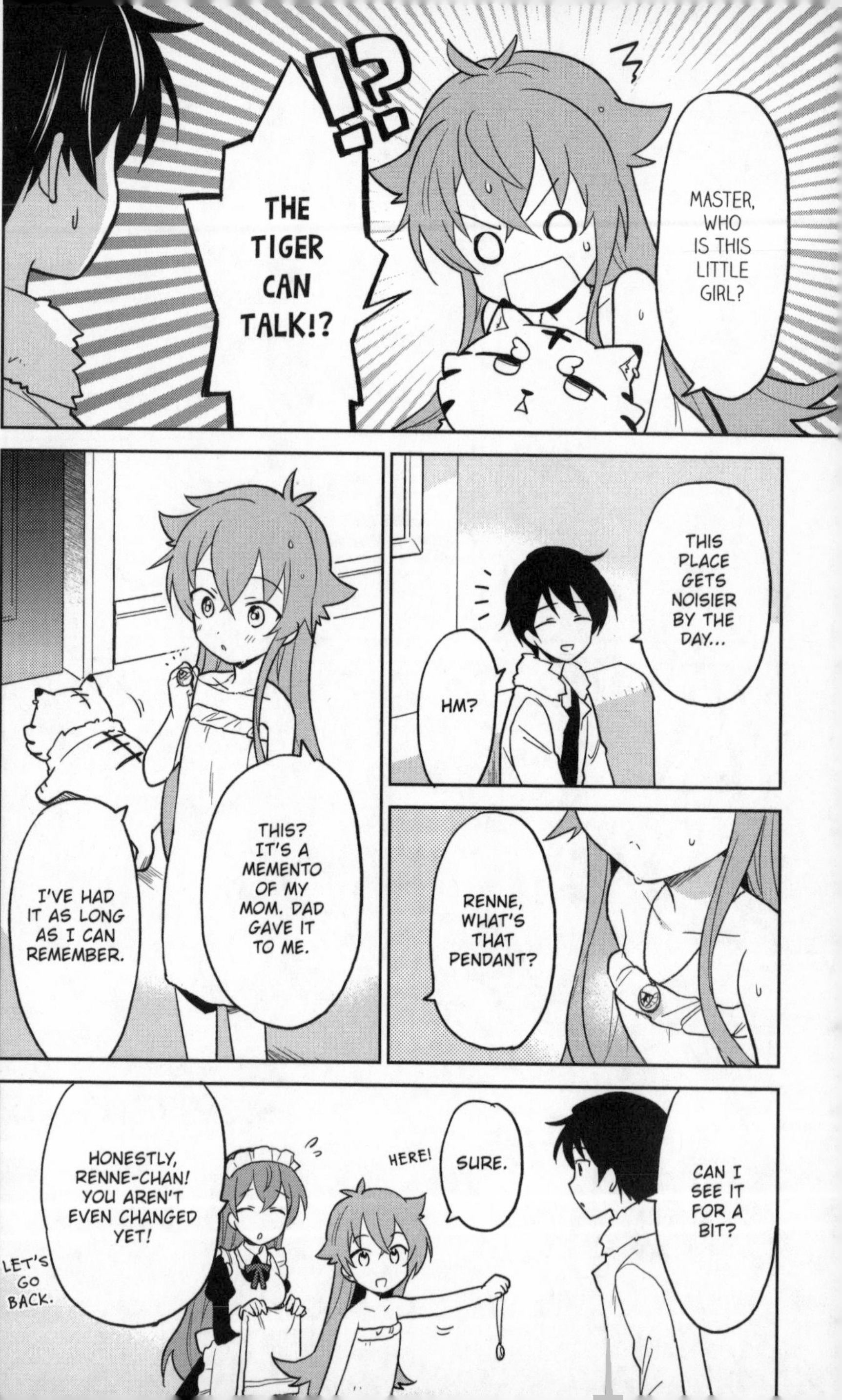
MASTER, WHO IS THIS LITTLE GIRL?
!?
THE TIGER CAN TALK!?
THIS PLACE GETS NOISIER BY THE DAY...
HM?
RENNE, WHAT'S THAT PENDANT?
THIS? IT'S A MEMENTO OF MY MOM. DAD GAVE IT TO ME.
I'VE HAD IT AS LONG AS I CAN REMEMBER.
CAN I SEE IT FOR A BIT?
SURE.
HERE!
HONESTLY, RENNE-CHAN! YOU AREN'T EVEN CHANGED YET!
LET'S GO BACK.

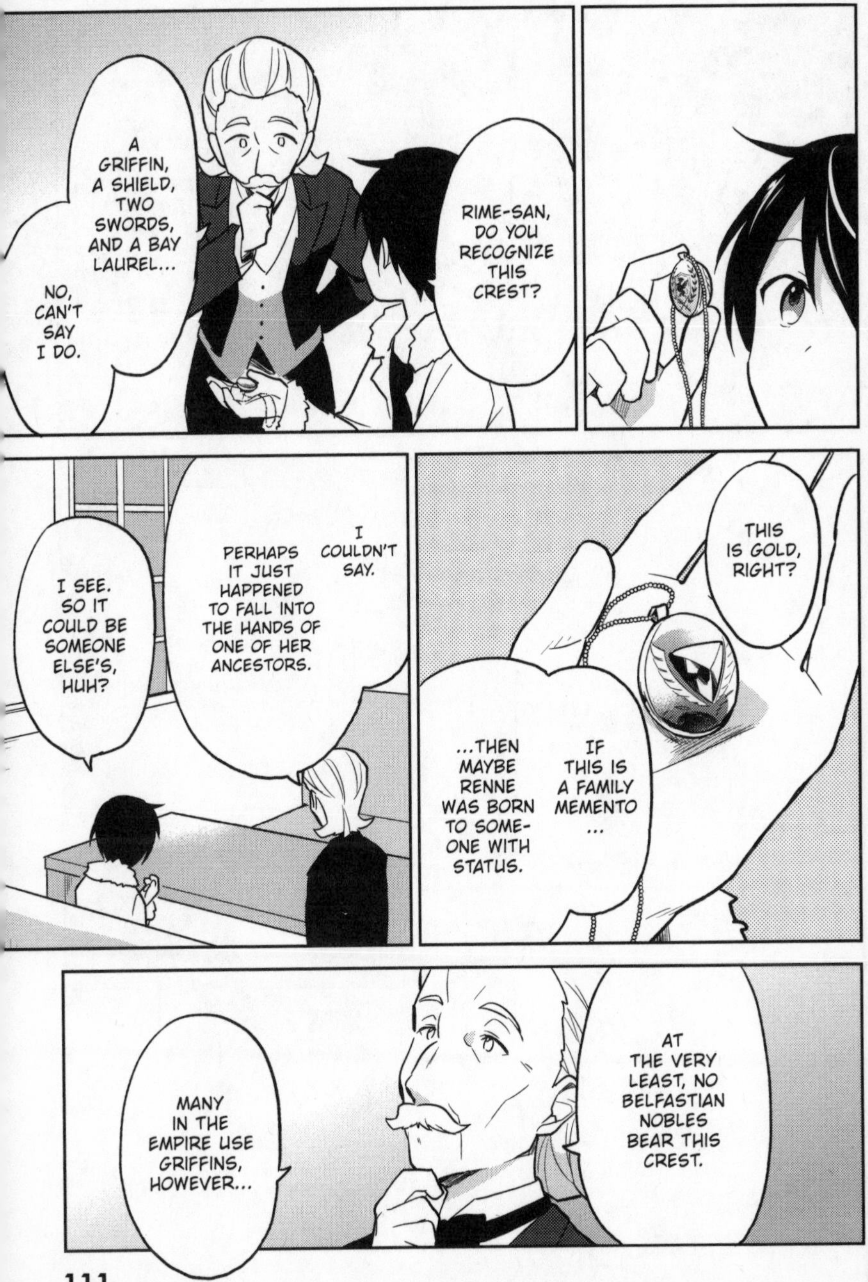
RIME-SAN, DO YOU RECOGNIZE THIS CREST?
A GRIFFIN, A SHIELD, TWO SWORDS, AND A BAY LAUREL...
NO, CAN'T SAY I DO.
THIS IS GOLD, RIGHT?
IF THIS IS A FAMILY MEMENTO...
...THEN MAYBE RENNE WAS BORN TO SOME-ONE WITH STATUS.
I COULDN'T SAY.
PERHAPS IT JUST HAPPENED TO FALL INTO THE HANDS OF ONE OF HER ANCESTORS.
I SEE. SO IT COULD BE SOMEONE ELSE'S, HUH?
AT THE VERY LEAST, NO BELFASTIAN NOBLES BEAR THIS CREST.
MANY IN THE EMPIRE USE GRIFFINS, HOWEVER...

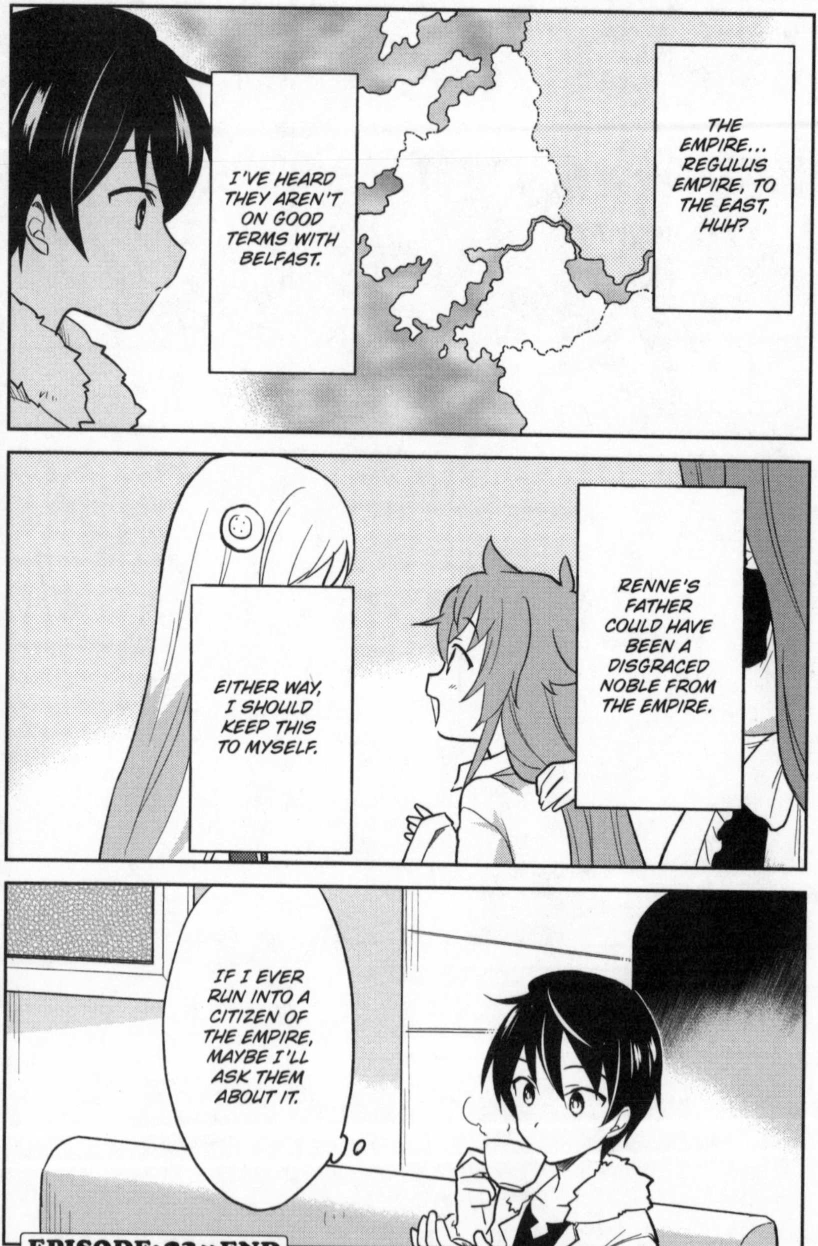
THE EMPIRE... REGULUS EMPIRE, TO THE EAST, HUH?
I'VE HEARD THEY AREN'T ON GOOD TERMS WITH BELFAST.
RENNE'S FATHER COULD HAVE BEEN A DISGRACED NOBLE FROM THE EMPIRE.
EITHER WAY, I SHOULD KEEP THIS TO MYSELF.
IF I EVER RUN INTO A CITIZEN OF THE EMPIRE, MAYBE I'LL ASK THEM ABOUT IT.

EPISODE: 23 » END

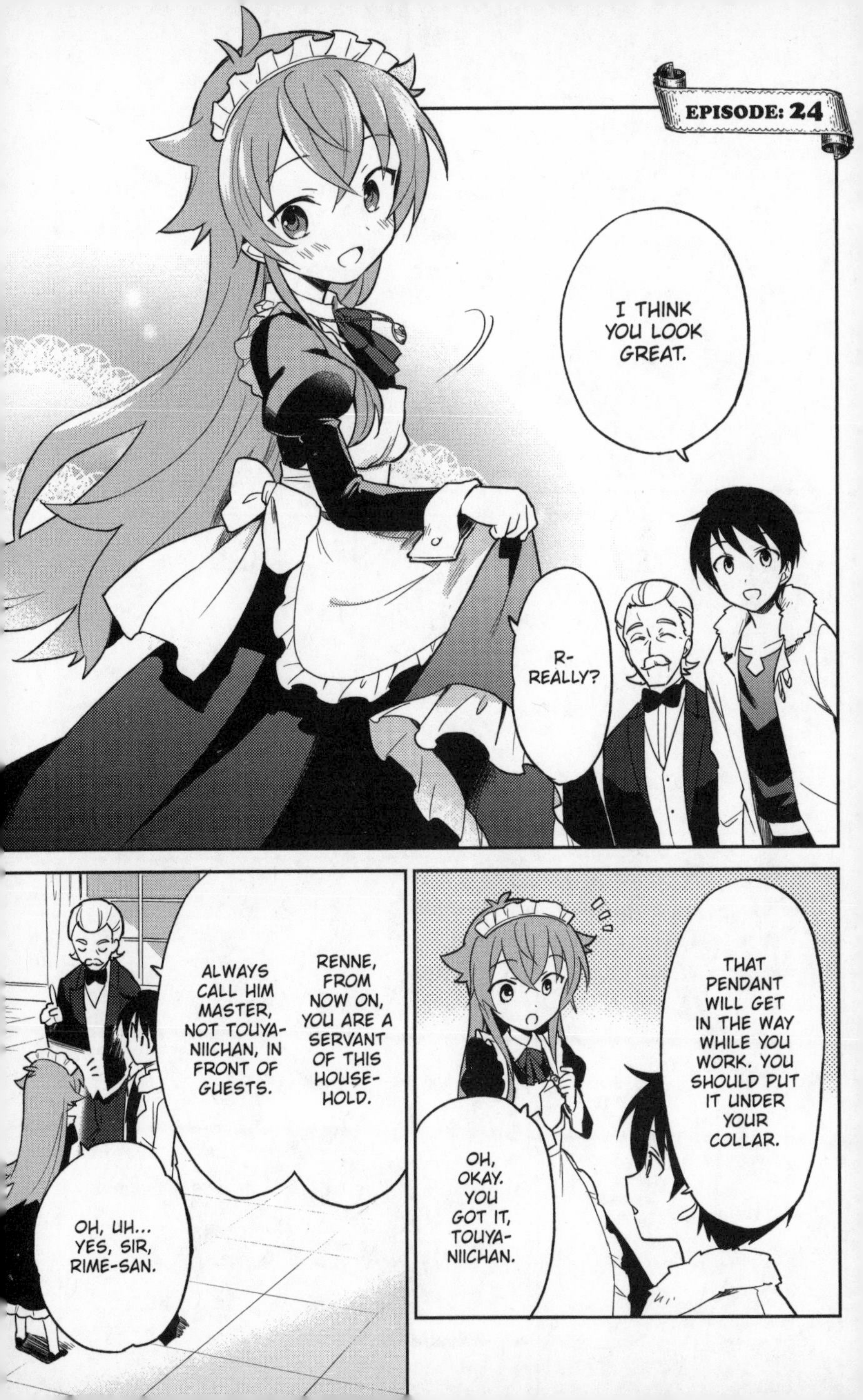
EPISODE: 24
I THINK YOU LOOK GREAT.
R-REALLY?
THAT PENDANT WILL GET IN THE WAY WHILE YOU WORK. YOU SHOULD PUT IT UNDER YOUR COLLAR.
OH, OKAY. YOU GOT IT, TOUYA-NIICHAN.
RENNE, FROM NOW ON, YOU ARE A SERVANT OF THIS HOUSE-HOLD.
ALWAYS CALL HIM MASTER, NOT TOUYA-NIICHAN, IN FRONT OF GUESTS.
OH, UH... YES, SIR, RIME-SAN.

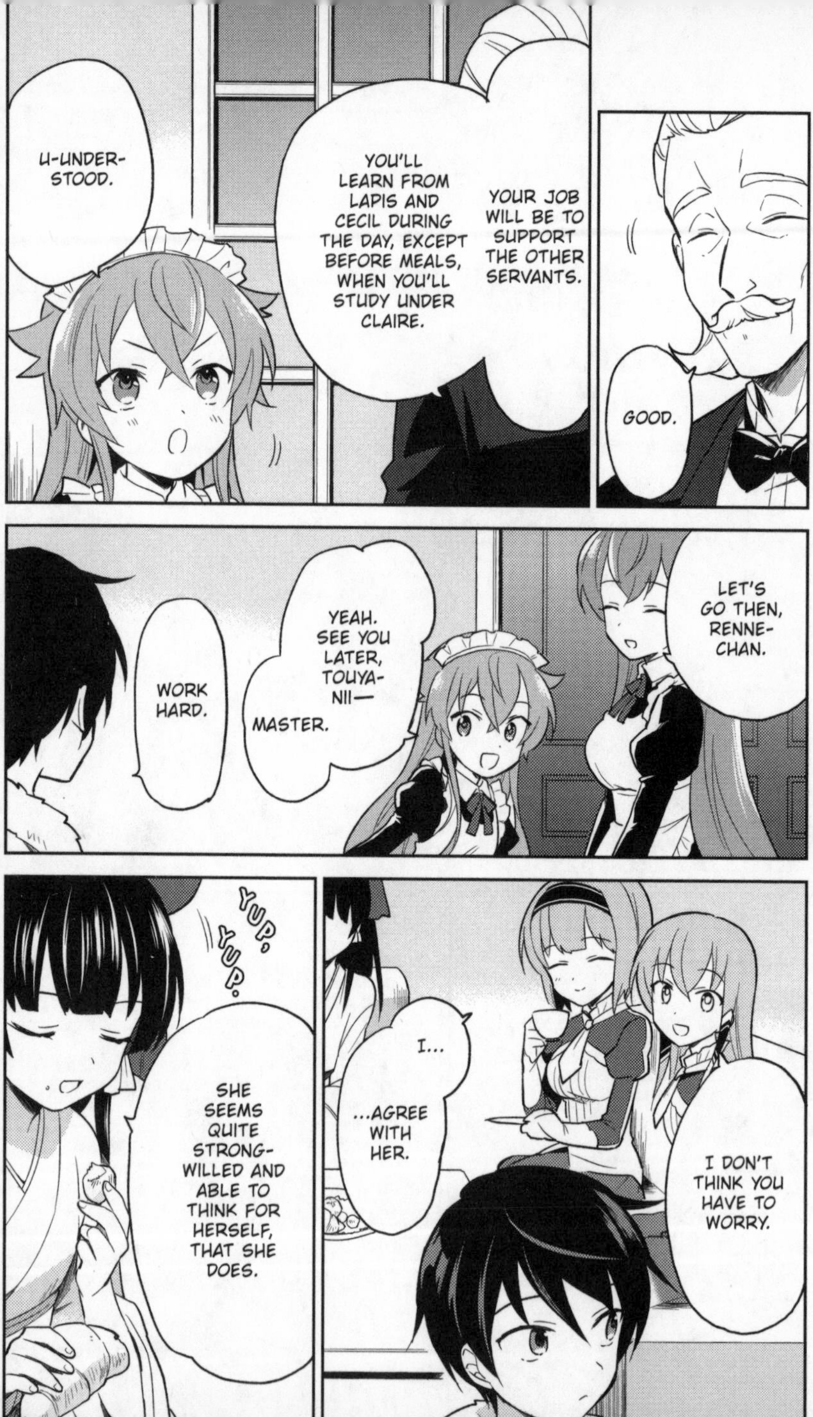
YOUR JOB WILL BE TO SUPPORT THE OTHER SERVANTS.
YOU'LL LEARN FROM LAPIS AND CECIL DURING THE DAY, EXCEPT BEFORE MEALS, WHEN YOU'LL STUDY UNDER CLAIRE.
U-UNDER-STOOD.
GOOD.
LET'S GO THEN, RENNE-CHAN.
YEAH. SEE YOU LATER, TOUYA-NII—
MASTER.
WORK HARD.
I DON'T THINK YOU HAVE TO WORRY.
I...
...AGREE WITH HER.
YUP, YUP.
SHE SEEMS QUITE STRONG-WILLED AND ABLE TO THINK FOR HERSELF, THAT SHE DOES.

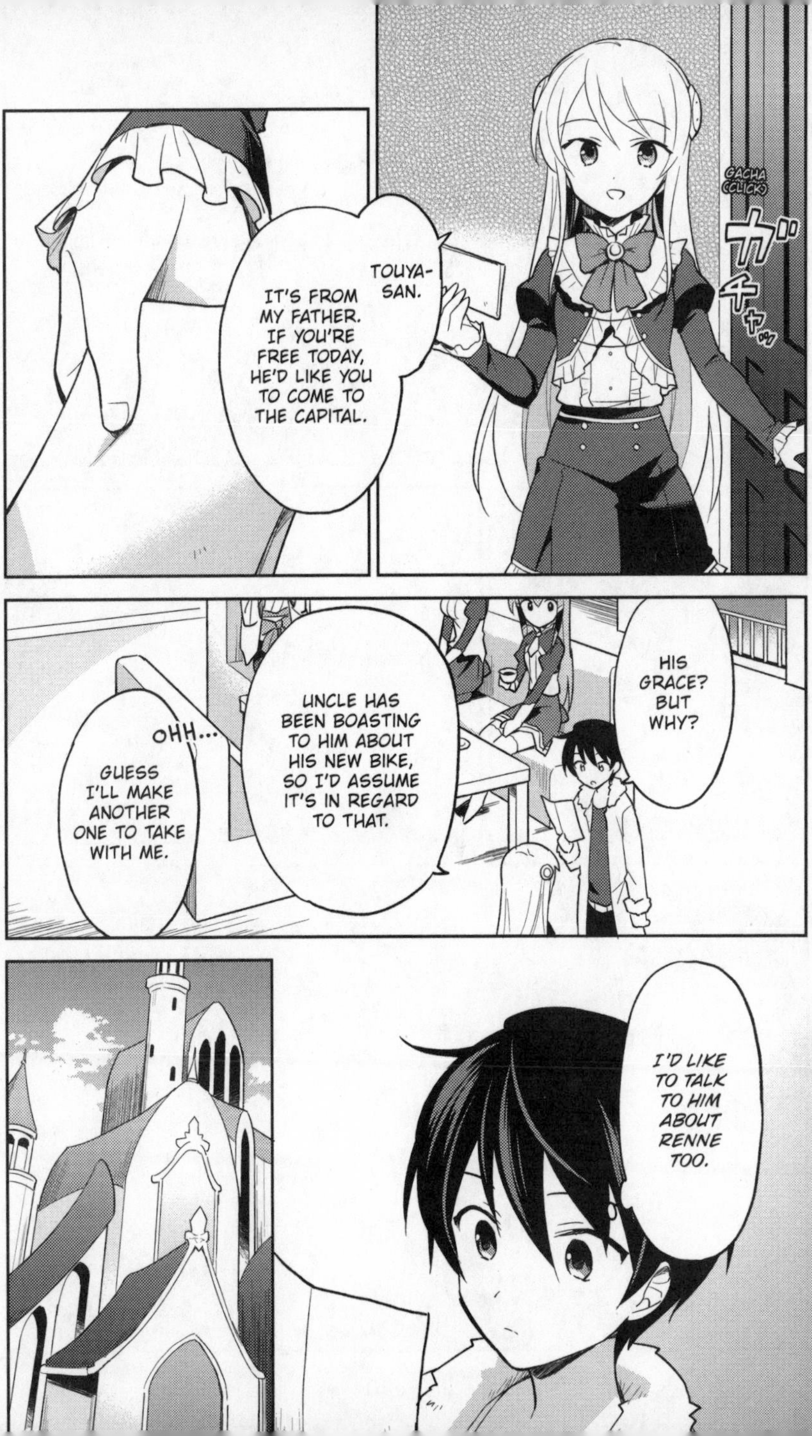
GACHA (CLICK)
ガチャッ
TOUYA-SAN.
IT'S FROM MY FATHER. IF YOU'RE FREE TODAY, HE'D LIKE YOU TO COME TO THE CAPITAL.
HIS GRACE? BUT WHY?
UNCLE HAS BEEN BOASTING TO HIM ABOUT HIS NEW BIKE, SO I'D ASSUME IT'S IN REGARD TO THAT.
OHH...
GUESS I'LL MAKE ANOTHER ONE TO TAKE WITH ME.
I'D LIKE TO TALK TO HIM ABOUT RENNE TOO.

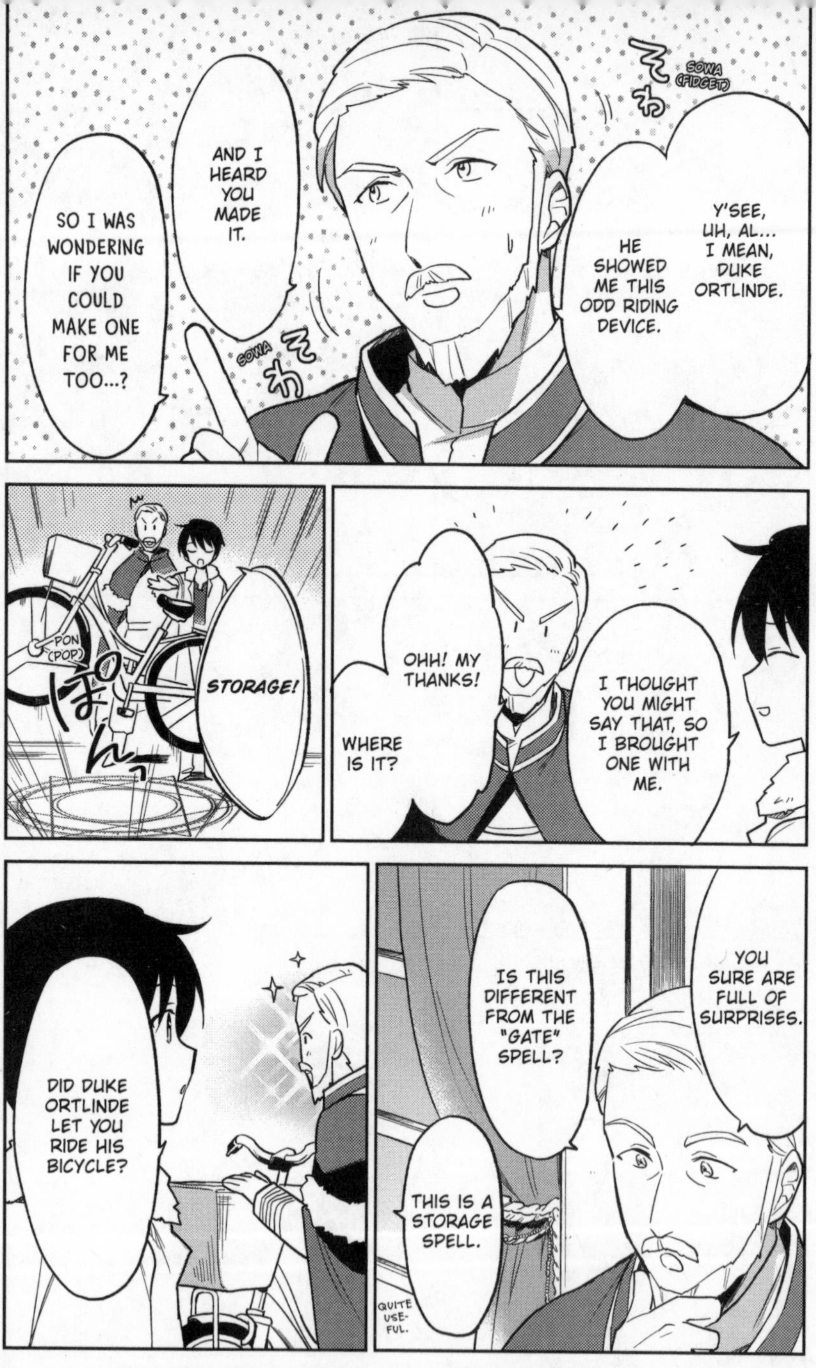
Y'SEE, UH, AL... I MEAN, DUKE ORTLINDE.
HE SHOWED ME THIS ODD RIDING DEVICE.
SOWA (FIDGET)
AND I HEARD YOU MADE IT.
SOWA
SO I WAS WONDERING IF YOU COULD MAKE ONE FOR ME TOO...?
I THOUGHT YOU MIGHT SAY THAT, SO I BROUGHT ONE WITH ME.
OHH! MY THANKS!
WHERE IS IT?
STORAGE!
PON (POP)
YOU SURE ARE FULL OF SURPRISES.
IS THIS DIFFERENT FROM THE "GATE" SPELL?
THIS IS A STORAGE SPELL.
QUITE USE-FUL.
DID DUKE ORTLINDE LET YOU RIDE HIS BICYCLE?

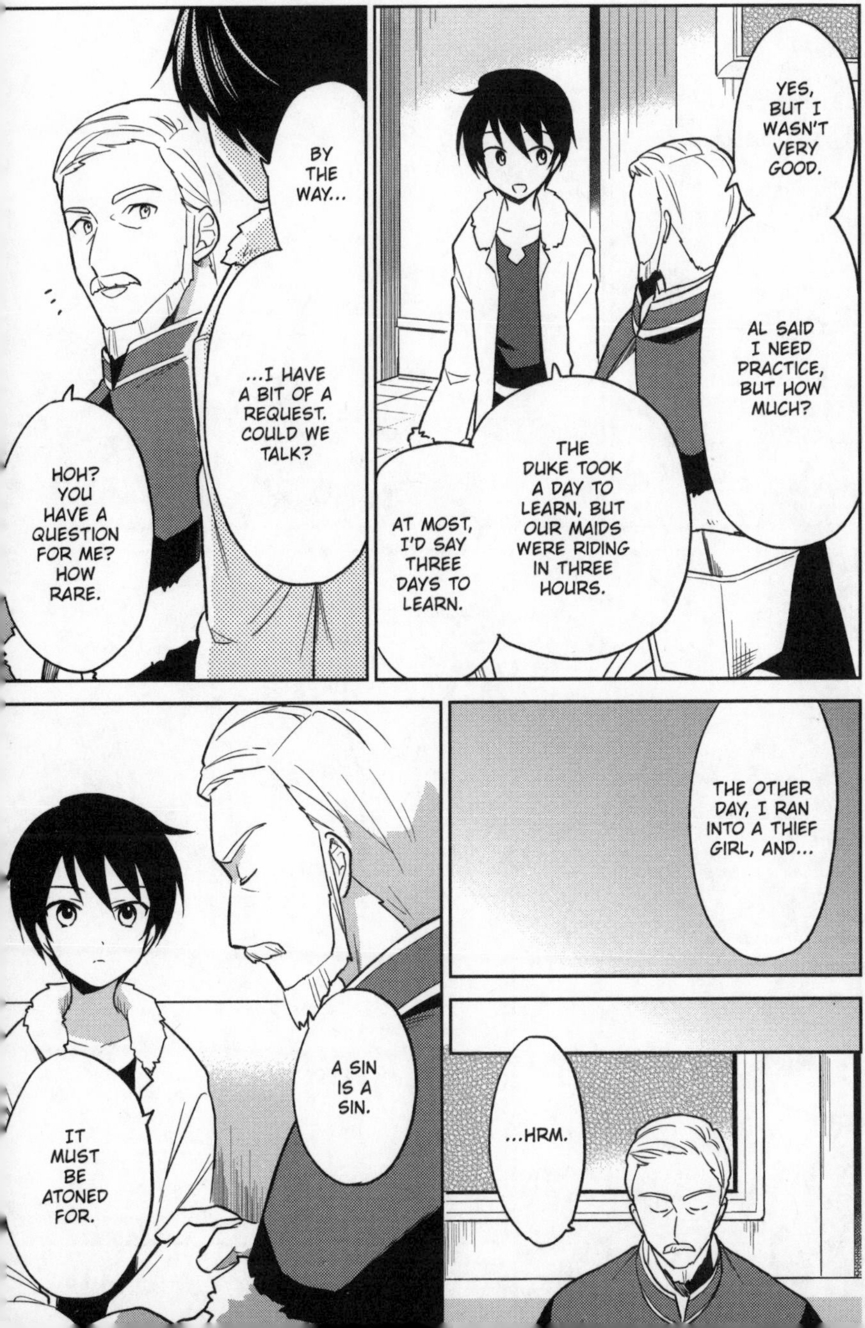
YES, BUT I WASN'T VERY GOOD.
AL SAID I NEED PRACTICE, BUT HOW MUCH?
THE DUKE TOOK A DAY TO LEARN, BUT OUR MAIDS WERE RIDING IN THREE HOURS.
AT MOST, I'D SAY THREE DAYS TO LEARN.
BY THE WAY...
...I HAVE A BIT OF A REQUEST. COULD WE TALK?
HOH? YOU HAVE A QUESTION FOR ME? HOW RARE.
THE OTHER DAY, I RAN INTO A THIEF GIRL, AND...
...HRM.
A SIN IS A SIN.
IT MUST BE ATONED FOR.

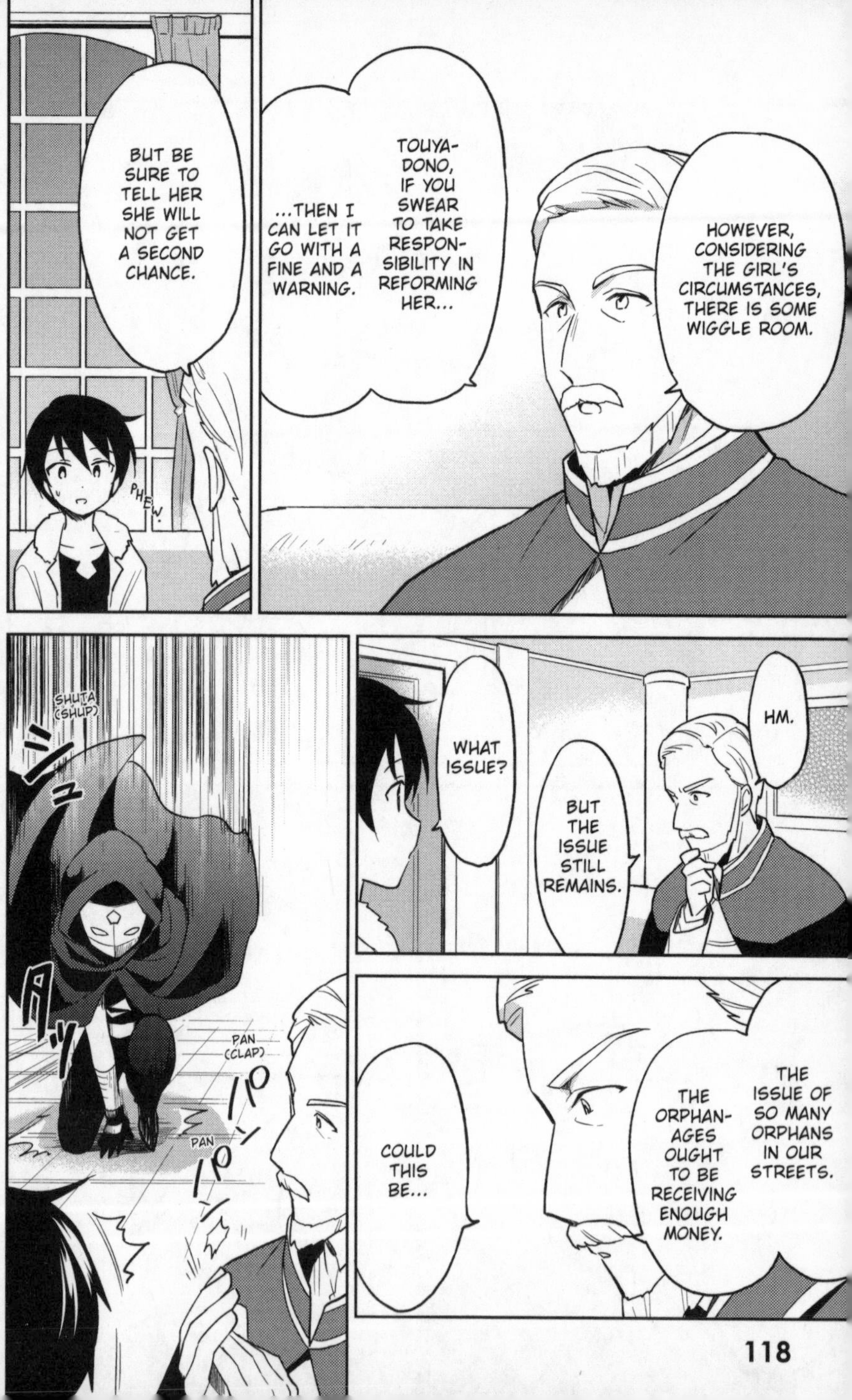
HOWEVER, CONSIDERING THE GIRL'S CIRCUMSTANCES, THERE IS SOME WIGGLE ROOM.
TOUYA-DONO, IF YOU SWEAR TO TAKE RESPONSIBILITY IN REFORMING HER...
...THEN I CAN LET IT GO WITH A FINE AND A WARNING.
BUT BE SURE TO TELL HER SHE WILL NOT GET A SECOND CHANCE.
PHEW.
HM.
BUT THE ISSUE STILL REMAINS.
WHAT ISSUE?
THE ISSUE OF SO MANY ORPHANS IN OUR STREETS.
THE ORPHANAGES OUGHT TO BE RECEIVING ENOUGH MONEY.
COULD THIS BE...
SHUTA (SHUP)
PAN (CLAP)
PAN

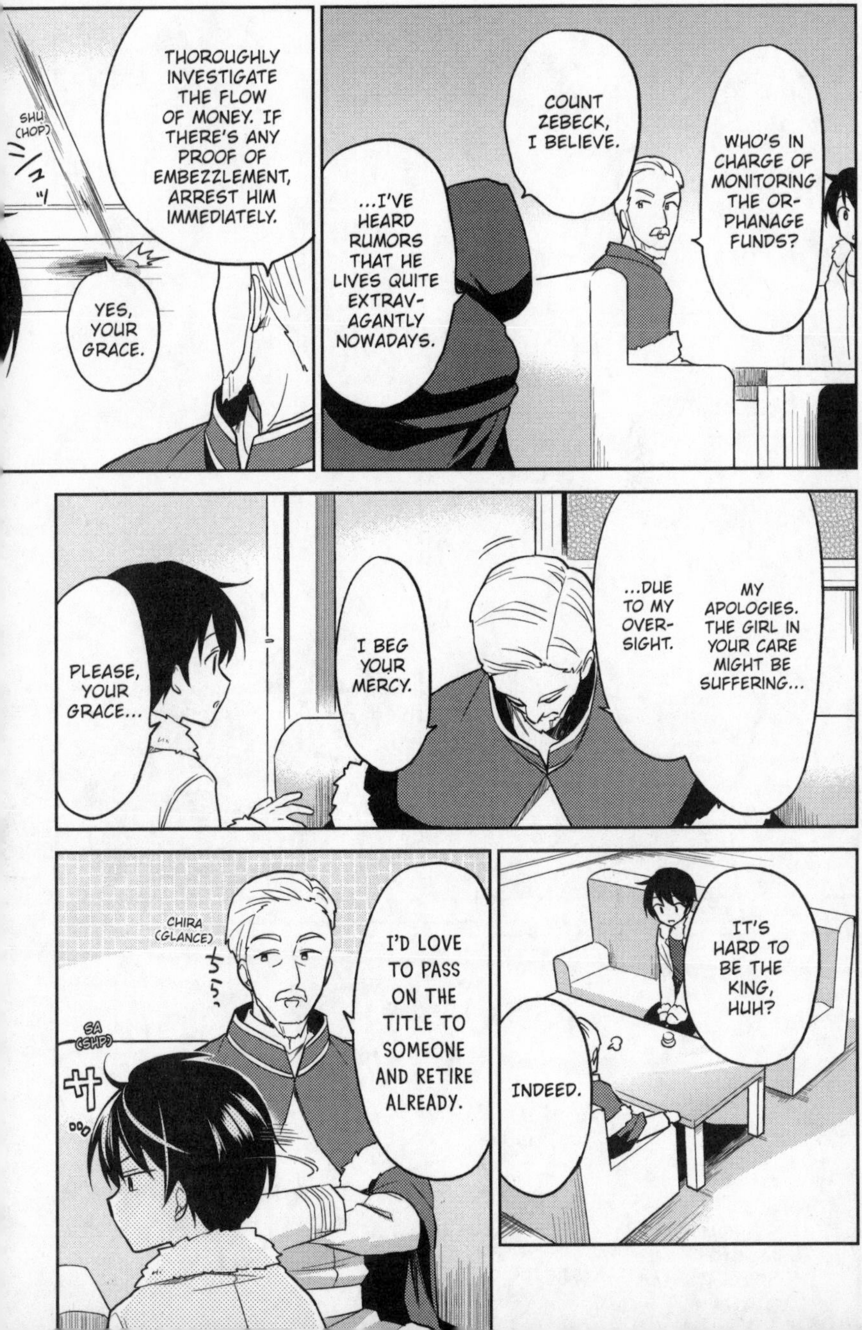
WHO'S IN CHARGE OF MONITORING THE OR-PHANAGE FUNDS?
COUNT ZEBECK, I BELIEVE.
...I'VE HEARD RUMORS THAT HE LIVES QUITE EXTRAV-AGANTLY NOWADAYS.
THOROUGHLY INVESTIGATE THE FLOW OF MONEY. IF THERE'S ANY PROOF OF EMBEZZLEMENT, ARREST HIM IMMEDIATELY.
SHU (CHOP)
YES, YOUR GRACE.
MY APOLOGIES. THE GIRL IN YOUR CARE MIGHT BE SUFFERING...
...DUE TO MY OVER-SIGHT.
I BEG YOUR MERCY.
PLEASE, YOUR GRACE...
IT'S HARD TO BE THE KING, HUH?
INDEED.
I'D LOVE TO PASS ON THE TITLE TO SOMEONE AND RETIRE ALREADY.
CHIRA (GLANCE)
SA

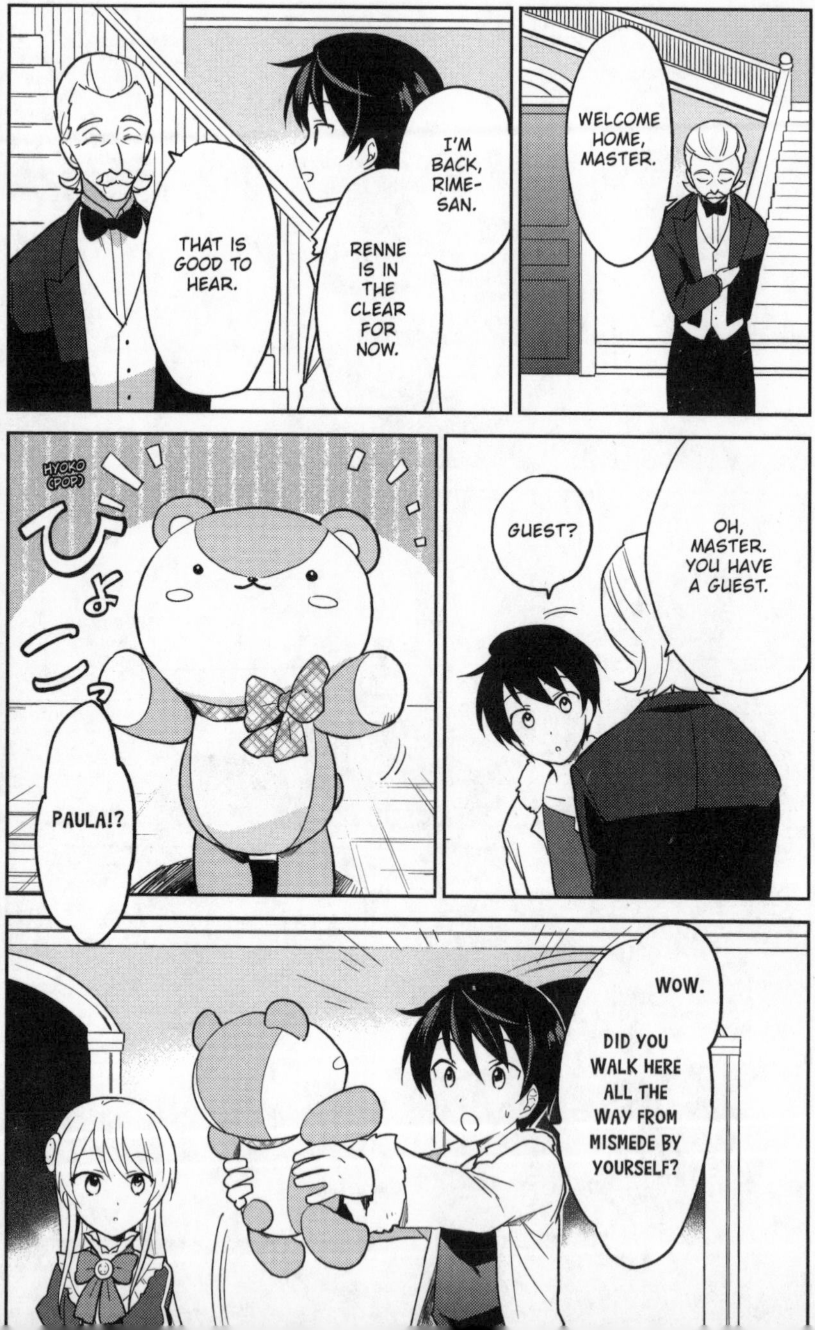
WELCOME HOME, MASTER.
I'M BACK, RIME-SAN.
RENNE IS IN THE CLEAR FOR NOW.
THAT IS GOOD TO HEAR.
OH, MASTER. YOU HAVE A GUEST.
GUEST?
HYOKO (POP)
ぴょこっ
PAULA!?
WOW.
DID YOU WALK HERE ALL THE WAY FROM MISMEDE BY YOURSELF?

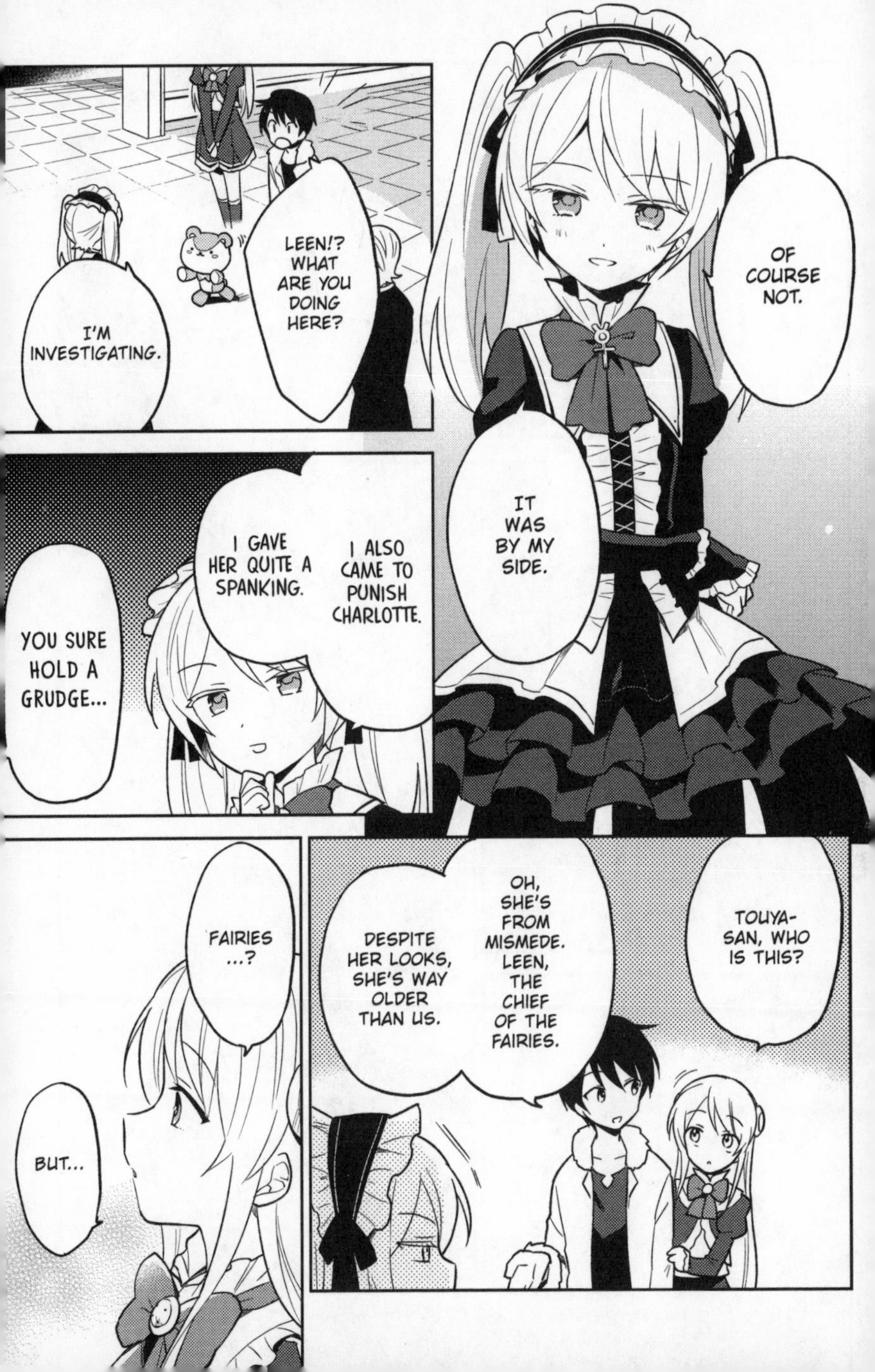
OF COURSE NOT.
IT WAS BY MY SIDE.
LEEN!? WHAT ARE YOU DOING HERE?
I'M INVESTIGATING.
I ALSO CAME TO PUNISH CHARLOTTE.
I GAVE HER QUITE A SPANKING.
YOU SURE HOLD A GRUDGE...
TOUYA-SAN, WHO IS THIS?
OH, SHE'S FROM MISMEDE. LEEN, THE CHIEF OF THE FAIRIES.
DESPITE HER LOOKS, SHE'S WAY OLDER THAN US.
FAIRIES ...?
BUT...

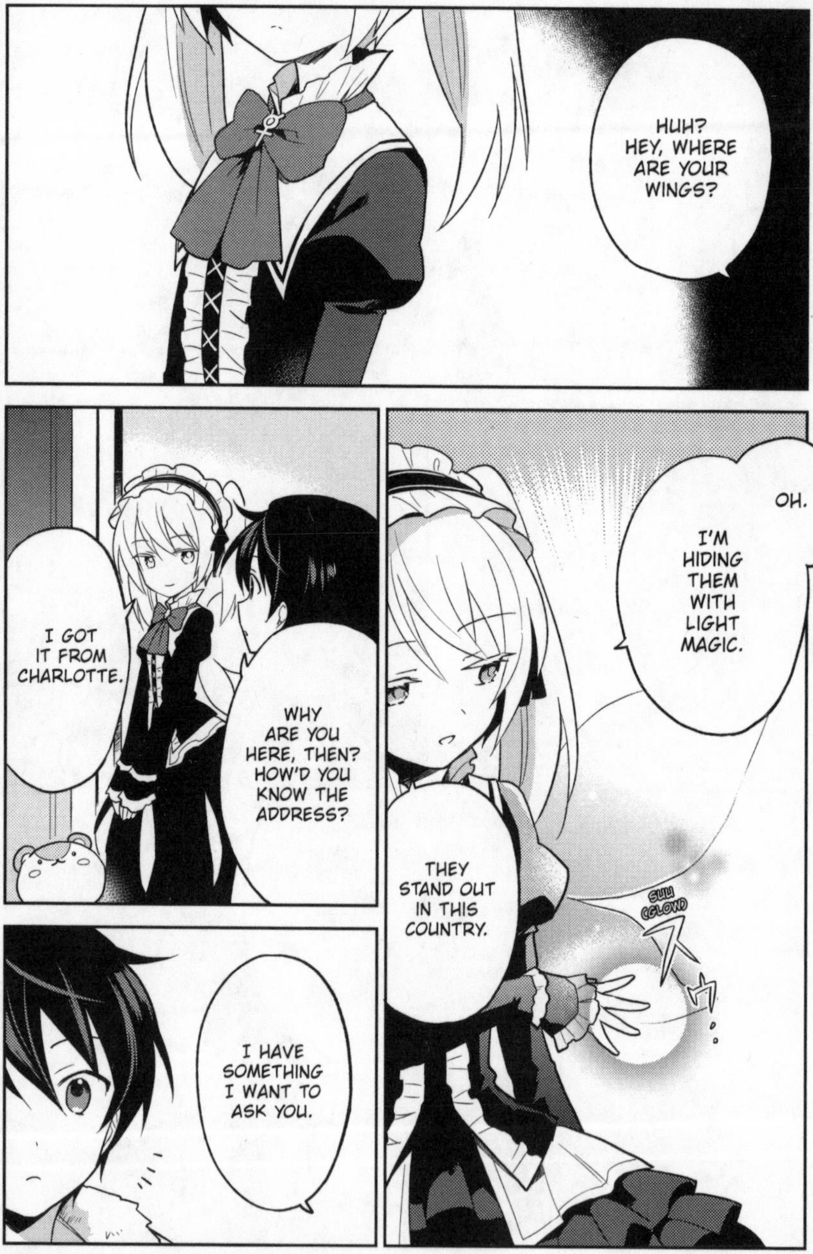
HUH? HEY, WHERE ARE YOUR WINGS?
OH.
I'M HIDING THEM WITH LIGHT MAGIC.
THEY STAND OUT IN THIS COUNTRY.
SUU (GLOW)
WHY ARE YOU HERE, THEN? HOW'D YOU KNOW THE ADDRESS?
I GOT IT FROM CHARLOTTE.
I HAVE SOMETHING I WANT TO ASK YOU.

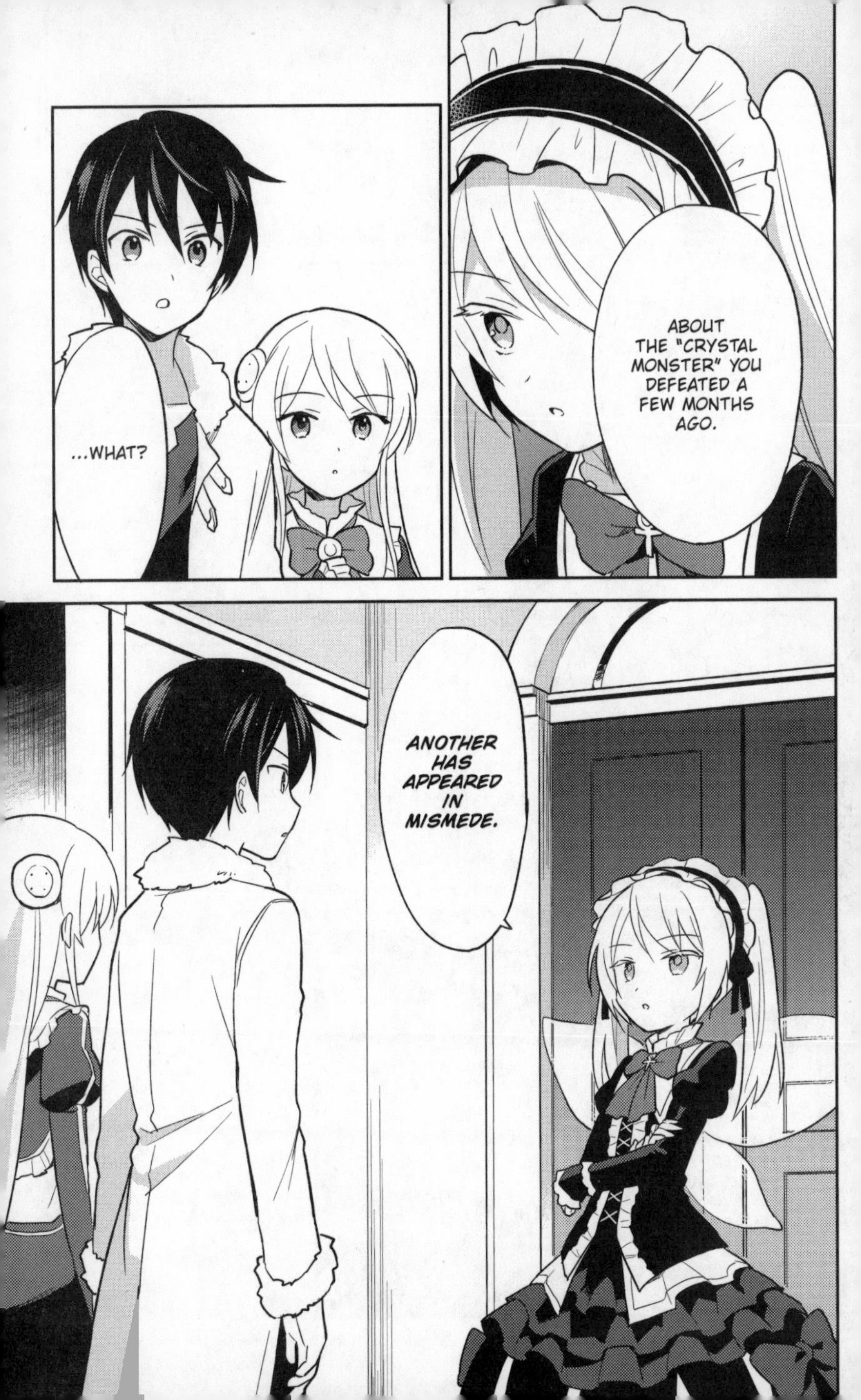
ABOUT THE "CRYSTAL MONSTER" YOU DEFEATED A FEW MONTHS AGO.
...WHAT?
ANOTHER HAS APPEARED IN MISMEDE.

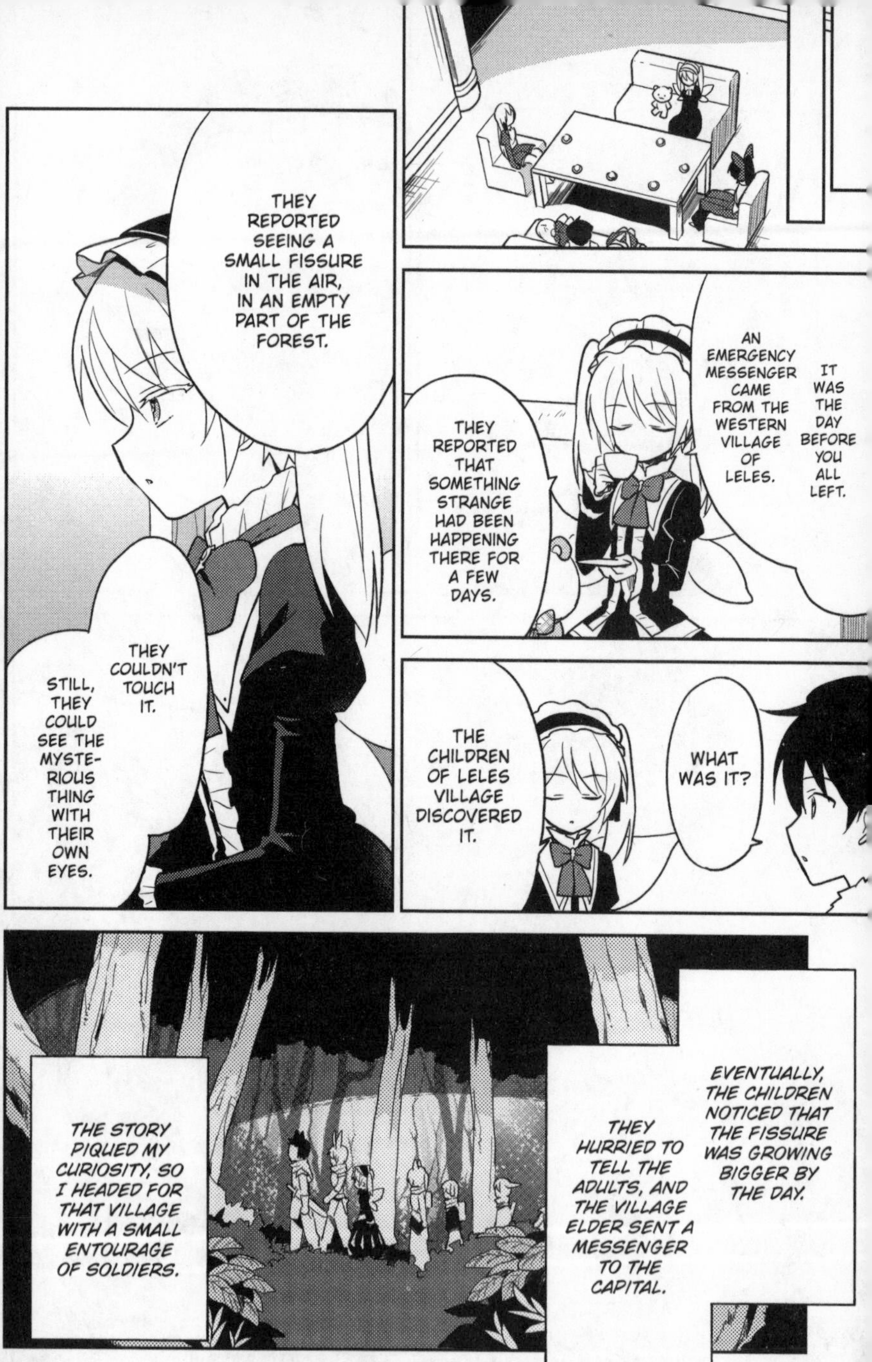
IT WAS THE DAY BEFORE YOU ALL LEFT.
AN EMERGENCY MESSENGER CAME FROM THE WESTERN VILLAGE OF LELES.
THEY REPORTED THAT SOMETHING STRANGE HAD BEEN HAPPENING THERE FOR A FEW DAYS.
WHAT WAS IT?
THE CHILDREN OF LELES VILLAGE DISCOVERED IT.
THEY REPORTED SEEING A SMALL FISSURE IN THE AIR, IN AN EMPTY PART OF THE FOREST.
THEY COULDN'T TOUCH IT.
STILL, THEY COULD SEE THE MYSTE-RIOUS THING WITH THEIR OWN EYES.
EVENTUALLY, THE CHILDREN NOTICED THAT THE FISSURE WAS GROWING BIGGER BY THE DAY.
THEY HURRIED TO TELL THE ADULTS, AND THE VILLAGE ELDER SENT A MESSENGER TO THE CAPITAL.
THE STORY PIQUED MY CURIOSITY, SO I HEADED FOR THAT VILLAGE WITH A SMALL ENTOURAGE OF SOLDIERS.

BUT WHAT I ARRIVED TO FIND WAS A VILLAGE TORN TO PIECES.

THE CRYSTAL MONSTER HAD KILLED THE VILLAGERS. NOT A STONE WAS LEFT UNTOUCHED BY ITS CURSE.

THE SOLDIERS AND I DID BATTLE WITH IT, BUT WE STOOD NO CHANCE.

THE MONSTER REFLECTED SWORDS AND ABSORBED MAGIC. ON THE RARE CHANCE WE BROKE A PIECE, IT REGENERATED.

IT WAS A TRUE NIGHTMARE.

HALF OF THE SOLDIERS ARE BEYOND RECOVERY. THE VILLAGE WAS COMPLETELY WIPED OUT.

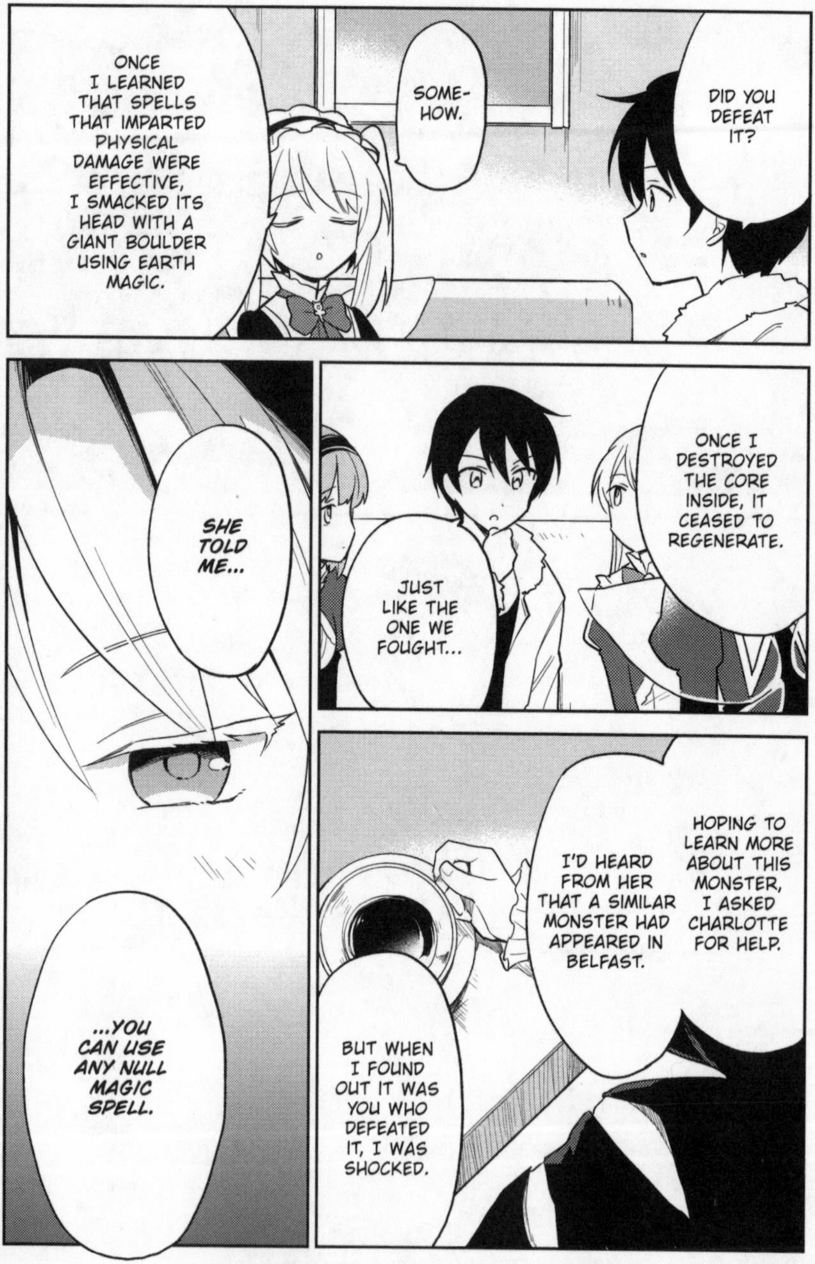
DID YOU DEFEAT IT?
SOME-HOW.
ONCE I LEARNED THAT SPELLS THAT IMPARTED PHYSICAL DAMAGE WERE EFFECTIVE, I SMACKED ITS HEAD WITH A GIANT BOULDER USING EARTH MAGIC.
ONCE I DESTROYED THE CORE INSIDE, IT CEASED TO REGENERATE.
JUST LIKE THE ONE WE FOUGHT...
HOPING TO LEARN MORE ABOUT THIS MONSTER, I ASKED CHARLOTTE FOR HELP.
I'D HEARD FROM HER THAT A SIMILAR MONSTER HAD APPEARED IN BELFAST.
BUT WHEN I FOUND OUT IT WAS YOU WHO DEFEATED IT, I WAS SHOCKED.
SHE TOLD ME...
...YOU CAN USE ANY NULL MAGIC SPELL.

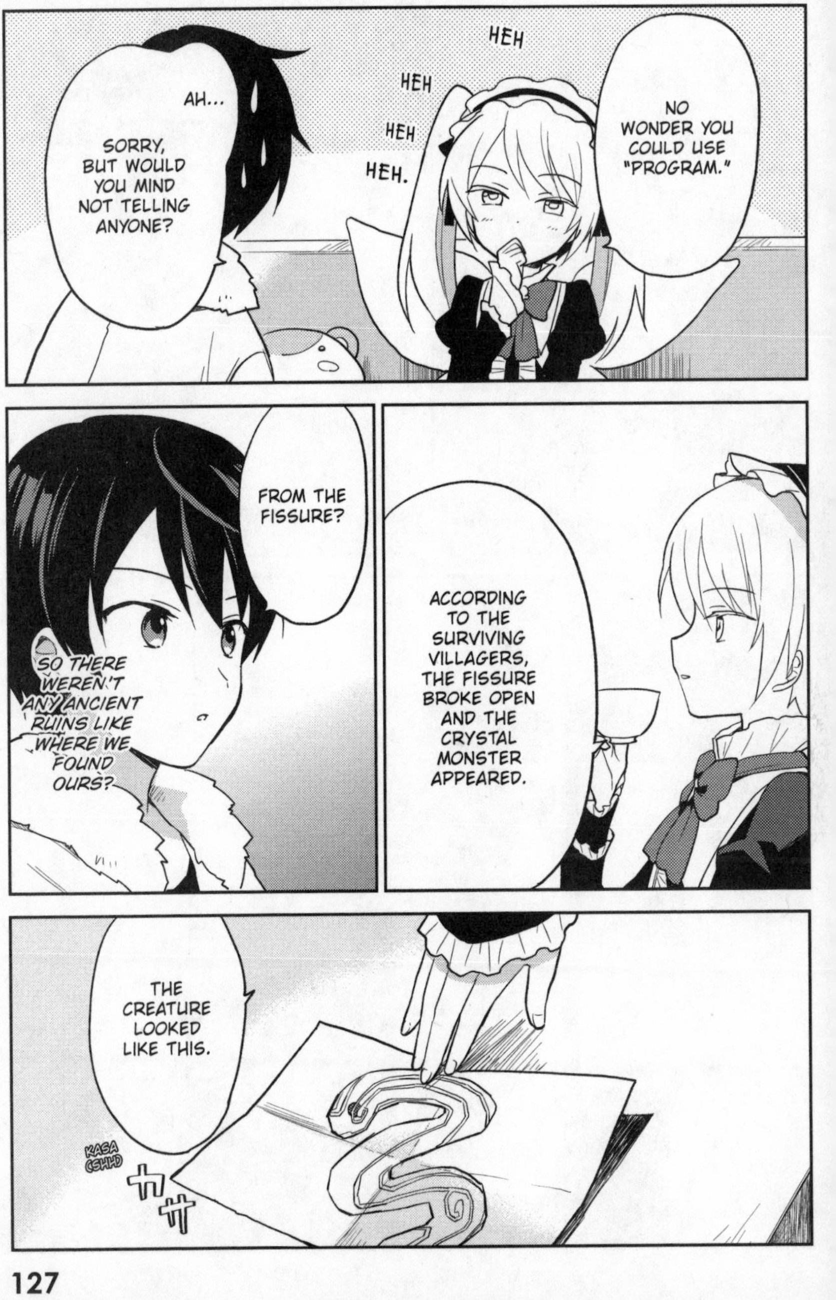
NO WONDER YOU COULD USE "PROGRAM."
HEH HEH HEH HEH.
AH... SORRY, BUT WOULD YOU MIND NOT TELLING ANYONE?
ACCORDING TO THE SURVIVING VILLAGERS, THE FISSURE BROKE OPEN AND THE CRYSTAL MONSTER APPEARED.
FROM THE FISSURE?
SO THERE WEREN'T ANY ANCIENT RUINS LIKE WHERE WE FOUND OURS?
THE CREATURE LOOKED LIKE THIS.
KASA CSHHD

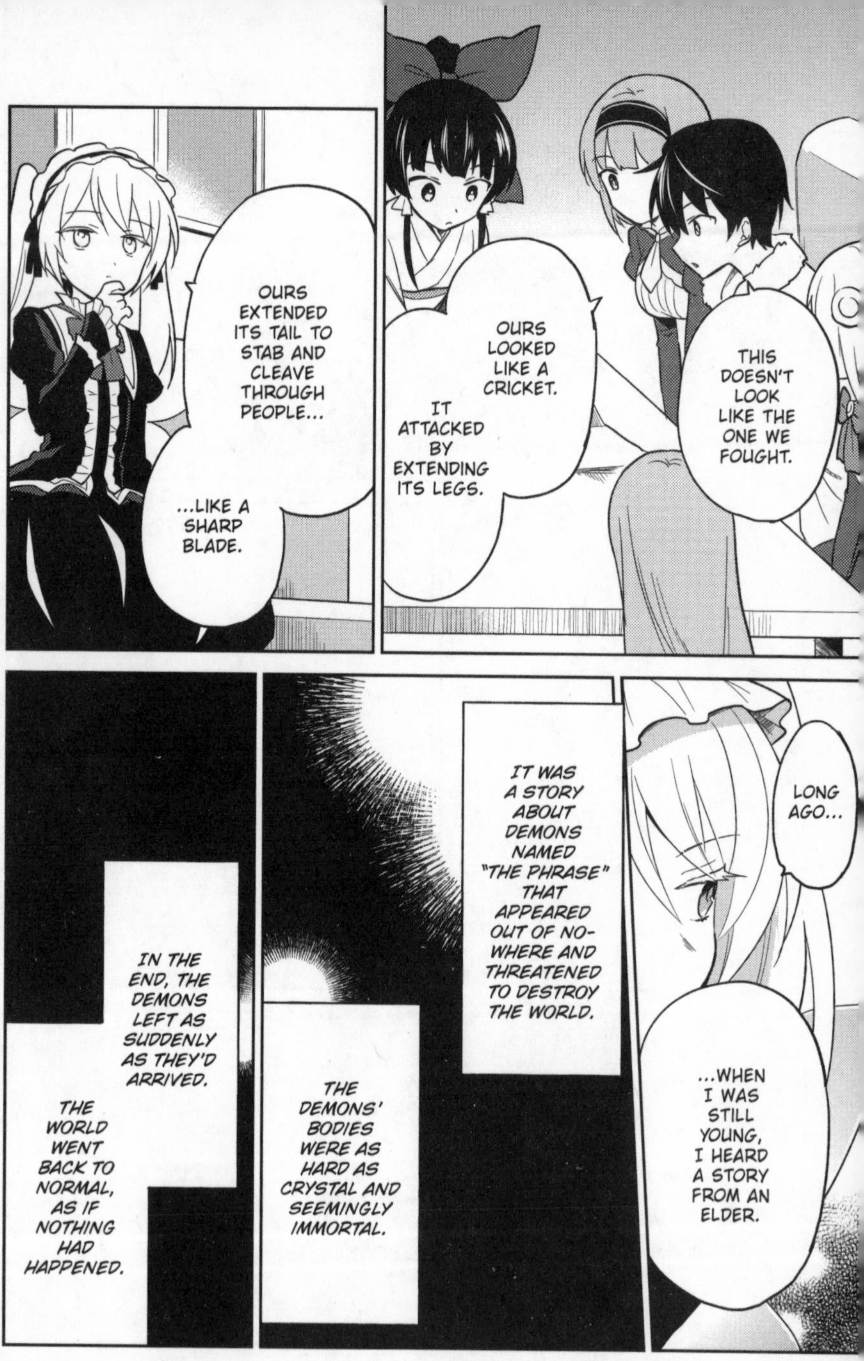
THIS DOESN'T LOOK LIKE THE ONE WE FOUGHT.
OURS LOOKED LIKE A CRICKET.
IT ATTACKED BY EXTENDING ITS LEGS.
OURS EXTENDED ITS TAIL TO STAB AND CLEAVE THROUGH PEOPLE...
...LIKE A SHARP BLADE.
LONG AGO...
...WHEN I WAS STILL YOUNG, I HEARD A STORY FROM AN ELDER.
IT WAS A STORY ABOUT DEMONS NAMED "THE PHRASE" THAT APPEARED OUT OF NO-WHERE AND THREATENED TO DESTROY THE WORLD.
THE DEMONS' BODIES WERE AS HARD AS CRYSTAL AND SEEMINGLY IMMORTAL.
IN THE END, THE DEMONS LEFT AS SUDDENLY AS THEY'D ARRIVED.
THE WORLD WENT BACK TO NORMAL, AS IF NOTHING HAD HAPPENED.

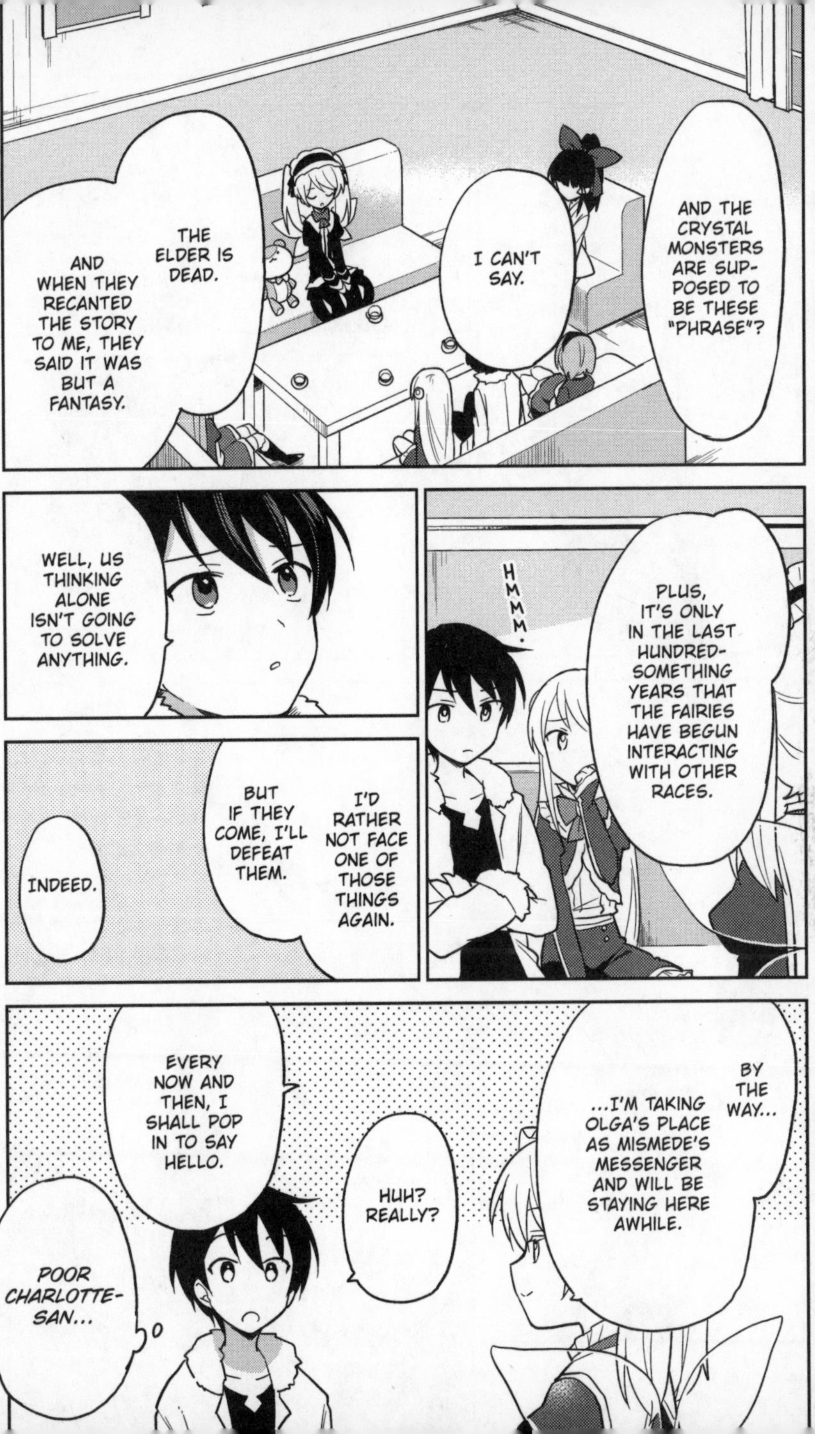
AND THE CRYSTAL MONSTERS ARE SUPPOSED TO BE THESE "PHRASE"?
I CAN'T SAY.
THE ELDER IS DEAD.
AND WHEN THEY RECANTED THE STORY TO ME, THEY SAID IT WAS BUT A FANTASY.
PLUS, IT'S ONLY IN THE LAST HUNDRED-SOMETHING YEARS THAT THE FAIRIES HAVE BEGUN INTERACTING WITH OTHER RACES.
HMMM.
WELL, US THINKING ALONE ISN'T GOING TO SOLVE ANYTHING.
I'D RATHER NOT FACE ONE OF THOSE THINGS AGAIN.
BUT IF THEY COME, I'LL DEFEAT THEM.
INDEED.
BY THE WAY...
...I'M TAKING OLGA'S PLACE AS MISMEDE'S MESSENGER AND WILL BE STAYING HERE AWHILE.
HUH? REALLY?
EVERY NOW AND THEN, I SHALL POP IN TO SAY HELLO.
POOR CHARLOTTE-SAN...

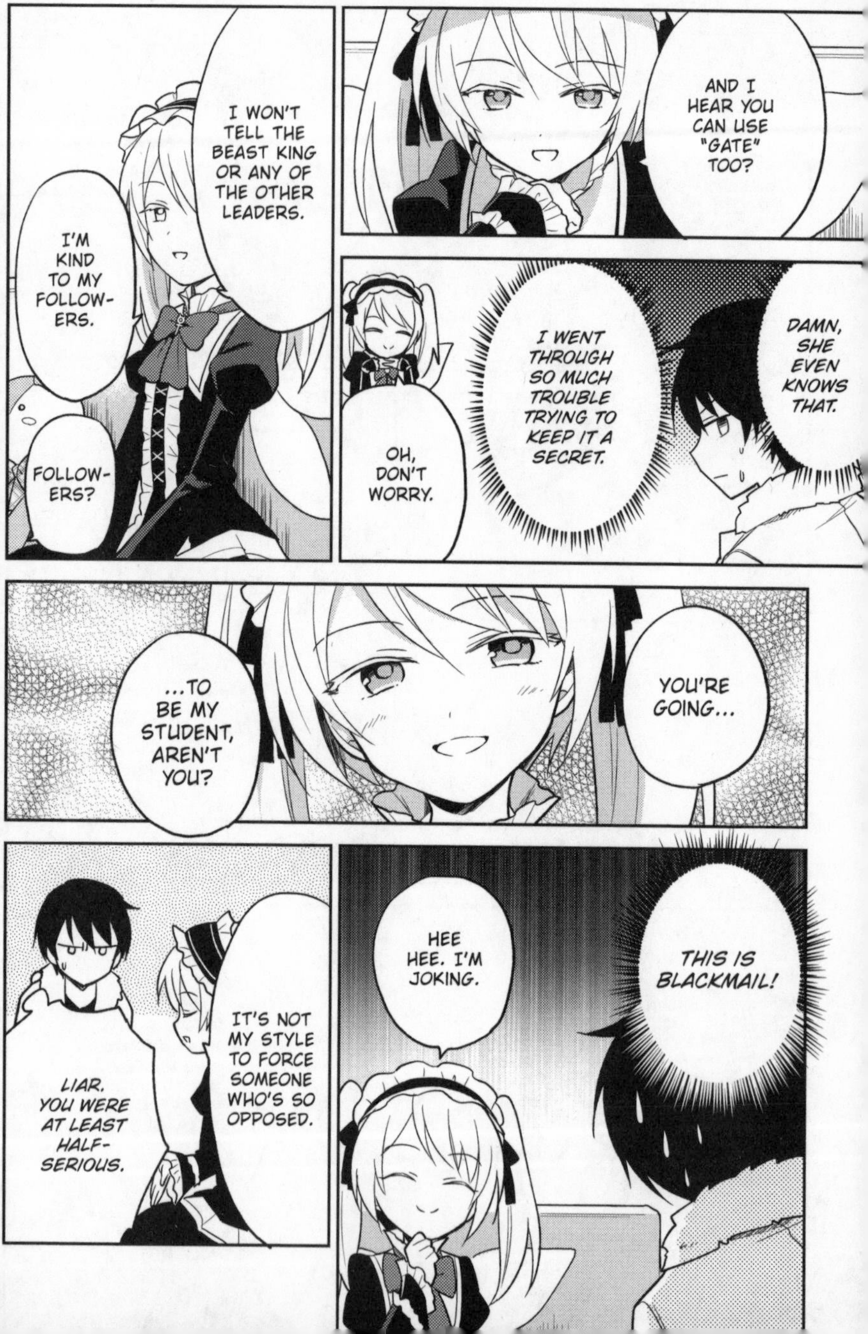
AND I HEAR YOU CAN USE "GATE" TOO?
DAMN, SHE EVEN KNOWS THAT.
I WENT THROUGH SO MUCH TROUBLE TRYING TO KEEP IT A SECRET.
OH, DON'T WORRY.
I WON'T TELL THE BEAST KING OR ANY OF THE OTHER LEADERS.
I'M KIND TO MY FOLLOW-ERS.
FOLLOW-ERS?
YOU'RE GOING...
...TO BE MY STUDENT, AREN'T YOU?
THIS IS BLACKMAIL!
HEE HEE. I'M JOKING.
IT'S NOT MY STYLE TO FORCE SOMEONE WHO'S SO OPPOSED.
LIAR. YOU WERE AT LEAST HALF-SERIOUS.

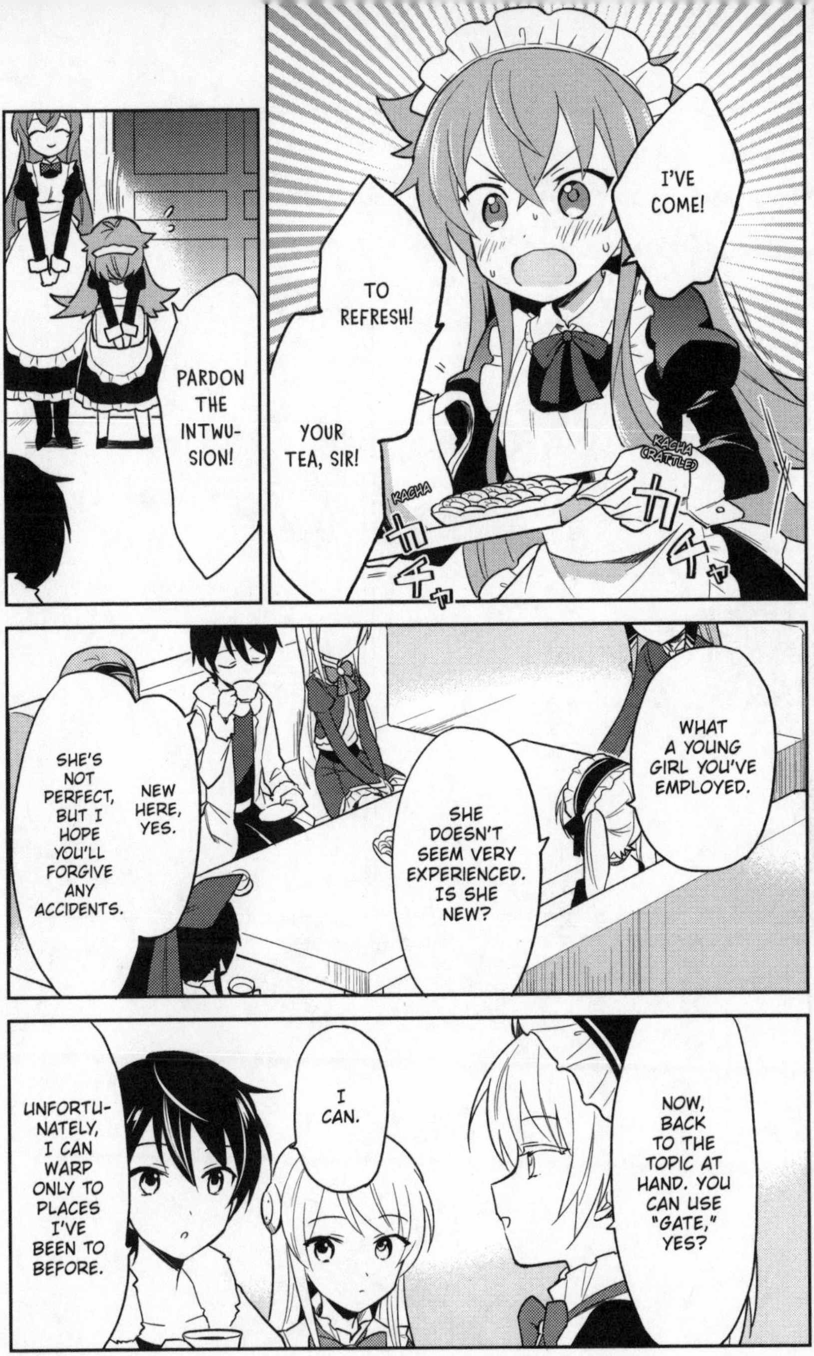
I'VE COME!
TO REFRESH!
YOUR TEA, SIR!
KACHA (RATTLE)
KACHA
PARDON THE INTWUSION!
WHAT A YOUNG GIRL YOU'VE EMPLOYED.
SHE DOESN'T SEEM VERY EXPERIENCED. IS SHE NEW?
NEW HERE, YES.
SHE'S NOT PERFECT, BUT I HOPE YOU'LL FORGIVE ANY ACCIDENTS.
NOW, BACK TO THE TOPIC AT HAND. YOU CAN USE "GATE," YES?
I CAN.
UNFORTUNATELY, I CAN WARP ONLY TO PLACES I'VE BEEN TO BEFORE.

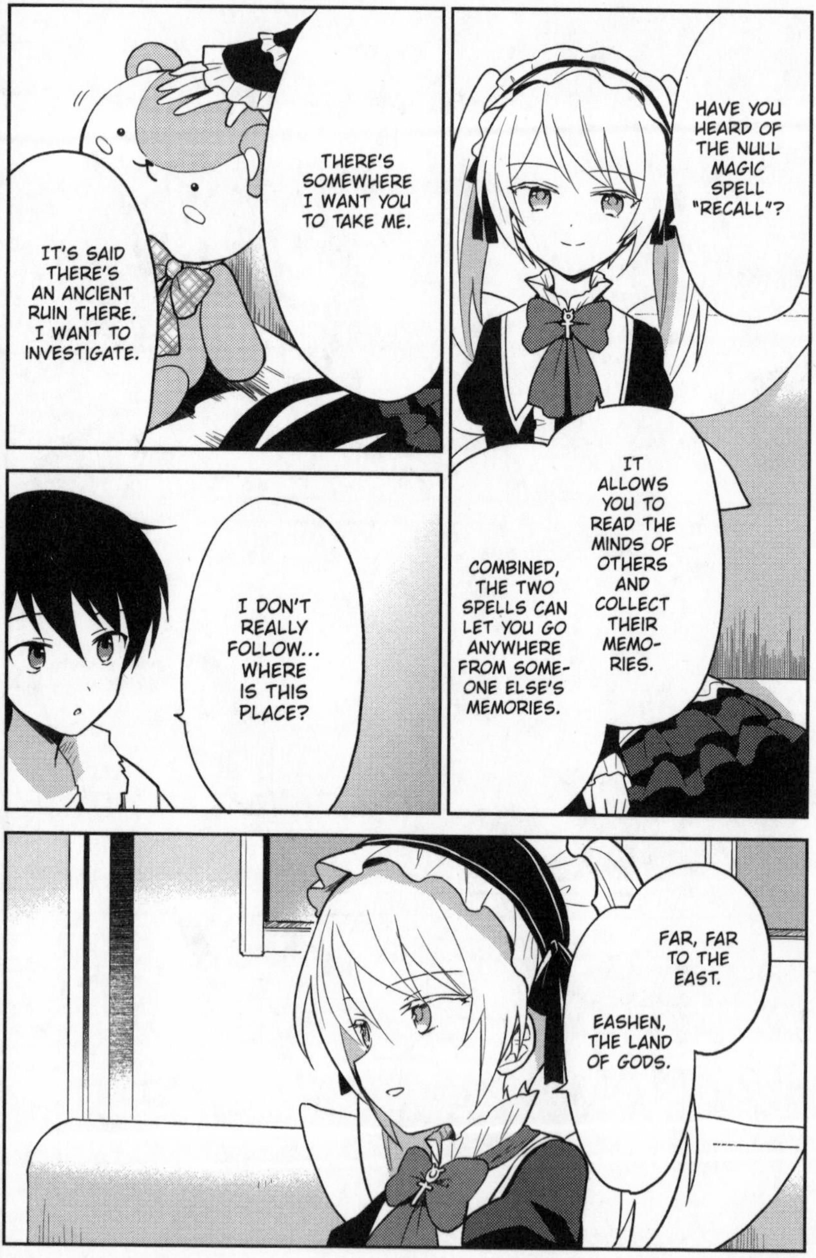
HAVE YOU HEARD OF THE NULL MAGIC SPELL "RECALL"?
THERE'S SOMEWHERE I WANT YOU TO TAKE ME.
IT'S SAID THERE'S AN ANCIENT RUIN THERE. I WANT TO INVESTIGATE.
IT ALLOWS YOU TO READ THE MINDS OF OTHERS AND COLLECT THEIR MEMORIES.
COMBINED, THE TWO SPELLS CAN LET YOU GO ANYWHERE FROM SOMEONE ELSE'S MEMORIES.
I DON'T REALLY FOLLOW... WHERE IS THIS PLACE?
FAR, FAR TO THE EAST.
EASHEN, THE LAND OF GODS.

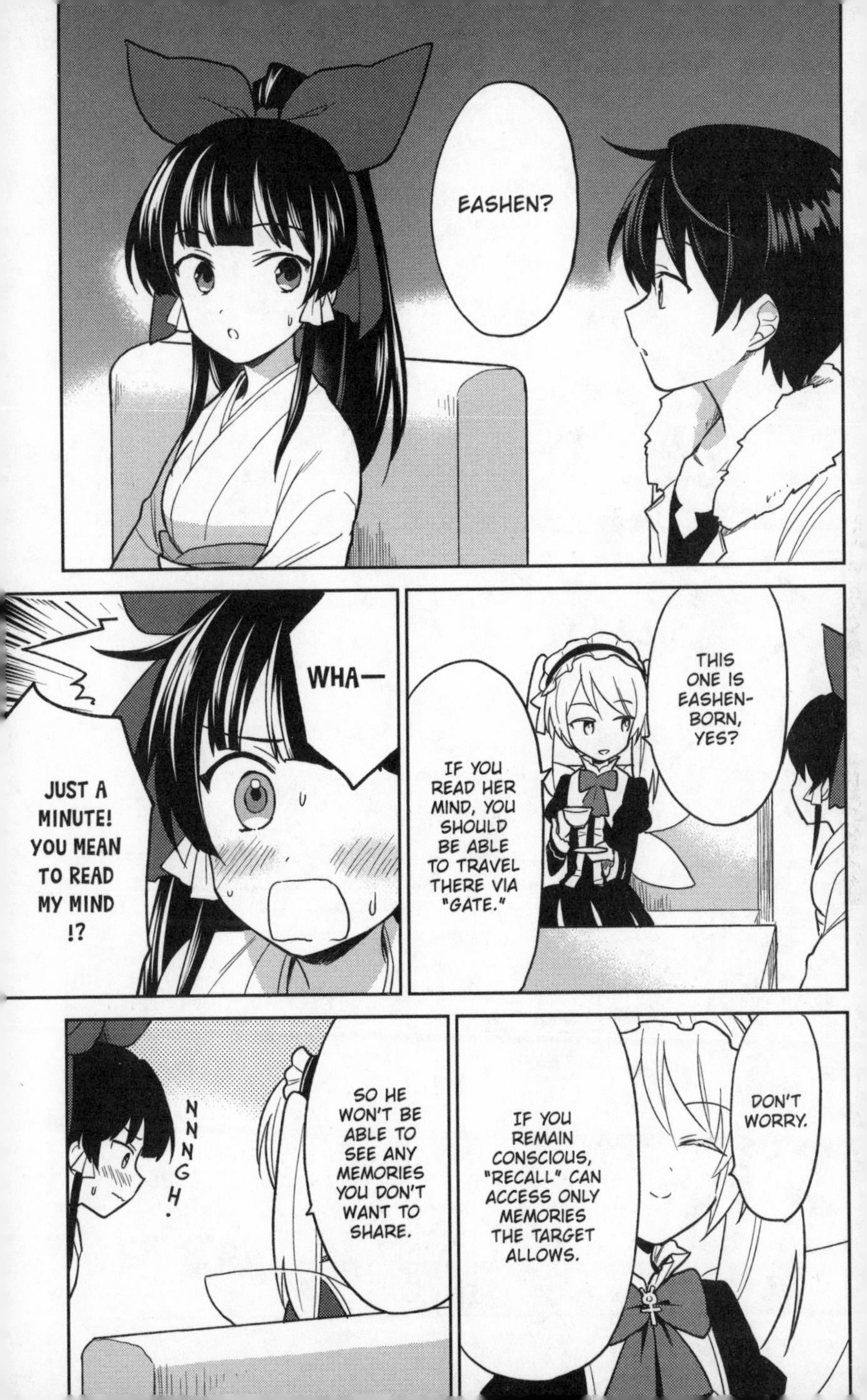
EASHEN?
THIS ONE IS EASHEN-BORN, YES?
IF YOU READ HER MIND, YOU SHOULD BE ABLE TO TRAVEL THERE VIA "GATE."
WHA—
JUST A MINUTE! YOU MEAN TO READ MY MIND !?
DON'T WORRY.
IF YOU REMAIN CONSCIOUS, "RECALL" CAN ACCESS ONLY MEMORIES THE TARGET ALLOWS.
SO HE WON'T BE ABLE TO SEE ANY MEMORIES YOU DON'T WANT TO SHARE.
NNNGH!

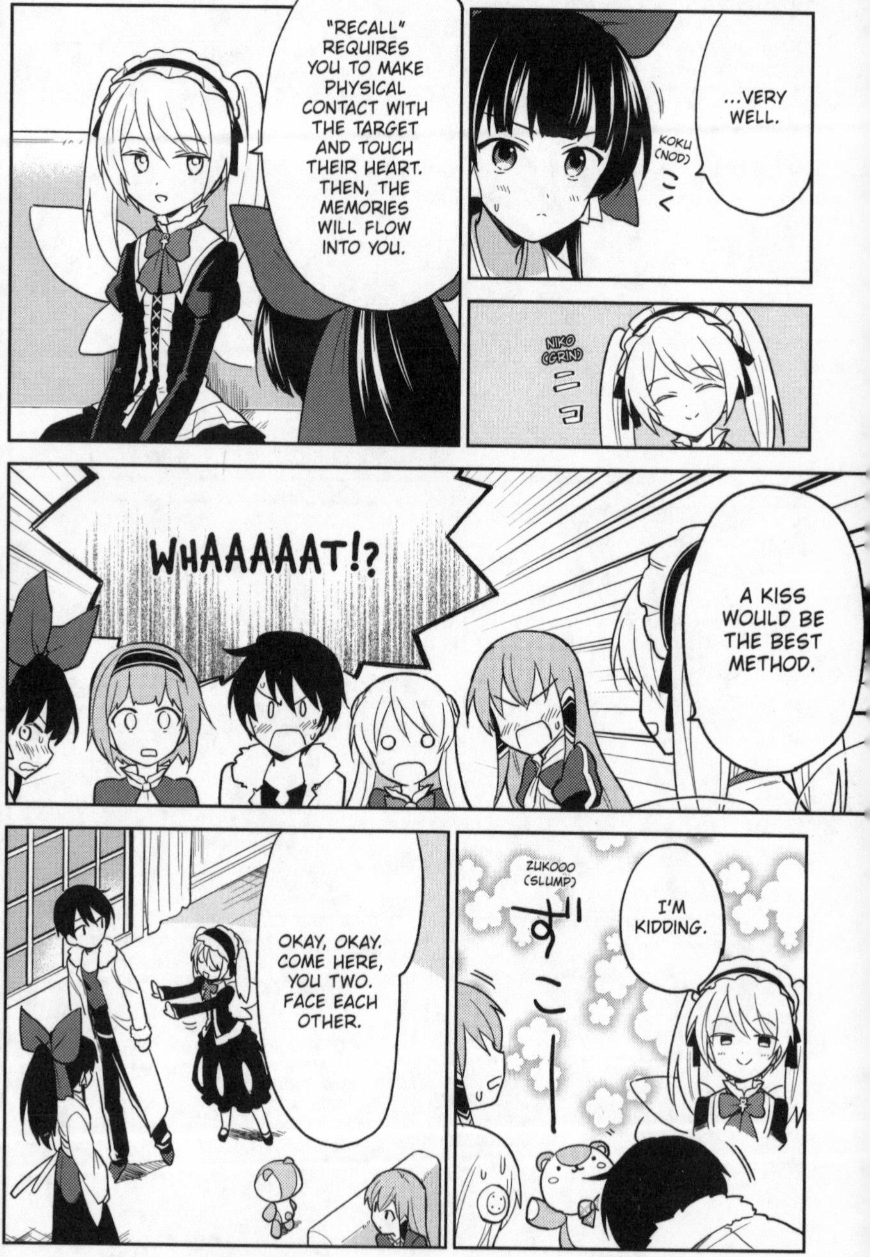
...VERY WELL.
KOKU (NOD)
こく
NIKO (GRIN)
ニコ
"RECALL" REQUIRES YOU TO MAKE PHYSICAL CONTACT WITH THE TARGET AND TOUCH THEIR HEART. THEN, THE MEMORIES WILL FLOW INTO YOU.
A KISS WOULD BE THE BEST METHOD.
WHAAAAAT!?
I'M KIDDING.
ZUKOOO (SLUMP)
ずこー
OKAY, OKAY. COME HERE, YOU TWO. FACE EACH OTHER.

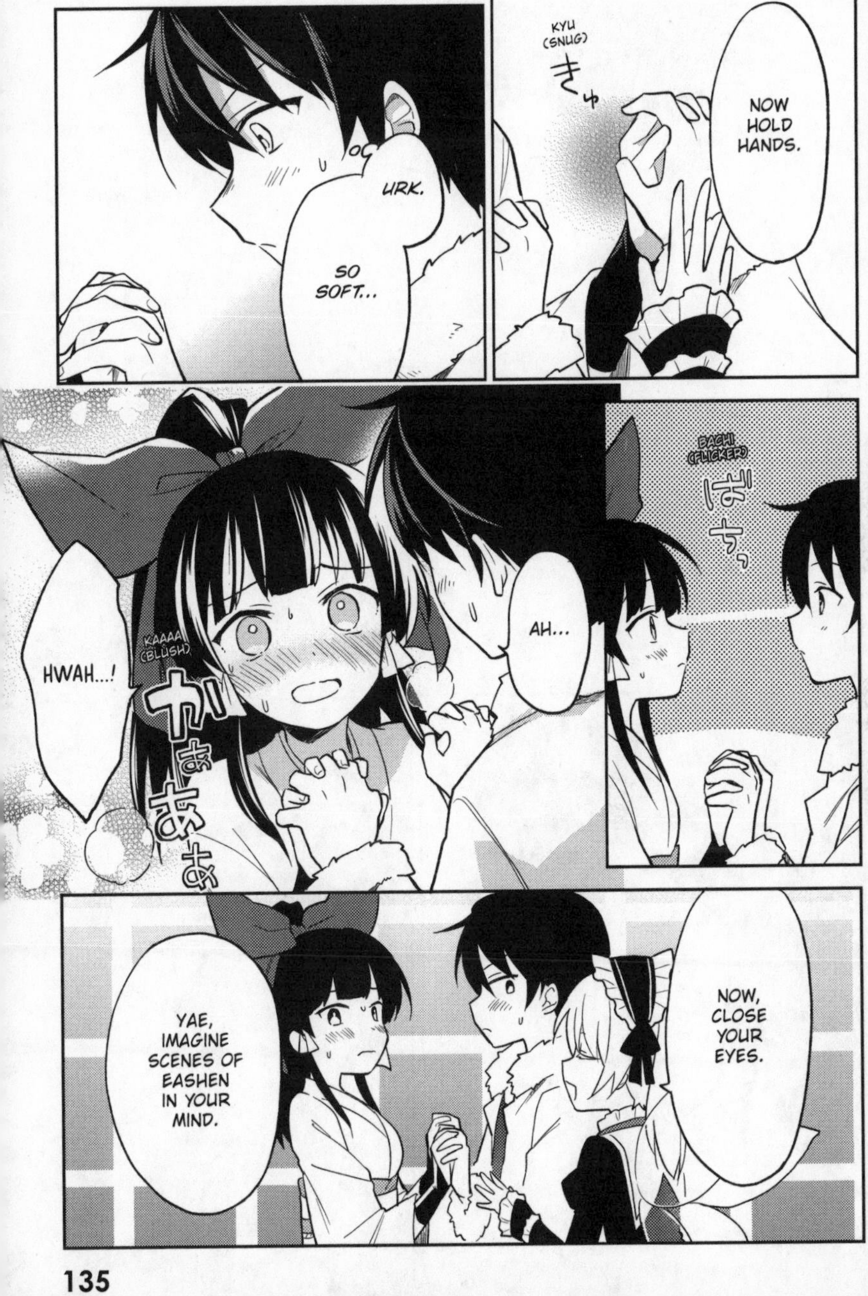
NOW HOLD HANDS.
KYU (SNUG)
きゅ
URK.
SO SOFT...
BACHI (FLICKER)
ぱちっ
AH...
KAAAA (BLUSH)
かぁあぁ
HWAH...!
NOW, CLOSE YOUR EYES.
YAE, IMAGINE SCENES OF EASHEN IN YOUR MIND.

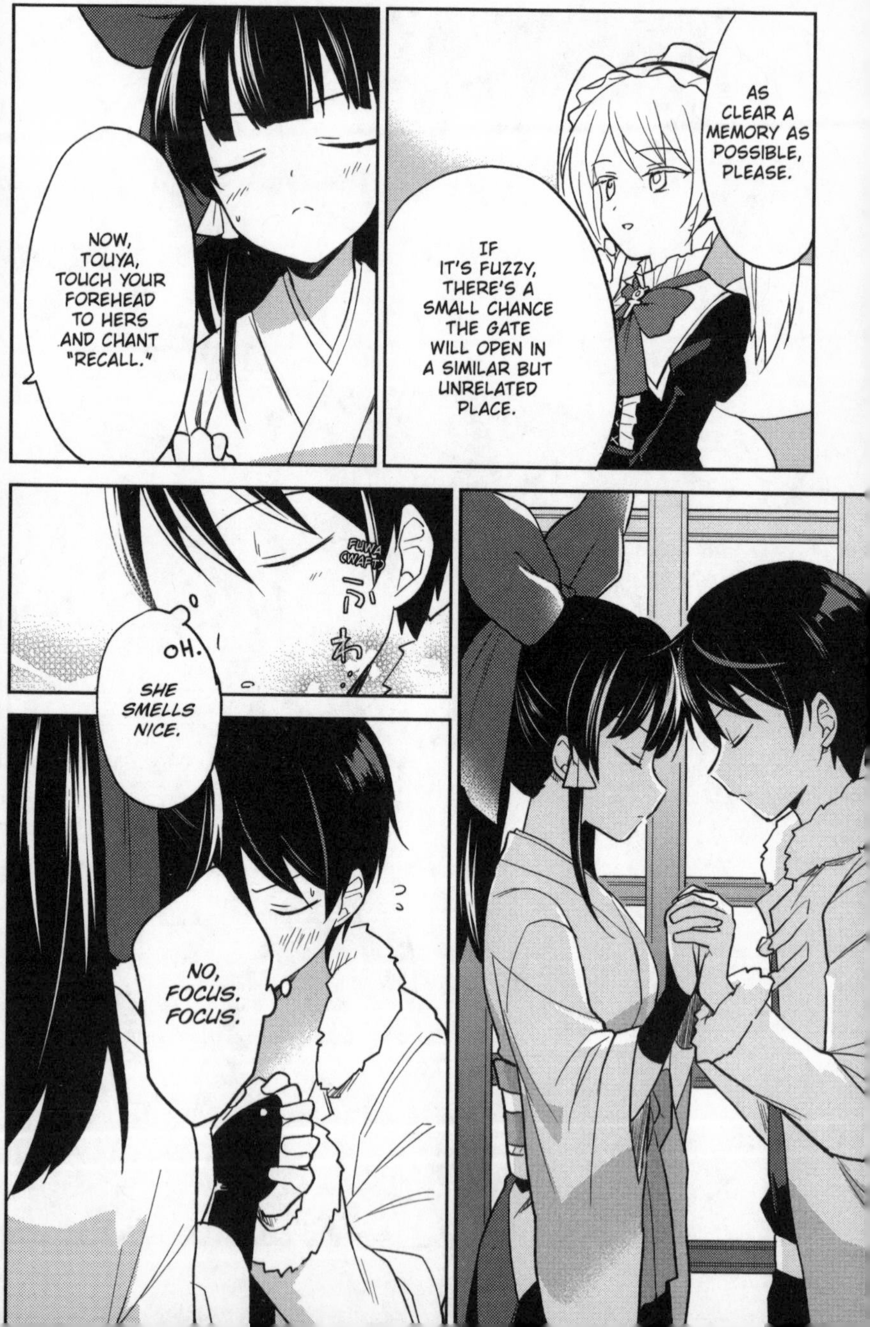
AS CLEAR A MEMORY AS POSSIBLE, PLEASE.
IF IT'S FUZZY, THERE'S A SMALL CHANCE THE GATE WILL OPEN IN A SIMILAR BUT UNRELATED PLACE.
NOW, TOUYA, TOUCH YOUR FOREHEAD TO HERS AND CHANT "RECALL."
FUWA (WAFT)
ふわ
OH.
SHE SMELLS NICE.
NO, FOCUS. FOCUS.

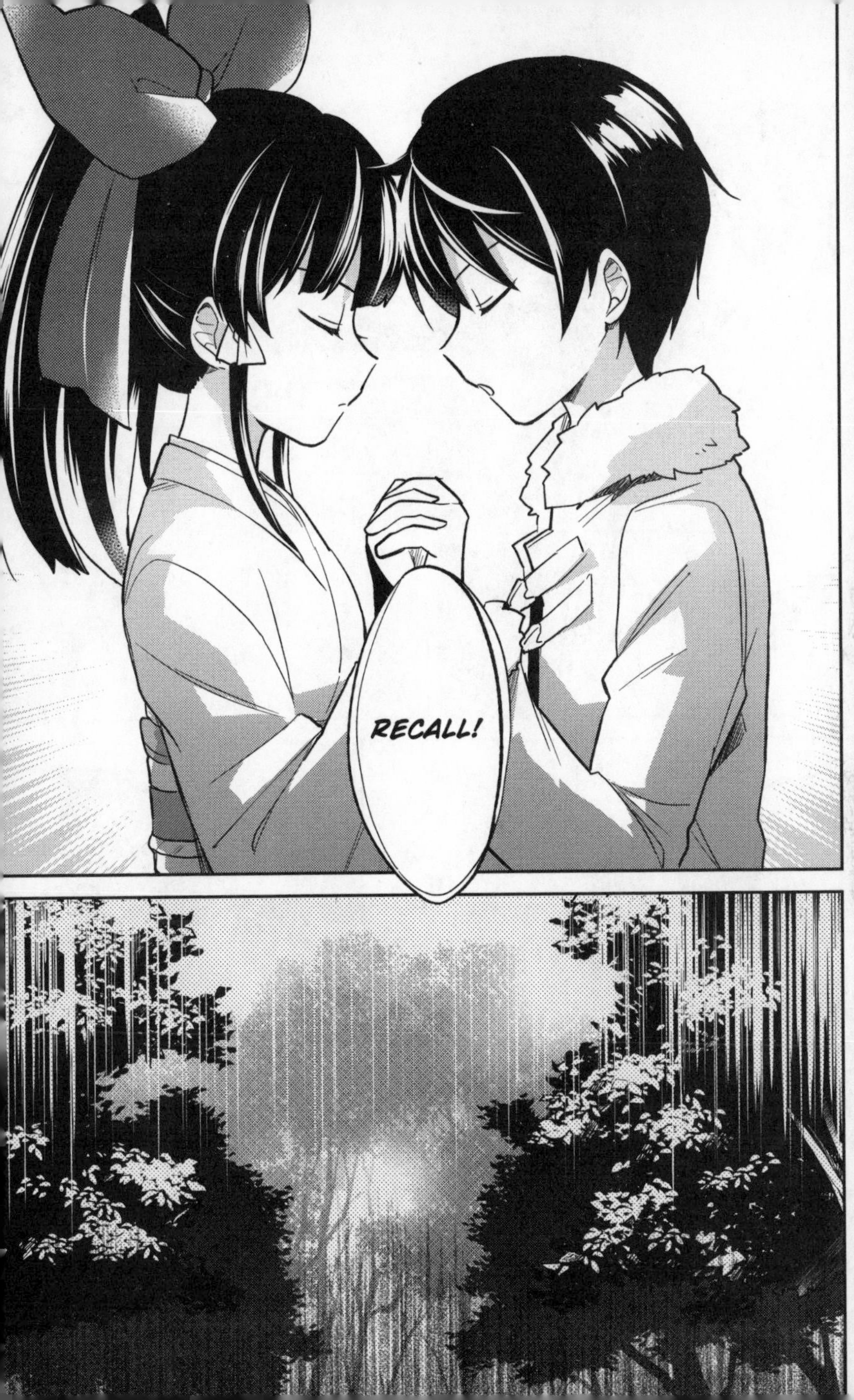
RECALL!

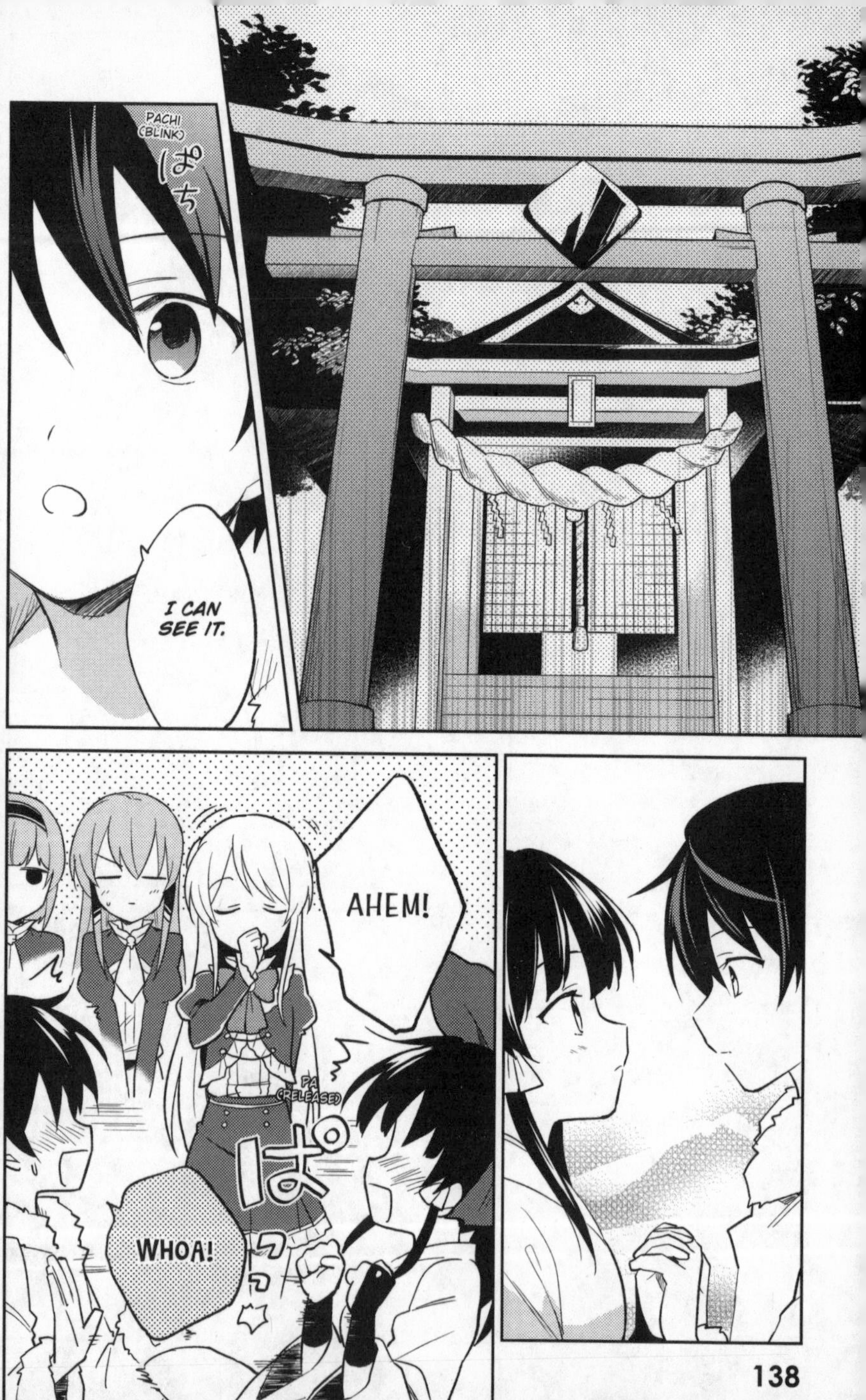
PACHI (BLINK)
ぱち
I CAN SEE IT.
AHEM!
PA (RELEASED)
ぱっ
WHOA!

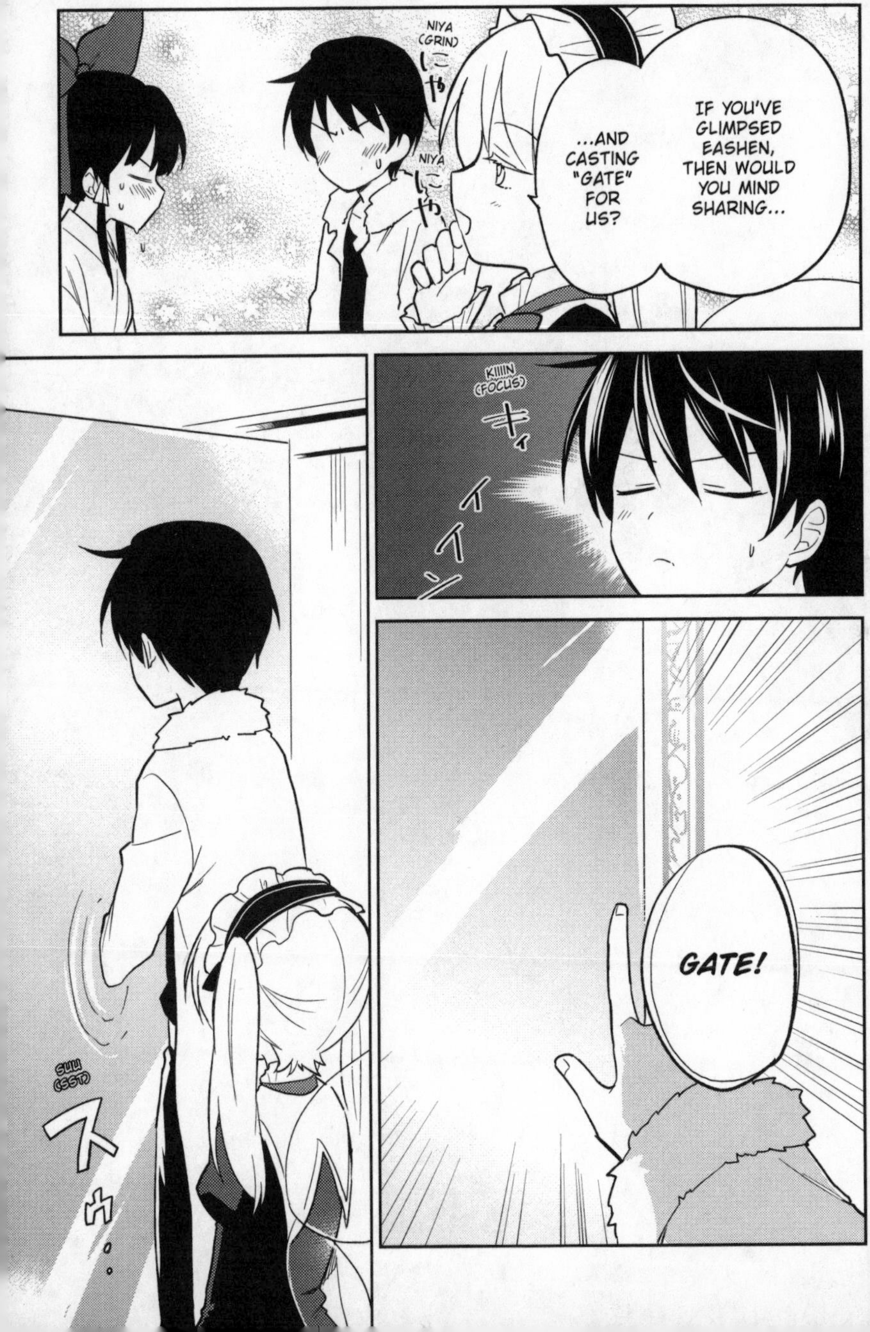
IF YOU'VE GLIMPSED EASHEN, THEN WOULD YOU MIND SHARING...
...AND CASTING "GATE" FOR US?
NIYA (GRIN) にや
NIYA にや
KIIIN (FOCUS) キィイイン
GATE!
SUU (SSST) スゥ…

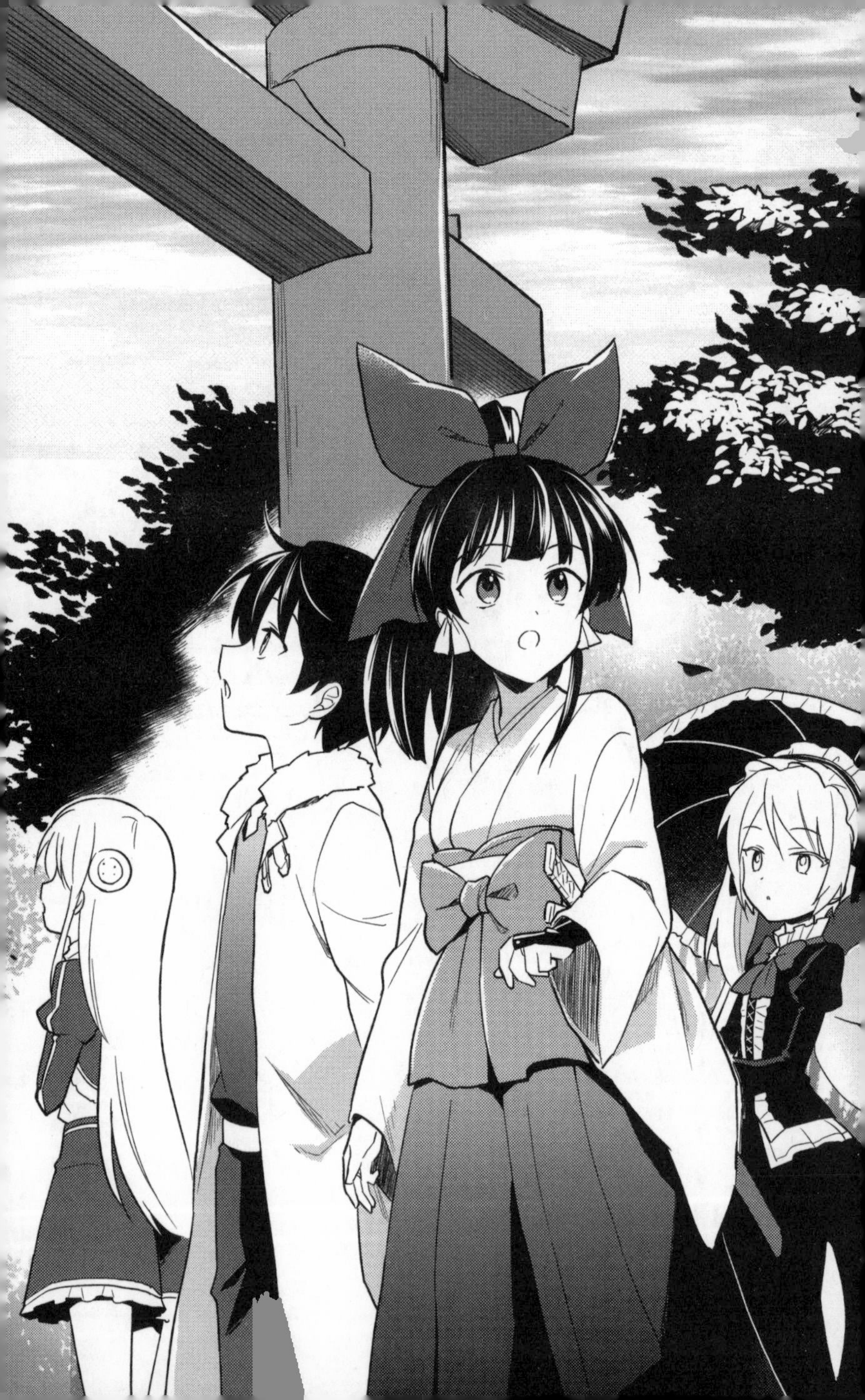

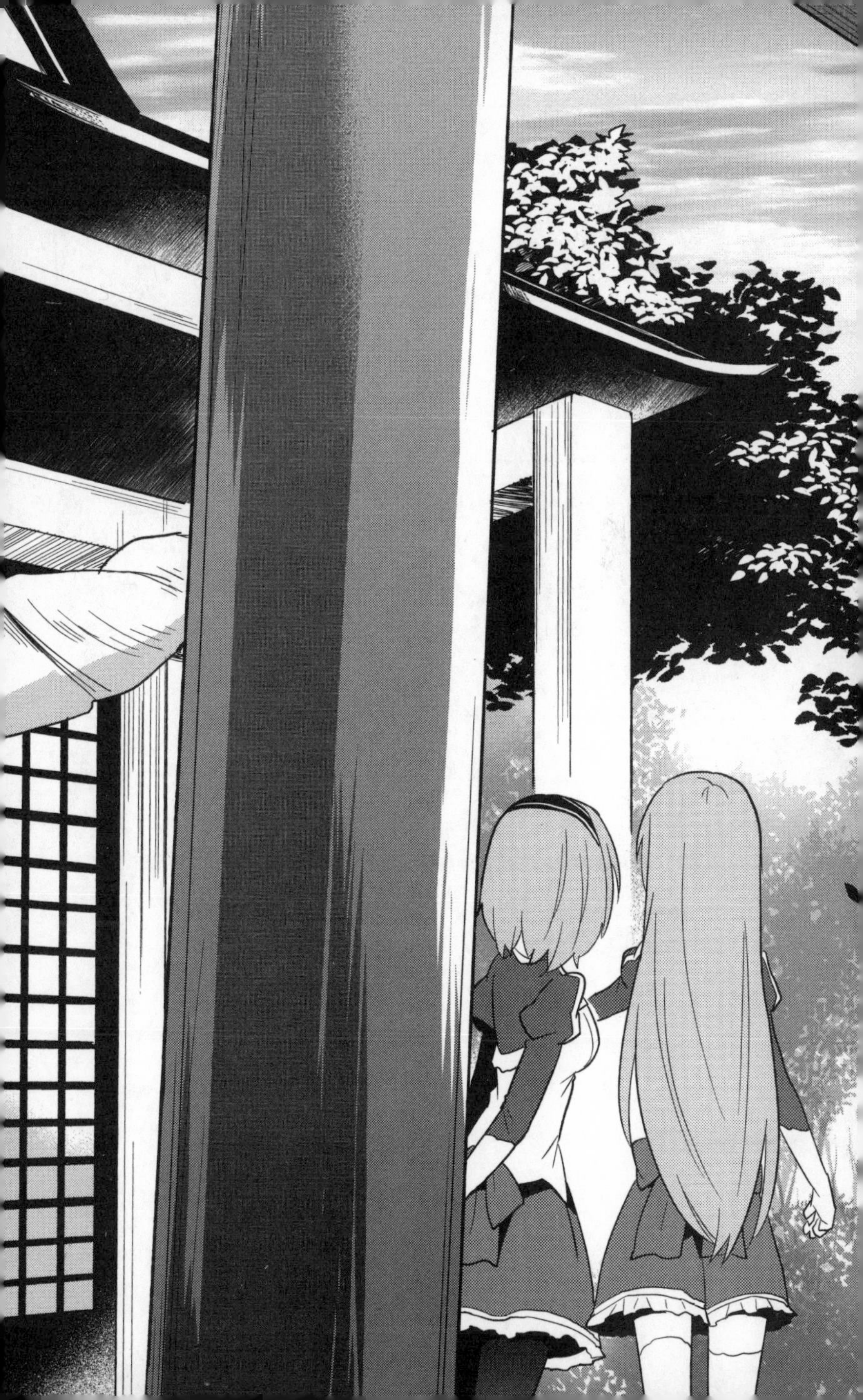

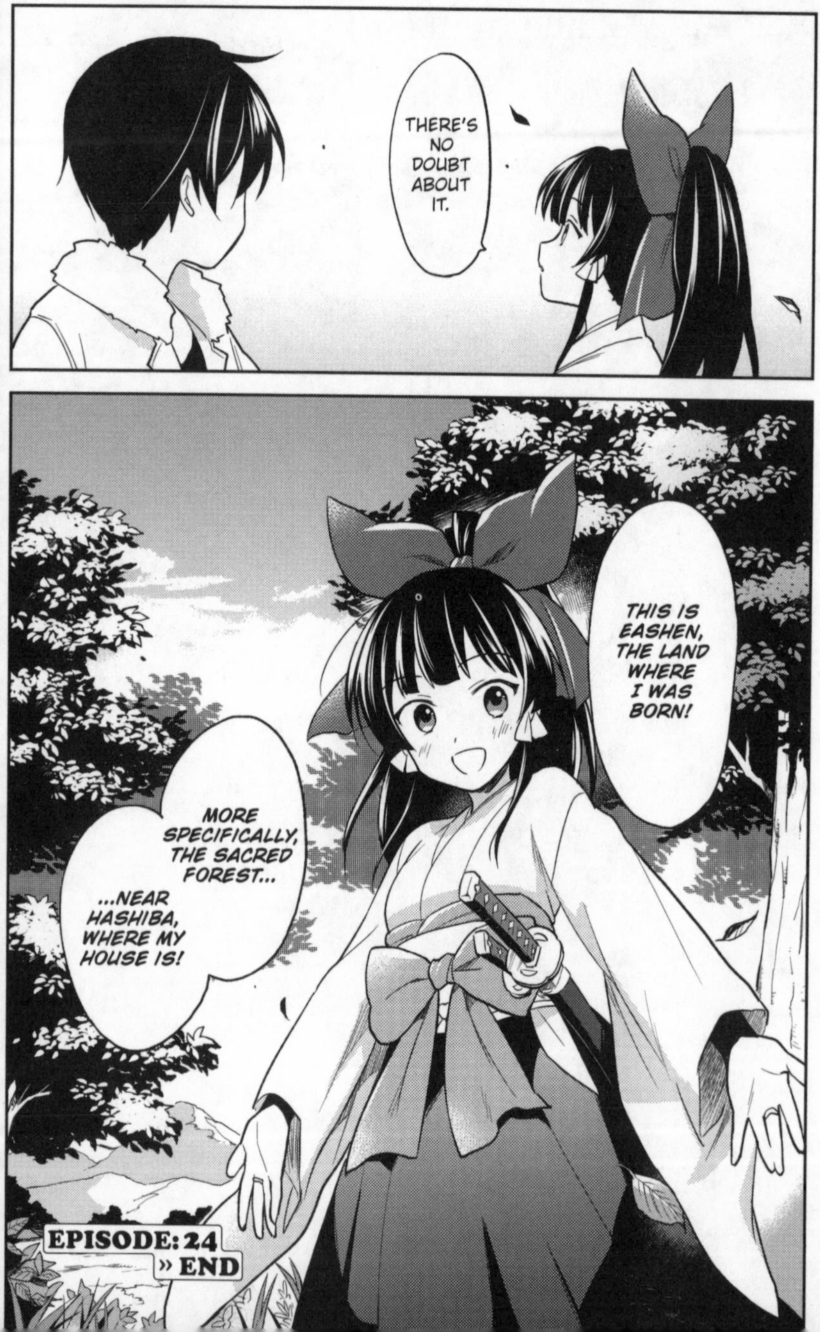
THERE'S NO DOUBT ABOUT IT.
THIS IS EASHEN, THE LAND WHERE I WAS BORN!
MORE SPECIFICALLY, THE SACRED FOREST...
...NEAR HASHIBA, WHERE MY HOUSE IS!
EPISODE: 24 » END

In Another World With
My Smartphone

In Another World with My Smartphone 5

Art • Soto Original Story • Patora Fuyuhara

Character Design: Eiji Usatsuka

Translation: Alexander Keller-Nelson | Lettering: Chiho Christie

ISEKAI WA SMART PHONE TO TOMONI. Vol. 5

First published in Japan in 2018 by KADOKAWA CORPORATION, Tokyo. English translation rights arranged with KADOKAWA CORPORATION, Tokyo through Tuttle-Mori Agency, Inc., Tokyo.

Yen Press
150 West 30th Street, 19th Floor
New York, NY 10001

Visit us!
yenpress.com • facebook.com/yenpress • twitter.com/yenpress
yenpress.tumblr.com • instagram.com/yenpress

First Yen Press Edition: April 2022

Yen Press is an imprint of Yen Press, LLC.
The Yen Press name and logo are trademarks of Yen Press, LLC.

The publisher is not responsible for websites (or their content) that are not owned by the publisher.

Library of Congress Control Number: 2020951871

ISBNs: 978-1-9753-2111-6 (paperback)
978-1-9753-2112-3 (ebook)

10 9 8 7 6 5 4 3 2 1

WOR

Printed in the United States of America